Juniata College
Beeghly Library

*Aaron and Clara
Rabinowitz*

Memorial Library Fund

How the Incas Built Their Heartland

History, Languages, and Cultures of the
Spanish and Portuguese Worlds

This interdisciplinary series promotes scholarship
in studies on Iberian cultures and contacts from the premodern
and early modern periods.

SERIES EDITOR

Sabine MacCormack, Theodore M. Hesburgh Professor of Arts and Letters,
Departments of Classics and History, University of Notre Dame

SERIES BOARD

J. N. Hillgarth, emeritus, Pontifical Institute of Mediaeval Studies
Peggy K. Liss, Independent Scholar
David Nirenberg, Johns Hopkins University
Adeline Rucquoi, École des Hautes Études en Sciences Sociales

TITLES IN THE SERIES

How the Incas Built Their Heartland

*State Formation and the
Innovation of Imperial Strategies
in the Sacred Valley, Peru*

R. ALAN COVEY

THE UNIVERSITY OF MICHIGAN PRESS
Ann Arbor

Copyright © by the University of Michigan 2006
All rights reserved
Published in the United States of America by
The University of Michigan Press
Manufactured in the United States of America
⊛ Printed on acid-free paper

2009   2008   2007   2006   4   3   2   1

No part of this publication may be reproduced, stored
in a retrieval system, or transmitted in any form
or by any means, electronic, mechanical, or otherwise,
without the written permission of the publisher.

A CIP catalog record for this book is available from the British Library.

Library of Congress Cataloging-in-Publication Data

Covey, R. Alan, 1974–
    How the Incas built their heartland : state formation and the innovation of imperial
strategies in the Sacred Valley, Peru / R. Alan Covey.
        p. cm. — (History, languages, and cultures of the Spanish and Portuguese worlds)
    Includes bibliographical references and index.
    ISBN-13: 978-0-472-11478-8 (cloth : alk. paper)
    ISBN-10: 0-472-11478-6 (cloth : alk. paper)
        1. Incas—Politics and government.   2. Incas—Kings and rulers.   3. Incas—
Antiquities.   4. Political culture—Peru—Cuzco Region.   5. Cuzco Region (Peru)—
Politics and government.   6. Cuzco Region (Peru)—Territorial expansion.   7. Cuzco
Region (Peru)—Antiquities.   I. Title.
    II. Series.
    F3429.3.P65C69   2006
    985'.019—dc22   2005026027

F
3429.3
.P65
C69
2006

Preface

In the 1550s, Bartolomé de Las Casas wrote a history of the Incas of South America's Andean region, part of a massive treatise on indigenous cultures of the Americas and their rights as civil societies. Las Casas never visited Peru, and the twenty-seven Inca chapters in his *Apologética historia sumaria* drew from the reports that travelers and clergy sent back to Spain following the invasion of the Inca empire in 1532. This was arguably the first scholarly treatment of primary sources from the Andes, and in the 450 years since then, hundreds of documents have been written about the Incas, advancing our understanding of the largest native empire to develop in the Americas.

Although new colonial-period manuscripts occasionally have been discovered in European or Peruvian archives, some of the most important advances in Inca studies in the past century have come from the field of archaeology, where the physical remains of the Inca empire—its cities, roads, and shrines—have been studied. Inca archaeology has flourished since the 1960s, with a scholarly literature that seems to grow exponentially.

Inca scholarship today finds itself at a crossroads, faced with the question of how historians and archaeologists are to collaborate to reconstruct the Inca past. Working as they do with documents written after the fall of the Inca empire, historians tend to project backward in time as far as they feel that they can rely on the historicity of the primary sources—typically to the middle of the fifteenth century, but rarely earlier than AD 1400. Inca archaeology has traditionally been closely tied to the study of the Spanish chronicles, and much has been learned by collecting data that pertain to the period that the documentary record addresses most explicitly. For archaeology to contribute to Inca studies as an equal to the historical record, however, archaeologists must explain how Inca civilization relates to earlier states and empires in the Andean highlands, and they thus ought to work forward in time from AD 1000 or earlier. Recent investigations by Peruvian, European, and North American archaeologists have begun to explore processes occurring in

the Cusco region after the decline of the Wari empire and leading up to
Inca imperial expansion (ca. AD 1000–1400). A large body of archaeological data has only recently begun to be employed to bridge the divide
between pre-Inca archaeology and historically oriented Inca studies.

The principal aim of this book is to unite the historical and archaeological evidence to describe how the Incas became sufficiently powerful
to embark on their unprecedented campaigns of territorial expansion,
as well as to consider how such developments related to earlier patterns
of Andean statecraft. To do so, I propose a new reading of the Spanish
chronicles, one that focuses on processes—rather than singular events—
occurring throughout the region surrounding Cusco, the Inca capital.
The historical record can be used to discuss the kinds of interactions that
allowed the Incas to subordinate neighboring groups living in a region
of considerable ethnic, political, and economic diversity.

The process-based reading of the Inca past can be studied in comparison with a large body of archaeological data, including new data
that my colleagues and I collected in 2000 as part of the Sacred Valley
Archaeological Project (SVAP). SVAP research consisted of a regional
archaeological survey in Peru's "Sacred Valley of the Incas," a stretch of
the Vilcanota-Urubamba Valley that is famous for its Inca monuments.
The regional survey work employed the same field methodology used
in two previous archaeological surveys directed by Brian Bauer in the
Cusco Basin and areas to its south. Survey crews of three to five Peruvian and American archaeologists walked in parallel lines of approximately 50 meters through all passable areas of a study region of roughly
400 square kilometers, registering over four hundred archaeological
sites on the basis of surface artifacts or architectonic features. Surface
collections of pottery were analyzed in the laboratory to identify the locations and sizes of settlements for all phases of the pre-Hispanic occupation of the region.

Following the survey research, several important sites were mapped
under the direction of Kenneth Sims, and the largest preimperial site,
Pukara Pantillijlla, was selected for broad horizontal excavations. Working with crews of twelve to fifteen men from the nearby town of Cuyo
Grande, we succeeded in excavating five complete structures, as well as
several test units in exterior trash deposits and building interiors. The
artifacts and radiocarbon dates from this research permitted us to date
Inca expansion into a previously independent area, one that is mentioned

in several Inca histories. The new data also provide a portrait of life at an early Inca administrative center.

Archaeological data allow us to identify the physical evidence for regional developments occurring over several centuries, and by reading the Inca histories in a compatible way, it is possible to construct two independent versions of how the Inca heartland was transformed after AD 1000. When synthesized into a single narrative, these two lines of evidence provide us with a detailed account of the rise of Inca civilization.

It would be disingenuous to promote a process-based reading of the Inca past without acknowledging that such work would not be possible without the efforts of earlier scholars, as well as a host of people who made the SVAP research possible. I would like to thank the many friends and colleagues who have helped me to develop as an anthropologist and supported me as I conducted the research on which this book is based.

My interest in anthropology and archaeology developed while I was an undergraduate at Dartmouth College, and my work with Paul Goldstein, Deborah Nichols, Roberta Stewart, John Watanabe, and Roger Ulrich introduced me to archaeology, anthropological theory, and the critical study of documentary sources. An initial interest in Maya and Roman archaeology led me to graduate studies at the University of Michigan, but fieldwork opportunities in Bolivia and Peru happily diverted me to the Cusco region and, eventually, to the SVAP research.

At Michigan, I was fortunate to study under a number of distinguished scholars, many of whom also proved to be generous mentors. Kent Flannery, Jeff Parsons, and Henry Wright taught courses that influenced my thinking about social evolution, the development of political complexity, and processes of state formation. Bruce Mannheim offered a year of Quechua the year before I conducted my fieldwork, which has proven invaluable for studying colonial dictionaries. Sabine MacCormack introduced me to the early colonial documents of non-Andean South America and has provided much-needed support and research opportunities throughout the dissertation process. Joyce Marcus deserves special mention, acting as my adviser throughout my doctoral studies. Joyce created courses tailored to her students' intellectual interests and is without rival for her dedication as a mentor and adviser. My doctoral project would not have succeeded without the guidance and criticism of these and other professors.

While Michigan provided the academic and theoretical background for the present study, I owe a debt of gratitude to a number of archaeologists for helping me to become a proficient field archaeologist. I was fortunate to work with Brian Bauer for four field seasons in Bolivia and Peru. While working on his Cusco Valley survey project, I learned survey methodology from Brian, who has provided encouragement, feedback, and advice as I have ventured out to direct my own fieldwork. Other archaeologists who helped me to develop as a field researcher include Paul Goldstein, Mike Moseley, Chip Stanish, and Adán Umire. Chip has been especially generous with his support and advice and instrumental in helping me to develop manuscripts and grant proposals successfully.

The Sacred Valley Archaeological Project received funding from several sources. Predissertation research was supported by the Latin American and Caribbean Studies Program at the University of Michigan, as well as a National Science Foundation Graduate Research Fellowship. The fieldwork itself was funded by a Fulbright-Hays Fellowship, a Wenner-Gren Foundation Individual Grant, the Department of Anthropology at the University of Michigan, the James Griffin Fund of the Museum of Anthropology at the University of Michigan, and a Discretionary Grant from the Horace H. Rackham Graduate School. Additionally, a National Science Foundation Dissertation Improvement Grant (BCS #0135913) provided funds to process thirty radiocarbon dates collected during field research.

The execution of the research would not have been possible without the participation and support of a number of Peruvian colleagues. The staff of the Cusco and Lima offices of the National Institute of Culture (INC) were helpful and patient in reviewing permit proposals and supervising the field research. The Fulbright office in Lima made it possible to process paperwork and get into the field without major complications, and Cecilia Esparza (the director at the time) made me feel like I had a real support network as I did my research. In the field, I was fortunate to work with an experienced crew of Peruvian archaeologists. Werner Delgado, Ricardo Huayllani, Amelia Pérez, René Pilco, and Herberth Reynaga participated in the survey project, and Ricardo and René supervised excavation crews from Cuyo Grande during the excavations at Pukara Pantillijlla. Dionisio Jancco, the president of Cuyo Grande, helped to organize our excavation crews and was instrumental in the success of the excavations. Wilfredo Yépez served as the Peruvian co-director of the project, offering sage advice on how to conduct the research. The Yépez family helped out with the project in many ways and has provided friendship and support during my visits in Cusco.

Following the fieldwork, I wrote my dissertation at the American Museum of Natural History while working with Craig Morris on data analysis from his work at the Inca city of Huánuco Pampa. During my time at the museum, Craig, Bob Carneiro, Elsa Redmond, and Chuck Spencer have given encouragement and criticism that have improved my work. I could not ask for a better environment for thinking through the dissertation and completing the writing.

Finally, I would like to thank my fellow graduate students for everything I have learned from them outside the classroom and in the field. There are too many to name them all, but I would especially like to thank Brad Jones, Stella Nair, Kenny Sims, Tiffiny Tung, Steve Wernke, and Karina Yager for help, support, and good company along the way. In addition to all of these names, I save Christina Elson's for last. She supported every step leading to the production of this book: the challenges of graduate school, the field research, and the laborious write-up process. Christina offered comments on grant proposals, directed an excavation crew at Pukara Pantillijlla, and read early drafts of text that wasn't ready for the dissertation committee. Her patience, generosity, and good company helped to make a challenging project possible.

Contents

Figures

Tables

CHAPTER ONE

A New Orientation for Inca Studies

When a small contingent of Spaniards led by Francisco Pizarro and Diego de Almagro invaded the Andean highlands in 1532, the Inca empire was the largest native polity to develop in the Americas. Inca territory included parts of the modern nations of Peru, Bolivia, Chile, Argentina, Ecuador, and Colombia, an area spanning coastal deserts, tropical jungles, montane valleys, and alpine tundra (fig. 1.1). That one polity could unite this region and rule a hundred or more distinct ethnic groups and local polities was remarkable to the invading Spaniards. This achievement was made all the more impressive when indigenous informants told them that Inca campaigns of expansion had been made over the span of only a few generations. Many Inca conquests were attested to by eyewitnesses who had fought in Inca armies or were among the conquered. In the decades following the conquest, European interest in the Inca past developed as Spain consolidated its colonial control over the Andean region, and oral histories and eyewitness accounts were collected and edited to describe the Inca past and justify or criticize the Spanish Conquest.[1]

For several hundred years, the historical and administrative texts collected in the first century or so after the conquest provided the sole means for discussing Inca territorial expansion and imperial administration. Many of the most reliable Spanish chroniclers explained Inca imperial origins as the result of the actions of a single dynamic individual named Inca Yupanqui (fig. 1.2).[2] According to these authors, the Inca capital, Cusco, was invaded by an ethnic group called the Chancas around AD 1438. Viracocha Inca, the Inca ruler, fled Cusco with the town's populace and his favorite son, leaving behind a young prince named Inca Yupanqui and a few of his friends and supporters. Before the Chancas could reach Cusco, the creator deity (also called Viracocha) appeared to Inca Yupanqui and promised him victory. Viracocha animated stones on the nearby hillsides, creating a host of warriors who fought in support of the

Fig. 1.1. Map of Inca territory, ca. AD 1532. Tawantinsuyu, the Inca realm, was the largest native empire to form in the Americas.

Inca prince. The Chanca invaders were repulsed, and Inca Yupanqui then personally crafted a new imperial order. The transformations credited to this ruler—construction of a magnificent urban capital, leadership in ambitious military campaigns, the creation of a legal code, and the establishment of a new religion—were so substantial that he assumed the title Pachacutic (*Pachakutiq*), "The One Who Brings a New Universal Cycle."[3] Having defeated dangerous enemies and established an imperial order, Pachacutic and his military commanders launched a lightning war upon the Andes that continues to impress modern historians.

Although this version of Inca imperial origins makes for compelling reading, it is rather unsatisfactory for explaining how one remarkable

Fig. 1.2. Pachacutic Inca Yupanqui. Pachacutic is commonly credited with innovating Inca imperial order. (Redrawn from Guaman Poma de Ayala 1980 [1615].)

and charismatic man could forge a mighty empire out of a village-level society. In trying to separate historical fact from imperial ideology, propaganda, and myth, anthropologists are left asking a number of questions that the Chanca invasion story does not explain adequately. How could a simple group of maize farmers transform themselves suddenly into committed imperialists? Without a centralized government and a large subject population, how could a large army have been assembled and provisioned for long campaigns? If we discount the divine assistance Pachacutic is said to have received from the creator deity, how and why would a group of farmers develop military strategies, a conquest ideology, and administrative policies for subjugating and governing new provinces whose populations outnumbered theirs? If we consider the story of the Chanca invasion carefully, it becomes clear that even the most brilliant and charismatic leader could not have created such a mighty empire single-handedly. Conditions beyond the control of a single individual must have played a significant part.

Complicating issues of how the story of imperial origins could be possible is the fact that the Pachacutic account is in part created by selective readings of the Inca histories. While certain Spanish chronicles do glorify the actions of Pachacutic above other Inca rulers, several scholars have noted recently that this is because the chroniclers relied on life histories told by certain Inca lineages intent on maximizing their own prestige during the colonial period. The lineages of Pachacutic's father, Viracocha Inca, and his son, Topa Inca Yupanqui, also presented versions of the past in which *their* ancestors were credited with the most important imperial developments.[4] These rival accounts also fail to explain the processes that made rapid territorial expansion and imperial administration possible.

The Inca histories cannot be treated as a complete and factual chronology of events performed by historical individuals. The life stories of individual Inca rulers and their repeated reorganization as state histories led to substantial revisions even before the Spanish Conquest.[5] Spanish transcriptions of Inca histories were executed with political ends in mind, and the reconfiguration of Inca narratives to fit European notions of universal history represents a further manipulation of already problematic materials. The comparison of the sequences of rulers in the Inca empire with that in other states and empires reveals the entire king list to be historically suspect, and not just in the preimperial period, as has generally been assumed by many historians.[6]

Considering that Inca histories are laden with the biases of Spanish and Andean writers, riddled with inconsistencies, and produced to meet specific political and ideological aims, how are modern scholars to discern what really happened? Historians have worked backward in time using the colonial-period documents, leaving off their narratives as they become inextricably intermingled with myth and legend. In this book, I propose an alternate method: rather than attempt to unravel the intricacies of Inca historiography, I propose that we cut this Gordian knot by adopting a process-based interpretive stance that treats Inca archaeology and ethnohistory as equals. The colonial historical documents can be used to describe how the Incas interacted with neighboring groups in the generations leading up to the first sustained campaigns of expansion outside the Cusco region. Regional archaeology and excavation data provide an independent perspective on the same period, permitting us to evaluate the historical accounts using the physical remains of actual human activities from that time.

A Process-Based Approach to the Study of Inca State Formation

This book begins with a comparative look at other early states and empires, as anthropological theory sets the parameters for our interpretive expectations. Rapid territorial expansion like that described for the Incas is not unknown for other empires, but a brief discussion of the Roman and Aztec empires demonstrates that rapid growth is most successful in cases where a centralized state government had already coalesced in the heartland of the emerging empire. Indicators of state formation can be identified in the oral histories and archaeological remains from other known states, and these indicators are used to evaluate the evidence for Inca state formation in the Cusco region.[7]

Studying Inca state formation encourages a process-based reading of the Inca histories. Rather than focus on the singular actions of quasi-historical individuals, this new reading identifies a suite of long-term, qualitative changes occurring throughout the Cusco region over the span of several generations (fig. 1.3). These include the development of a centralized and internally specialized government, the spread of a new religion that reflects and justifies a more hierarchical society, and the emergence of an ideology supporting the permanent conquest of new territories. When looking for evidence for similar processes in the Inca

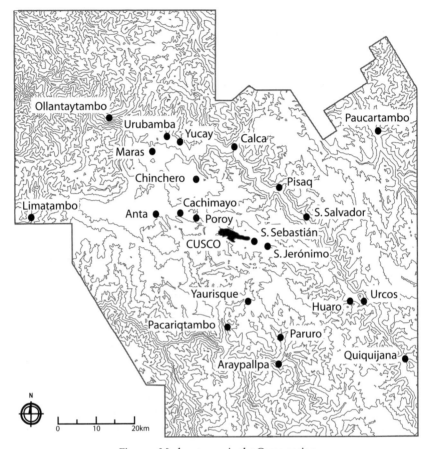

Fig. 1.3. Modern towns in the Cusco region

histories, I present information from independent historical sources where possible, privileging those that provide the most detailed discussion of incidents occurring in Cusco and its immediate vicinity prior to the accession of Pachacutic.

The Impact of Pre-Inca Civilizations in the Cusco Region

While historical studies of the Incas work backward in time using colonial-era documents, this book uses archaeological data to move forward chronologically from around AD 600. At that time, Wari settlers from the Ayacucho region in the central highlands immigrated to the region and established colonies or enclaves about 35 to 45 kilometers to the southeast of the modern city of Cusco. Wari colonists transformed the area immediately surrounding their settlements over a period of several hundred years, constructing agricultural fields and irrigation canals and investing substantial amounts of labor into building an imperial installation at the site of Pikillacta. The largest Wari sites in the Cusco region were abandoned by AD 1000, at which time any formal political relationship between the Cusco and Ayacucho regions appears to have ended.

Excavations at Pikillacta and other Wari sites have led investigators to conclude that the Cusco region was a province of an imperial polity and that the Wari tradition of statecraft and imperial administration must have enabled the rapid rise and expansion of the Inca empire. It is true that Pikillacta was a massive site, one that was probably constructed with the labor of Wari colonists and the local populations of the Cusco region. This would-be provincial capital was never completed or fully occupied, however, making a Cusco province seem more like an unrealized goal than an administrative reality.

Archaeological surveys of the Cusco Basin and areas to the north and south of Cusco have yielded a very different view of the local effects of the Wari colonial system in the Cusco region. Although the arrival of foreign colonists dramatically transformed the area immediately surrounding new Wari settlements, local groups in other locations continued to live in the same villages and farm the same fields as they had since around AD 400. Survey archaeologists have not found evidence of any Wari administrative sites outside of the Lucre Basin and Urcos area. The survey evidence fails to support a provincial model for the Wari occupation of the Cusco region.

This is not to say that Wari settlers living near the Cusco Basin were not influential. We know that local people obtained exotic goods like obsidian and turquoise through Wari long-distance exchange networks. Despite the rarity of pottery from the Ayacucho region at sites located more than about 10 kilometers from Wari settlements, local groups in the Cusco Basin produced and distributed pottery that emulated Wari design motifs. Even if many local groups were not directly governed by the Wari state, there is evidence that they participated in religious rituals and perhaps public feasts that were sponsored by Wari officials.

The Wari polity does not appear to have administered the Cusco

region as a province, and the centuries-long hiatus between the abandonment of major Wari installations and the formation of the Inca state
makes it unlikely that the Incas simply remobilized a Wari model of
statecraft. We must instead look to more indirect influences contribut-
ing to the rise of Inca civilization. Wari settlers probably introduced intensive agricultural practices to the Cusco region, as well as social structures whereby labor service was given for public construction projects,
then reciprocated through religious rituals and public feasts. The centuries of Wari settlement in the Cusco region must have reconfigured
how local groups conceived of the authority of their elite leaders, and
such developments set the stage for the political competition that cul-
minated in Inca state formation.

The Cusco Region after AD 1000

The abandonment of large Wari sites around AD 1000 was part of a
major settlement shift throughout the Cusco region at that time. Former
occupants of the Wari colonies resettled in a series of towns located near
the valley-bottom maize lands that they would have continued to farm.[8]
Although systematic survey data have not been collected for this region,
it appears that the new towns were probably the principal settlements
of small complex polities. The elite leaders of such settlements appear to
have organized the same kinds of public works as their Wari predecessors, including defensive walls and religious architecture. The absence
of obvious defenses at some towns indicates that these settlements were
probably large enough to discourage raiding by hostile groups, but the
abandonment of productive farmland in the area between the former
Wari colonies and the Cusco Basin has been interpreted as evidence that
the balkanized polities that succeeded the Wari colonial system were not
necessarily allies of the emerging Inca polity.[9]

The Cusco Basin underwent major settlement changes after AD
1000.[10] The population grew dramatically as new groups immigrated
into the basin, and the city of Cusco grew over time to become the Inca
capital. New irrigation canals and agricultural terraces were built in
areas that were previously too marginal for agriculture, and the growing population settled new villages near these fields. Most villages in the
Cusco Basin were located on low ridges just above fertile valley-bottom
farmland, and these do not appear to have been defended. The overall

settlement system of the Cusco Basin was much more complex and hierarchical than other parts of the Cusco region. Not all sites near Cusco were necessarily under the direct administration of the emerging Inca state; several small fortified villages and ridgetop settlements were occupied in remote areas in the southernmost reaches of the Cusco Basin, most of which appear to have been abandoned before AD 1400.

A pattern of high-elevation ridgetop settlement and the construction of defensive works are much more pronounced in the Sacred Valley to the north of Cusco. After AD 1000, settlement became more hierarchical, with a number of small and large villages established at elevations of 4000 meters or higher. Some villages were settled in locations offering natural protection—steep-sided ridges or precipitous cliffs—while others were fortified through the construction of defensive walls and ditches. Where local leadership managed to organize the labor of a community or small polity, defensive projects seem to have taken priority over agricultural intensification or the construction of public or ritual buildings.

The largest settlements in the Sacred Valley were located close to a very different set of resources than those in the Cusco Valley, and local populations probably farmed higher-elevation crops (generally, without the benefit of irrigation) and herded camelids. No large settlements were situated near the valley bottom, where some of the world's most productive maize land is farmed today. Differences in domestic architecture, local pottery decoration, and burial treatment indicate that the Sacred Valley was home to multiple political and ethnic groups at this time. Populations living on the south side of the valley appear to have interacted frequently with the Incas, while those to the north did not.

Groups living to the west of the Cusco Basin also maintained relations with the Incas. Although regional survey work has not been completed in this area, the historical documents describe a number of distinct ethnic and political units. One group, the Ayarmacas, is said to have been a complex polity, with a paramount ruler who owned camelid herds and various agricultural lands and who at some point in the past rivaled the Inca paramount for regional preeminence. The Ayarmacas practiced a mixed herding and maize-farming economy, while several village-level polities are also said to have lived near valley-bottom maize lands located along the important caravan route running west from Cusco to the Apurímac River.

It is likely that the villages to the west of the Cusco Basin were

organized similarly to those located to the south of Cusco.[11] This area
is characterized by low population density, and the inhabitants of the
small villages in the region lived near their farmlands in communities
that lacked artificial defenses. Groups living between the Cusco Basin
and Apurímac River commonly used pottery acquired from the Cusco
Basin, and their local settlement and economy remained stable after AD
1000, indicating that their incorporation into the Inca state probably
occurred early on and did not result in major transformations of local
economies.

The entire Cusco region experienced the transformation of settlement patterns, political integration, and local economy after AD 1000.
The Inca state thus formed in a region characterized by a high degree of
ethnic diversity, on a landscape where a variety of different herding and
agricultural strategies were pursued. The maize-farming population of
the Cusco Basin grew dramatically, and by AD 1200 or so, there is evidence that the Incas of Cusco were emerging as the most powerful polity
in the region—a group that governed a large population and had access
to substantiated surpluses of agricultural products with which it could
fund state projects. The Incas may have been the dominant group in the
Cusco region by the thirteenth century, but they did not rule over most
of their neighbors. Many small villages may have lived under Inca protection, and polities of moderate complexity intermarried with the Inca
elite and contracted alliances. The strongest rivals to Inca dominance
lived to the northwest and southeast of the Cusco Basin. Groups in the
latter area were probably descendants of Wari settlers who had their
own large settlements and monumental architecture, but they appear to
have lacked the large subject population seen in the Cusco Basin.

The Formation of the Inca State

Given the diversity of the ecological, political, and ethnic landscape after
AD 1000, it is not surprising that the Incas employed many strategies to
incorporate their neighbors into a single centralized state. Having used
the archaeological record to work forward to roughly AD 1200, we can
begin to apply our process-based reading of the Inca past for comparison with the archaeological record.

The rapid population growth in the Cusco Basin after AD 1000 would
have created new administrative needs for the Inca polity, while simul-

taneously presenting opportunities for Inca leaders to increase their power and authority. Labor service provided to the Inca elite was used to build new agricultural lands and irrigation canals, resources that could feed the increasing population but were thought of as the personal estates of Inca rulers and their lineages. The allocation of newly improved farmland would have increased the political power of Inca leaders, undercutting the traditional kin-based authority of local leaders. Some groups may have resisted Inca dominance, but the Cusco Basin ultimately came under the direct control of Inca rulers.

As rural populations in the Cusco Basin came to be dominated by Inca paramounts, the growing population living in Cusco would have become increasingly dependent on the Inca elite for organizing an urban food supply. The city grew, flourishing as a center of ceremonial and ritual life for the Cusco Basin, and its sizeable nonfarming population must have grown to include religious specialists, artisans, and officials who served the Inca state. A state religion based on the worship of the sun—to grow the precious maize crop produced on new agricultural terraces—was organized under the auspices of the Inca nobility.

As Inca rulers grew more powerful, they began to espouse an ideology justifying the conquest or subordination of neighboring groups. The Inca histories indicate that the first territorial expansion outside the Cusco Basin occurred around the time that the Inca elite consolidated its local control over the basin. It is unclear whether military action was required to incorporate the villages and small polities living to the south of Cusco. Given that people in that area used the Cusco Basin ceramic style and that there is no evidence of major modification of the regional settlement system under Inca rule, it is likely that the incorporation of small groups living near Cusco did not require extended military campaigns.

The situation in the Sacred Valley provides a marked contrast. Forts and fortifications were constructed, and as the Incas came to control new territory, they settled new villages in areas between the Cusco Basin and neighboring polities that had been depopulated. Evidence of Inca influence among neighboring groups includes the construction of special architecture and prevalence of Cusco Basin pottery in areas where these were previously lacking. The permanent incorporation of groups living to the north of the Sacred Valley provides evidence that Inca society had developed a central administration with specialized offices for governing groups not sharing kin ties with the Inca elite.

Inca Expansion Practices and Local Reactions

As the Incas began to incorporate the different political and ethnic groups living in the Cusco region, they often resorted to military action, but many groups living to the north and west of the Cusco Basin were initially integrated through more peaceful means. In these cases, marriage alliances prevented major hostilities between groups while at the same time promoting Inca power among these groups. Marriages between Inca rulers and elite women from neighboring groups created lasting bonds in which the wife's kin bore the responsibility of providing service to her children and their descendants. This service was reciprocated through Inca sponsorship of festive events, many of which would have taken place in Cusco. As Inca rulers took multiple wives from neighboring ethnic groups, they increased the pool of labor service available for state projects because elite women continued to receive labor service, including the maintenance of lands and herds in their hometowns. The organization of feasts and ritual events to reciprocate labor would have helped to transform Cusco into the center of festive and ceremonial life for the region.

Stories of a small polity called the Huayllacans clearly illustrate how the Incas used marriage alliances to extend their dominance. The Huayllacans lived just to the north of the Cusco Basin, and archaeological settlement patterns indicate that their population comprised a group of small villages and hamlets whose leaders lived in the large village of Qhapaqkancha. Although elite Huayllacan women had customarily married men from the nearby Ayarmaca group, the Huayllacans broke with this tradition, and an elite woman married the sixth Inca ruler. This provoked a war between the Huayllacans and Ayarmacas, one in which the Incas appear to have remained neutral. Seeing that they were losing to the more powerful Ayarmacas, the local elite permitted the Ayarmacas to kidnap the son of the Inca ruler and his Huayllacan wife. The boy was eventually returned to his father in a sequence of events resulting in additional marriage alliances between the Incas and the Ayarmaca and Anta ethnic groups. Huayllacan treachery was forgiven, but when this group later attempted to meddle in Inca royal succession, the Huayllacans were decimated, and their lands were seized as a personal estate of the Inca ruler whose kidnapping they had arranged when he was a boy.

While elite marriage exchange provided a means for extending Inca rule over some of the groups of the Cusco region—particularly those that practiced herding and mixed agriculture in the region to the north-west of Cusco—groups of different ethnicity appear to have been con-quered militarily. One of the best-documented examples of conquest and early administration is the case of the Cuyos, a group living to the north of the Sacred Valley. Pre-Inca villages in the Cuyo area were situated at high elevations in the side valleys, an area where mixed farming and herding are likely to have been practiced. Not only does village location imply a different economic base for Cuyo society but this area also has decorated pottery, household architecture, and burial practices that are distinct from that of the Cusco Basin, suggesting real cultural differences.

The Cuyos are mentioned as one of the first groups conquered by the Incas, and an Inca governor was placed in the area even though Cuyo elites continued to hold local leadership positions. Archaeologically, the imposition of Inca administration is evident through the construction of special architecture and the prevalence of Cusco Basin pottery at certain villages to the north of the Sacred Valley. In particular, the Incas built religious and administrative architecture at the site of Pukara Pantillijlla, which grew rapidly as it developed into a secondary administrative cen-ter of the expanding state. Radiocarbon dates from excavations at this site indicate that the Inca reorganization of the Cuyo area began in the late thirteenth or early fourteenth century.

The Cuyos are said to have remained under Inca rule for several gen-erations but were accused of plotting the assassination of the ninth ruler, Pachacutic. In retaliation, Inca armies passed through Cuyo lands, burn-ing villages and killing a large number of the local people. The Cuyo area then became Pachacutic's personal estate, and valley-bottom lands were developed for intensive maize agriculture and resettled with retainers from conquered provincial regions.

The Consolidation of Inca Rule in the Cusco Region

If marriage alliances helped to extend Inca dominance and reduce hos-tilities between different polities, they often failed to produce a peaceful transition to direct Inca rule at the local level. Local rebellion is com-monly mentioned as the final phase by which the Inca state consoli-dated its control over groups in the Cusco region. Because our histori-cal perspective comes from Inca informants, we should be cautious about such accounts. While local leaders would have had good reasons for attempting to throw off the yoke of Inca rule, we must consider the likelihood that the Inca version of events was crafted after the fact to justify the reorganization of local economies and political systems to meet the goals of the Inca elite.

To understand why local elites would have rebelled, we should consider the long-term goals of the Inca leadership for the Cusco region. The Inca state had developed a conquest ideology that encouraged expansion, with its related desire to access large agricultural surpluses and exotic goods that were not available locally. Expansion into the Cuyo area provided direct access to caravan routes to the Amazonian lowlands, but it also gave the Inca state control over both sides of a valley where maize could be grown intensively. Sacred Valley groups like the Cuyos and Huayllacans did not farm the valley bottom intensively, so the Incas used labor tribute to canalize the Vilcanota River, construct hillside agricultural terraces, and build irrigation canals that could bring water several kilometers from the side valleys that they now controlled.

The transformation of valley-bottom lands for maize production involved massive investments in state infrastructure—not only for the terraces and canals for growing maize but also for storage structures, a road system to bind the area to the capital, and administrative buildings for governing the local population. Inca officials would have demanded most of the labor service that had previously been available to support local elites. Over time, Inca administrators became the principal authority for deciding how food was produced, loyalty was rewarded, religious rituals were performed, and conflicts were resolved. While cooperation with the Inca state would have been an attractive short-term strategy for local leaders, it undermined the authority and power of these individuals in the long term. From the Inca perspective, local leaders would be increasingly redundant in local administration, and they probably would have represented the principal means for organizing resistance to the complete subordination of local economies, politics, and religious life.

Whether the final consolidation of the Cusco region was executed in reaction to local rebellions or was initiated by the Incas themselves as part of a new policy to streamline local administration, it appears that the entire Cusco region was reduced to direct Inca control by around AD 1400. This corresponds to the first territorial conquests made outside the Cusco region—the first campaigns of an emerging empire.

From State to Empire:
Strategies for Expansion and Administration

By AD 1400, the Incas had been expanding their territory throughout the Cusco region for as much as two hundred years, a period in which they developed strategies for incorporating and governing new populations. Territorial expansion was justified by a sense that the Inca ruler could have no equal, and the Incas often described military action as being an acceptable reaction to hostile responses from local elites. New polities and ethnic groups were initially incorporated with as little use of direct force as possible, and local leaders were commonly left in charge with oversight from Inca officials. If the threat of war was the iron fist for intimidating resistant groups into subordinating themselves to Inca rule, marriage alliances with local leaders and gifts of exotic goods were the velvet glove that encouraged initial cooperation.

Once new groups had been brought under state governance, the Incas tended to leave local economies largely untouched, using labor tribute to intensify herding and agricultural production in areas that local communities were not using to their full potential. Facilities had to be constructed for storage, administrative activities, and rituals of the state religion, and newly incorporated territories were linked more closely to the capital through the construction of roads. Some new agricultural lands were allocated for local food production and the propitiation of sacred places and shrines (*wak'akuna*), but the majority went to support the Inca state, the cult of the sun, and the lineage of the Inca ruler.

Over time, state administration superseded many of the functions of local leaders, which may explain why these officials would have led rebellions against Inca rule when opportunities presented themselves. Whether or not the Incas were being truthful in their frequent descriptions of local rebellion, it is clear that over time they preferred to administer territory directly, with Inca officials managing the upper-level political and religious activities, the most important of which took place in Cusco.

These patterns of expansion and administration had to be modified as the Incas expanded throughout the Andean region. In the Titicaca Basin, local economies were dominated by herding, and local leaders were wealthy and powerful. On the Pacific coast, several polities already existed where local rulers commanded specialized labor, had a state religion, and were intensively farming most available agricultural land. In Ecuador, the Incas encountered groups that had specialized merchants and used shell ornaments in their exchanges. Inca imperial strategies evolved to meet local conditions, and while the maize-farming valleys of the central Andean highlands show strong evidence of direct administration, other regions saw more indirect means of government. It is likely that the Incas would ultimately have desired to implement direct administration throughout their empire, but they clearly lacked the means to do so at the time of the Spanish Conquest.

The Transformation of the Imperial Heartland

As the Incas conquered farther from the Cusco region, their heartland came to play a different role within the expanding empire. In short, the Inca heartland was promoted above provincial regions as a place apart from the rest of the empire. Most of the autochthonous ethnic groups of the Cusco region were granted honorary Inca status, providing a large population of low-level imperial officials who spoke Quechua, understood Inca state practices, and could be relocated to provincial regions to implement the development of provincial infrastructure and stabilize imperial administration. As local populations were moved throughout the Andes, provincial groups were resettled to the Cusco region as permanent retainers of the Inca elite.

The political economy of the Inca heartland was dominated by the royal Inca lineages and the state religion. The descendants of former rulers controlled estates that their ancestors had established, and the retainer population provided a range of services for the Inca elite, including herding, farming, transportation of goods between regions, and the production of cloth. The Cusco region was ethnically diverse, but the retainer population served royal Inca lineages directly. The population of the Inca elite burgeoned in the imperial period, and while some Inca nobles served as high-level imperial administrators, a large number lived on the estates built by their ancestors and meddled in the politics of the imperial heartland. Estates were developed to provide Inca nobles with relaxation and enjoyment but were probably also used to by powerful individuals—especially the wives and mothers of former Inca rulers—to support the influence of competing factions.

Process and the Study of Inca Origins

This book proposes that historical or structural readings of the Spanish chronicles alone cannot answer the question of how the Inca empire managed to expand so rapidly throughout the Andean region. Chronological problems in the histories and a "great man" interpretive focus have led to the assertion of social and political underdevelopment in the Inca heartland prior to the rise of Pachacutic. Such assumptions are hard to reconcile with what archaeologists and ethnohistorians in other parts of the world have observed about imperial expansion.

The new, process-based interpretation—summarized in the preceding and detailed in the following chapters of this book—can resolve many of the problems with interpreting the Inca past from colonial-period documents. Inspired by the comparative anthropological study of state formation in the archaeological and historical record, this new approach attempts to reconstruct the conditions that made rapid Inca imperial expansion possible. Paradoxically, it is only by turning our attention away from the legendary acts of a single Inca ruler that we can understand how the competing interests and deliberate acts of individuals enabled Inca imperialism. By expanding our interpretive vista beyond Pachacutic's world-changing deeds, we can begin to describe the local effects of Inca expansion, as well as the strategies by which non-Inca elites attempted to maintain local autonomy. A focus on state formation and territorial expansion in the Cusco region permits us to consider how the Inca state came to control large populations and resources, a process through which the strategies used in imperial expansion and administration were developed, tested, and refined.

CHAPTER TWO

State Formation, Imperial Expansion, and the History of Inca Research in the Cusco Region

In promoting a new relationship between historical documents and archaeological data in Inca studies, it is important to state how a focus on regional processes can be preferable to the research orientations that have been influential in recent decades. The Inca empire is one of the best-known pre-Hispanic cultures of the Americas thanks to the research of anthropologists and historians, and a new interpretive paradigm would not be possible without such research. The process-oriented approach advocated here is not intended to negate or replace the existing scholarly literature on historiography or the structural characteristics of imperial Inca society.

Where an interdisciplinary study of long-term regional processes can prove useful is in providing a narrative of the kinds of changes that are most likely to have occurred in the Cusco region, developments that enabled the trajectory of rapid territorial growth throughout the Andean region after AD 1400. While the interpretations presented in this book are based on sixteenth-century historical accounts and archaeological data, its expectations and interpretation are driven by propositions derived from the comparative study of other ancient states and empires. This chapter describes the comparative anthropological approach pursued in this book, presenting a suite of archaeological and historical indicators that guide the interpretive process. Once the theoretical expectations have been articulated, a brief overview of Inca studies in the imperial heartland demonstrates the intellectual debt that this book owes to previous researchers, as well as the ways that it diverges in its conclusions.

Anthropological Perspectives on Imperial Expansion

Many authors remark at the rapidity of Inca imperial expansion, as though it stands out distinctly from that of other early empires.[1] In fact, comparisons with other empires indicate that rapid territorial expansion is a common characteristic of empire building but that the conditions making such expansion possible require an anthropological explanation.[2] While the official histories of imperial societies often focus on the agency of a single individual in establishing an empire—an Alexander the Great, Genghis Khan, or Pachacutic Inca Yupanqui—anthropologists recognize that to achieve monumental results, the actions of even the most brilliant and charismatic individuals are dependent on prevailing ecological and social conditions.[3] In short, it is more significant to understand the development of particular conditions favoring social transformation than to develop biographies of the charismatic individuals who come to be credited with such changes. Rather than debate the historical role of Pachacutic or any other Inca emperor, we should attempt to understand how an Inca polity developed that could take advantage of particular political and ecological conditions in the Andes to expand so rapidly. A cursory look at a few other empires that achieved rapid territorial expansion provides some important clues for reconstructing the conditions under which the Inca empire developed.

Early Roman Imperial Expansion (ca. 264–134 BC)

The first wave of Roman imperial expansion followed several hundred years of warfare and alliance building between Rome and its Etruscan, Latin, and Samnite neighbors (among others).[4] During the early third century BC, Rome defeated rebellions by Etruscan towns, repulsed Gallic invasions, and fought a prolonged war with the Samnites, becoming mired in the politics of southern Italy, which had been dominated by Greek colonies for several hundred years.[5] As Rome continued to consolidate its control over central Italy, Roman armies were sent to southern Italy in support of allies and were garrisoned in several towns. A fear of growing Roman power led some Greeks living in southern Italy to seek the aid of Pyrrhus, the king of Epirus, who invaded the Italian peninsula in 280 BC. Pyrrhus marched to within 60 kilometers of Rome with a professional army of twenty-five thousand men—and twenty elephants—and the support of the Greek cities of Tarentum, Metapontum, and Heraclea, as well as the Samnites, Lucanians, Bruttians, and Messapians. Most Roman allies failed to defect to the Greek cause, however, and after several costly victories over Roman armies, Pyrrhus abandoned Italy, leaving Rome the undisputed power on the peninsula.

The first war with the Carthaginian empire began just a decade later.[6] Erich Gruen provides a brief description of Rome's position in 265 BC, on the eve of its first major territorial expansion outside of the Italian peninsula:

> The Italian peninsula was now united under Roman hegemony. Through absorption, annexation, common citizenship, or treaty the Italian states were bound to Rome in common policy. . . . The relative isolation of Italy from the areas conquered by Alexander gave Rome the time needed to extend her influence and consolidate her holdings at home. The city's central location in the peninsula, astride the Tiber, afforded a unique position for dominion and control. And Italy's central position in the Mediterranean basin enabled Rome to face both east and west. By 265 Roman legions, drawn from the peasantry and fighting for their city and homes, had already proved their skill under fire for generations. Rome won the loyalty of Italy, not only through force of arms, but through extension of the franchise and sharing of institutions.[7]

From 264 to 134 BC, Rome expanded rapidly, conquering a rival empire, Carthage, and incorporating its territories as new provinces. It also annexed the city-states of Greece and Asia Minor into this developing imperial order. In roughly the same span of time that Inca territory expanded to control much of the Andean region, Rome rose from a leading power in the Italian peninsula to become the preeminent power in the Mediterranean world.[8] The critical invasion of Pyrrhus (280–75 BC) may have been important for determining the tempo by which the final resistance to Roman order in Italy was defeated, but like the Chanca invasion of the Cusco region—said to have been the stimulus for Pachacutic's transformation of the Inca polity—this appears to have occurred toward the *end* of a long regional integration process.[9]

The Aztec Triple Alliance (c. AD 1428–1520)

The period leading up the rise of Aztec civilization remains shrouded in myth and imperial propaganda.[10] Like the Incas, the Mexica elite recounted what Michael E. Smith describes as a "rags-to-riches story," a myth involving migration from a distant origin place by a small group that was destined to rise to dominance over the many Postclassic polities of central Mexico.[11] Through alliance manipulation and the use of force, the Mexica and their allies consolidated their control over most of the complex polities (*altepetl*) in the Basin of Mexico between about AD 1250 and 1430.[12] Stories of Mexica origins describe the initial settlement of their capital, Tenochtitlán, which grew rapidly and came to be supported by intensive raised-field agriculture. Although the Mexica were originally subordinates to the nearby Tepanec polity, they eventually appointed as ruler (*tlatoani*) a man said to be descended from the Toltecs. Smith describes the rule of Huitzilhuitl(r. AD 1391–1415) in the final decades leading up to the emergence of the Aztec Triple Alliance:

> Under his popular leadership, people came from all over the Valley of Mexico to live in Tenochtitlan, and the city expanded greatly. The Mexica became highly skilled as soldiers and diplomats in their dealings with neighbors. One of Huitzilhuitl's major accomplishments was the establishment of successful marriage alliances with a number of powerful dynasties. . . . In addition to his diplomatic success, Huitzilhuitl also led the Mexica to victory in a number of military campaigns.[13]

In 1428, when the Mexica under Itzcoatl successfully rebelled against Tepanec domination, their polity was already wealthy and powerful, with a reputation as able diplomats and fierce warriors. The Mexica and their allies quickly incorporated the complex polities of the Valley of Mexico, then extended their territory rapidly for roughly ninety years, incorporating large parts of Mesoamerica into their provincial system.[14] When Hernán Cortés reached the Gulf Coast in 1519, the Aztec empire was the largest polity to develop in Mesoamerica.

Prior to its short phase of imperial expansion, Mexica society developed several important features, including an urban capital, a system of intensive agriculture that could feed a large, nucleated population, and a government-supervised marketplace for acquiring and exchanging staples and exotic goods. The Mexica elite held specialized positions, achieving status as warriors, diplomats, and merchants. Marriages were the basis for many alliances with groups in the Valley of Mexico, as well as polities beyond that region.

Conditions Enabling Rapid Imperial Expansion

We could discuss many other examples of rapid imperial expansion, but the preceding cases are sufficient to demonstrate not only that other early empires managed to incorporate vast new territories in 100–150 years but that the polities embarking on such campaigns had developed a certain degree of hierarchy and complexity.[15] Many anthropologists would identify the kinds of changes described for the preimperial Roman and Mexica polities as processes resulting in the formation of a centralized state.

State Formation and Its Archaeological Indicators

Anthropological archaeologists have debated the nature of state formation and have presented several means for evaluating political complexity in the archaeological record.[16] For this book, I define a state as a polity characterized by a centralized and internally specialized government.[17]

Archaeological indicators of state formation can be identified at several different interpretive levels, and such identifications are most secure when multiple indicators are present.[18] State formation often takes place within a relatively small region and is often followed by territorial expansion (table 2.1). At the regional level, the development of a four-tier settlement hierarchy and a log-normal or primate rank-size graph have been interpreted as evidence for increasingly hierarchical and centralized organization,[19] an apparatus settlement system considered to be consistent with an administrative hierarchy that is more complex than those

TABLE 2.1.   Estimates of Integrated State Territory

Name	Integrated Territory	Dates	Source
Susa	Up to 20,000 km^2	Middle Uruk	Wright 1998
Warka	15,000+ km^2	Early Uruk	Johnson 1980, 248
Monte Albán	20,000 km^2	MA II	Marcus and Flannery 1996
Tikal	20,000+ km^2	Early Classic	Adams and Jones 1981
Teotihuacán	25,000–50,000 km^2	Early Classic	Marcus 1998
Rome	20,000+ km^2	Fourth to third century BC	Harris 1979
Maradi	8,000 km^2	1854–75	Smith 1967
Dahomey	24,000 km^2	Nineteenth century	Spencer 1990
Benin	About 10,000 km^2	Nineteenth century	Bradbury 1967

of prestate societies. Log-normal rank-size graphs are often taken as evidence of centrally coordinated regional economies, but in cases where the urban capital of the state is disproportionately large, the graph may be convex.[20]

At the site level, the construction of palaces and appearance of standardized religious and administrative building forms can indicate the establishment of state institutions.[21] The leaders of prestate polities are typically not capable of using labor tribute to construct palatial residences, and the standardization of religious and administrative architecture is thought to accompany the development of religious and administrative hierarchies. Qualitative changes in the presence of exotic materials and craft products might also be considered evidence of economic centralization or social stratification concomitant with state formation.

The archaeological evidence for other cases of state formation suggests that multiple indicators are needed to demonstrate such processes unambiguously.[22] The success of the archaeological model depends on the existence of sufficient data to identify multiple indicators of Inca state formation.

Oral Histories and Processes of State Formation

In chapter 1, several problems with the historicity of the Spanish chronicles were noted. Narratives of the past were reorganized repeatedly in Inca times, and their transcription decades after the conquest was often influenced by an author's political intentions, philosophical convictions, or notions of proper historiography. The colonial period documents describing the Inca past cannot be treated as a complete and factual chronology of events performed by historical individuals, and scholars ought to explore other useful ways of studying them. The archaeological record provides one means for evaluating what kind of society the Incas lived in at the time of their initial imperial expansion, and it is possible to read the historical documents in a compatible way to identify the same processes of state formation described in the archaeological record.

Just as the archaeological indicators of state formation enumerated in the preceding are derived from the comparative study of several archaeologically known states, it is possible to identify indicators of state formation in the oral histories of societies known to have experienced such processes. Using the same basic definition as for archaeological cases—a suite of qualitative changes involving the emergence of a centralized, internally specialized government—it is possible to identify state formation for several societies, including Dahomey in West Africa, the Betsileo and Merina of Madagascar, and Hunza in Kashmir. Some of the kinds of innovations mentioned in the oral histories of these cultures are presented in table 2.2, which lists the numbers of rulers credited with a particular development.

Kent Flannery has recently observed that the role of human agency becomes more pronounced when we consider historical cases of state formation.[23] In looking at long-term, regional processes, we do not focus on the "state makers" glorified in the oral histories but instead identify how a given polity changed internally and in relation to its neighbors. From the table, it is possible to see that emerging states often develop more intensive economies in which production is centrally managed through laws and religious ceremonies that are controlled by the elite.

TABLE 2.2.   Some Ethnohistoric Indicators of State Formation Processes

	Merina	Betsileo	Dahomey	Hunza
Territorial control of over 2000 km²	Ruler 3	Ruler 7	Ruler 4	Ruler 4
Reduction of local autonomy	3	4–7	4	4
Growth of capital (immigration)	3	4–7	2	4
Permanent military conquests	3	5	2	2
Codification of judicial system	N/A	4–5	3	4
Imposition of tribute requirements	N/A	5	3	4
Complex elite hierarchies with more titles	2	5	4	4
Asymmetrical marriage alliances	1	N/A	1	N/A
Construction of palaces or royal estates	3	N/A	3	N/A
Intensification of production	3	5–7	N/A	4
Sumptuary laws, direct state access to exotics	2	5	3	4
Calendrical reform, management of specialized production	1	N/A	N/A	4
Co-option of local religion or rituals	2–3	N/A	3	3
Development of state religion and religious hierarchy	2–3	5	3	3
Introduction of technological innovations	1	N/A	N/A	4
Introduction of military innovations	1–2	5	3	N/A

Note: Numbers indicate which ruler (or rulers) in a multigenerational sequence is credited with a given development. For the Merina, ruler 1 is Andriamanelo (see Brown 1979, 120–30 for sequence). Kottak (1980, 67–81) discusses Betsileo state formation, noting that the process began with rulers 3 and 4, a woman and her son. Herskovits (1938, 11, 13) discusses several ruler lists for Dahomey; for this table, ruler 1 is Dogbagri, and the account of Argyle (1866, 3–13) is used. The Hunza case uses information in Sidkey (1996) and considers Mir Silim Khan as ruler 4 in the process of state formation.

Immigration to the capital increases, and increased agricultural production feeds a growing urban population of retainers, craft specialists, and bureaucrats. The management of a centralized economy and large population requires special administrative and religious offices, and elite hierarchies become more complex as the state forms. New intermediate elites are supported by tribute, tax collection, or labor service, which is also used by the ruling elite to build palaces and private estates, as well as to acquire exotic goods not available locally. Externally, the emerging state begins to conquer or annex new territory, reducing previously autonomous neighboring elites to subordinates. Conquests are often made in order to acquire productive resources or control over important trade routes. The permanent incorporation of new territory requires that new provincial officials be appointed.

As with archaeological indicators for state formation, it is the identification of a whole set of changes—rather than the innovation of any single indicator—that will help us to recognize the development of a centralized state government. We are seeking evidence of a fundamental change in the nature of Inca society, as well as the ways that the Incas interacted with neighboring groups. Since multiple versions of the Inca past exist, we should be able to identify the same kinds of changes in independent sources.[24] The most useful sources for this analytical process will be those that provide detailed information on events occurring within about 50 kilometers of Cusco prior to the reign of Pachacutic. While the archaeological evidence provides the means for evaluating the historical sources, it is critical to avoid selecting only the information that corroborates our anthropological expectations.

Process-Based Perspectives and the Study of the Inca Past

Although the formation of an Inca state exhibiting the same traits as the cultures in the comparative study would have major significance for anthropologists focusing on long-term changes in regional databases, it would have had far less relevance to the sixteenth-century Incas and Europeans whose interest in the Inca past was oriented toward contesting the time depth of the imperial period. Many writers attempting to diminish the Inca imperial achievement recount incidents relevant to the study of state formation. The repeated reorganization of Inca histories certainly would have affected how the processes of state formation were remembered, but this becomes less important if multiple versions of the Inca past describe the same kinds of changes observed in other cases of state formation.

Even though the interpretive approach proposed in this book takes a methodological departure from most modern historical studies, there is a long tradition of process-based studies of the Incas. Polo de Ondegardo, one of the most astute early colonial administrators, observed that "these Incas conquered through violence and warfare . . . and thus the only difficulty was in conquering those neighboring polities in the Cusco region, because afterwards, all the conquered groups went with them [the Incas], and it was always a much larger force than the others [i.e., opposing local groups]."[25] In 1571, Ondegardo speculated that Inca imperialism had developed through processes occurring over 350–400 years in which the region within about 25 kilometers of Cusco was consolidated under Inca control.[26] Pedro Sarmiento de Gamboa concluded that Inca strategies for expansion and consolidation were transformed under Pachacutic's father following several generations of raiding and indirect control over the strongest rivals to the Inca polity.[27]

If some colonial writers—especially those who developed synthetic prespectives on the Inca past using multiple lines of evidence—recognized that local processes in the Cusco region had somehow made Inca imperial expansion possible, why have modern scholars fixed upon the story of Pachacutic and the Chanca invasion as the most reasonable explanation of imperial origins? The simplest answer to this question is that the Pachacutic story provides the most reasonable paradigm for describing Inca *imperial* expansion, regardless of its shortcomings in addressing the processes leading up to such expansion.

Although many of the most reliable colonial authors describe a rapid phase of imperial expansion by the last few Inca rulers, several chronicles offer a gradual perspective on Inca imperialism, generally describing a more steady imperial territorial expansion from the time of the founding Inca ancestor, Manco Capac.[28] Until the 1940s, scholars such as Philip Ainsworth Means suggested that the story of a rapid Inca imperial expansion was a Spanish invention, devised to discredit the Incas and portray them as parvenu tyrants outside of Cusco.[29] A series of influential publications in the 1940s by John H. Rowe reoriented the debate over Inca imperial expansion and firmly established the rapid expansion model as the one best supported by the available ethnohistoric and archaeological evidence from the Inca heartland and provinces.

In 1945, Rowe observed that archaeological evidence, coupled with different kinds of reliable ethnohistoric sources, pointed to a rapid and late Inca imperial expansion. His systematic study of Inca political origins using archaeology and a critical reading of documents shifted the question of Inca political origins from a historical to an anthropological one. The German archaeologist Max Uhle had advocated a more active interpretive role for archaeology several decades earlier, but Rowe was the first to develop artifact chronologies in coordination with documentary research on the Incas.[30] The rapid expansion paradigm for Inca imperialism still stands largely intact today, and most archaeologists agree with its general processes, if not the calendar dates presented in the Inca histories.[31] In the 1940s, Rowe did not attempt to push the available data to resolve the issue of *how* such rapid expansion was made possible, although he did suggest that some chronicles contained information on developmental processes after about AD 1200 and leading up to Inca imperial expansion.[32] Without a strong independent database from regional archaeology, the chronicle references to early developments in the Inca polity were considered too unreliable to be studied critically.[33]

Long-Term Change and Inca Origins

Shifting the interpretive focus to processes of long-term change is the first step in moving beyond "great man" paradigms of Inca origins to develop more anthropological perspectives on the Inca empire. Scholars following the paradigm of rapid Inca imperial expansion have attempted to explain the conditions that enabled (or necessitated) such rapid, punctuated expansion. Factors hypothesized to have influenced the Inca developmental trajectory include institutionalized exchange relationships, internal conflict and interregional hostility, the centralization of economic management and redistribution, and ideological innovations.[34] Even in the absence of new data, significant scholarship has shifted the interpretive focus from singular events and the deeds of heroes and kings to the long-term development of social, economic, military, and ideological power. Like these scholars, many archaeologists tend to explain rapid Inca imperialism as the result of long-term regional processes of state formation and political consolidation.[35]

Archaeological Inquiry in the Cusco Region

In the nineteenth century, Cusco was a destination for many European travelers exploring South America, and authors such as Charles Wiener and Ephraim Squier provide descriptions of some of the region's surviving archaeological monuments.[36] Aside from the acquisition of collections (probably from looted tombs), Max Uhle's excavations at Q'atan near modern Urubamba, and Hiram Bingham's work at Machu Picchu, little systematic excavation work was undertaken prior to the 1930s.[37] Archaeological research in the Cusco region began to flourish in the early 1930s, due to an increase in government funding to celebrate the four hundredth anniversary of the Spanish founding of the city of Cusco.[38] At this time, Peruvian archaeologists began to conduct large-scale excavations at such monumental Inca sites as Saqsaywaman.[39]

The interpretive power of Cusco archaeology improved with the establishment of a preliminary artifact sequence by Rowe in 1944. Since the 1940s, the archaeological understanding of the pre-Columbian past has expanded as researchers have elaborated the artifact chronology and explored important time periods in the region. Large-scale excavations have been conducted throughout the region and have addressed the full range of human occupation in the Cusco region.[40] The protection and study of monumental sites by the National Institute of Culture (INC) has led to the identification of hundreds of archaeological sites within the Inca heartland.

Systematic Surveys in the Inca Heartland

While excavation work has increased the interpretive power of relative artifact chronologies, regional systematic survey projects have begun to map changing settlement patterns in the Cusco region (fig. 2.1). Prior to the 1980s, numerous researchers had reconnoitered the region, making observations on the sites they encountered, but not systematically studying a defined region.[41] The first systematic regional survey project was conducted in the Paruro area by Brian Bauer, who directed a pedestrian survey of over 600 square kilometers in a region just south of the Cusco Basin, registering over four hundred sites in a region where only a handful had previously been known.[42] Based on settlement pattern continuities in Paruro after AD 1000, Bauer concluded that an Inca state had formed in Cusco well before AD 1400, extending its control over the

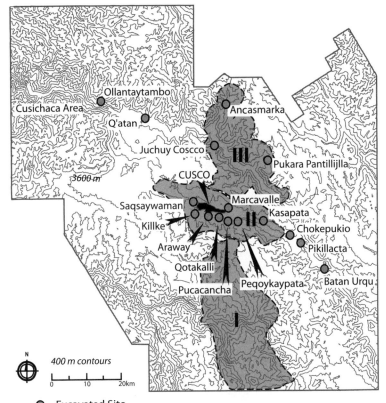

● Excavated Site

I. Paruro Archaeological Project, directed by Brian Bauer
II. Cusco Valley Archaeological Project, directed by Bauer
III. Sacred Valley Archaeological Project, directed by author

Fig. 2.1. Important sites and survey projects in the Cusco region. Although excavations have been conducted in the region for nearly a century, it was only in the
late 1980s that systematic regional settlement data made it possible to describe pre-
Inca settlement patterns.

Paruro region without substantial modification to local political and
economic organization.[43]

Testing the hypothesis of early Inca state formation led Bauer to direct a second major regional survey in the Cusco Basin, a region in which
approximately fourteen hundred sites were identified (fig. 2.2).[44] Settlement patterns in the Cusco Basin and to the east and west provided a
second major region for comparing settlement change over time, and the

Fig. 2.2. The Cusco Basin, ca. 1930. (Negative no. 334756, Courtesy Dept. of Library Services, American Museum of Natural History.)

presence of an early Inca state has been substantiated with the new data.[45] The same methodology and artifact sequence were used in both surveys, providing a foundation for expanding the regional database with subsequent survey projects.[46]

The Sacred Valley Archaeological Project

This book considers Bauer's data from the Paruro and Cusco Basin surveys, but it also presents new data on over four hundred archaeological sites identified by the Sacred Valley Archaeological Project (SVAP), a survey and excavation project conducted in 2000 to expand the results of earlier survey research. The data from the Paruro and Cusco Basin projects had indicated that the Cusco polity developed early political control over the Cusco Basin and modestly populated areas to the south; assessing the extent and timing of this control and its relationship to the Spanish chronicles required that further research be initiated.

The area selected for a third intensive settlement survey was a 30-kilometer stretch of the Vilcanota-Urubamba Valley, from just above the modern town of San Salvador to just below the town of Calca (fig. 2.3).[47] In addition to the main river valley, the study region also included the side valleys draining into the Vilcanota River, a total area of approximately 400 square kilometers. This area was chosen for several reasons. From a practical perspective, the Sacred Valley study region abuts Bauer's Cusco Basin survey, effectively connecting the three regional survey projects into a single 80-kilometer transect of the Inca heartland, a combined study region of about 1300 square kilometers in which over two thousand archaeological sites have been located. The continuities in artifact types made it possible to employ a similar field methodology with an experienced crew of Peruvian archaeology students who had studied the Cusco ceramic chronology.

Geographical and ecological considerations also influenced the definition of the study region. Because the aim of the project was to assess changing levels of influence and political control over the region, it was important to include areas that were close to the Cusco Basin, as well as lands that would have been beyond the administrative capabilities of an unspecialized government.[48] The Chit'apampa Basin is located about a half day's walk from Cusco, while walking to the Chongo and Qochoq valleys to the north of the Vilcanota River would involve a much greater

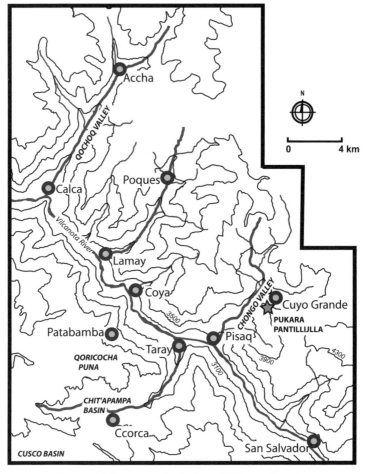

Fig. 2.3. Modern towns in the Sacred Valley study region

time and energy investment. Some sites in the Chongo Valley were over 25 kilometers from Cusco and would require over 2500 meters of vertical climbing in each direction. The site of Ancasmarca (in the Qochoq Valley) was even more distant, with a similar elevation change. Based on environmental constraints, it was hypothesized that complex polities in the southern part of the survey region could be governed without the need for a specialized administrative hierarchy, but that the successful incorporation of groups living to the north of the Vilcanota River would require state-level political organization.

Ecologically, the study region was designated to focus on all areas of agricultural production, with small areas of high-elevation grassland (*puna*) included in the survey. Based on the traditional ecozone identifications described in the following chapter, the study region included areas of maize production in the lowest areas of the survey—from about 2900 meters around Calca—up to approximately 3600 meters in irrigated areas. Elevations from 3300 to 3800 meters are used today to dry-farm a wide range of crops. Above this is a zone of tuber production, and areas of grassy *puna* are found above 4000 meters. As defined, the study region included an elevation range of 2900–4500 meters, where a variety of human activities would have occurred in prehistory. Data on land use patterns, crop yields, and cultivation practices were available from ecological studies of the Vilcanota Valley and some side valleys in the survey region.[49]

One final consideration, and certainly not an insignificant one, was that the study region is mentioned frequently in the Spanish chronicles and colonial archival documents. Archaeologists had already identified and studied several Inca and pre-Inca sites in the region (fig. 2.4), including Ancasmarca, Juchuy Coscco, Warq'ana, Muyu Muyu, and Pukara Pantillijlla.[50] Because earlier survey projects had identified where Inca state control was articulated early on—and without major disruption to existing settlement patterns—it was important to consider a region whose ethnic inhabitants had more complex, and often more contentious, interactions with the expanding Cusco state. Several Inca histories state that some local populations in the Sacred Valley were displaced during the Inca imperial period and their resources were developed as royal estates, four of which (Paullu, Caquia Xaquixaguana, Pisaq, Calca) were known to lie within the study area (fig. 2.5).

In addition to regional survey work, the Sacred Valley Archaeological Project included excavations at the site of Pukara Pantillijlla, a large ridgetop village that was probably called Cuyomarca in Inca times.[51] Five complete buildings were excavated at the site, as well as five test units, a total area of over 200 square meters that yielded a large sample of pottery and other artifacts. These excavations provide evidence of domestic occupation at the site prior to its incorporation into the Inca polity, as well as the period during which the site functioned as a secondary administrative site for the Inca state.

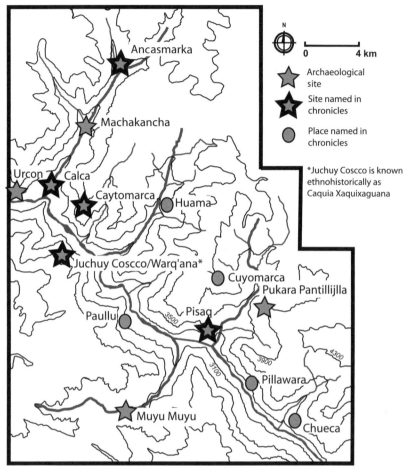

Fig. 2.4. Sacred Valley sites known from the Spanish chronicles and previous archaeological research

Summary

As we have seen in this chapter, many factors make rapid imperial territorial expansion possible, but one common feature of successful imperialism is the formation of a state that has begun to develop a centrally administered core region or heartland. Although long-distance conquests are known to precede the full administrative consolidation of this heartland, the state will have begun to unify previously independent groups

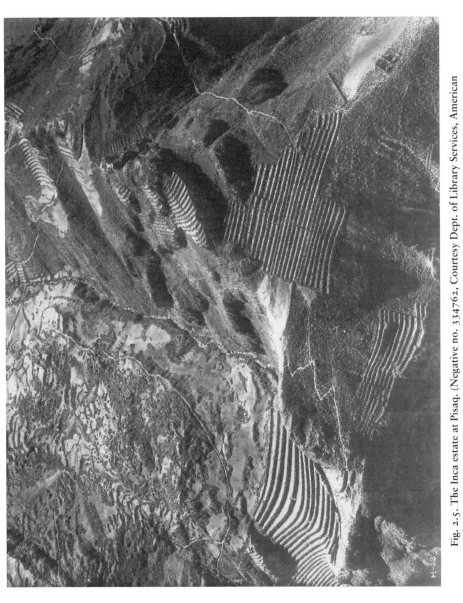

Fig. 2.5. The Inca estate at Pisaq. (Negative no. 334762, Courtesy Dept. of Library Services, American Museum of Natural History.)

under a centralized government that has a distinct ideology and shared ethnicity or citizenship. Within this region, the state will govern a large population and manage an intensified political economy, both of which provide the basis for a military force capable of, and ideologically inclined to, a program of extended conquest. Many of the strategies for expansion and territorial administration developed during the state formation and regional consolidation process become the means for rapid imperial expansion.

The proposition that state formation provided the means for rapid Inca imperial expansion not only accords with the regnant paradigm for rapid imperial expansion first articulated by Rowe but also offers an interpretive point of departure for the archaeological and historical study of Inca imperial origins. Regional settlement data and site-level excavations can be used to determine whether multiple indicators of Inca state formation are present before AD 1400, while a process-based reading of the Inca histories can identify some of the kinds of human interactions that would have occurred during the generations leading up to the first imperial campaigns.

Although this book's approach may depart from the methods and conclusions of some previous studies, it is consistent with the process-based approaches of other archaeologists and ethnohistorians. The collection of new archaeological data from the Sacred Valley study region permits a detailed analysis of the problem with reference to a huge volume of previous archaeological and documentary studies. The new data confirm the propositions of many researchers as well as the expectations of anthropological archaeologists.

CHAPTER THREE

Ecology and Risk Reduction
in the Inca Heartland

In seeking to identify whether Inca state formation provided the basis for imperial expansion, we should also consider why a state would form in the Cusco Basin when it did. To do so, the process-based study of the ethnohistoric and archaeological data must be grounded in an understanding of the effects of environmental variability and climatic fluctuation on processes of culture change. Environmental conditions in the Cusco region today are highly variable, and human groups have pursued different strategies to manage environmental risks under specific ecological parameters. Certain conditions might seem amenable to the development or persistence of centralized states, but others would encourage strategies requiring less complex social and economic organization.

In this chapter, the major ecological zones of the Cusco region are described, permitting us to consider two possible strategies that early sedentary farming groups could have used to reduce risk. Having looked at variations in the Cusco landscape, it is possible to address the question of climate change and its implications for human settlement patterns in the centuries leading up to Inca imperial expansion.

Environmental Zones of the Cusco Region

Many valuable studies of the ecology of the Cusco region have been published since the 1970s.[1] In addition, extensive ethnographic fieldwork has been conducted throughout the region, identifying local patterns of production and management of natural resources.[2] In order to understand how the political economy of the Inca imperial heartland related to preimperial ethnic and ritual divisions, it is important to consider native ecological divisions within this large region. This book follows the typology employed by Jeffrey Parsons and colleagues, which is based

TABLE 3.1.   Ecological Zones in the Cusco Region

Ecozone	Elevations and Human Use	SVAP Area (%)
Cordillera	4700–5700 meters; no economic use	0
Upper *puna*	4200–4700 meters; pastoralism	~5
Lower *puna*	3850–4200 meters; camelid pastoralism, tuber horticulture	~25
Upper *kichwa* (*suni*)	3500–3850 meters; mixed farming of tubers, grains, tarwi	~30
Lower *kichwa*	2700–3500 meters; maize agriculture	~40
Ceja de montaña	Below 2700 meters; cultivation of maize, tropical fruits, coca leaf	0

on a number of classic geographical studies of Andean ecology.[3] These researchers identify six principal ecological zones for the Andean highlands: *cordillera, puna* (separated into upper and lower subzones), *kichwa* (also separated into an upper subzone [*suni*] and a lower one), *ceja de montaña, montaña,* and *selva* (or *yunka*). The most important ecozones of the Cusco region are the first four, and their approximate elevations and general production characteristics are listed in Table 3.1.

Cordillera

By definition, the *cordillera* lies above elevations where widespread human subsistence activities are common. In the Cusco region, many snow-capped mountains lying in this zone were venerated by the Incas and their neighbors, including Pitusiray, Sawasiray, Salcantay, and Ausangate.[4] Today, pilgrimages to the glaciers of Ausangate during the Qoyllur Rit'i festival mark important ritual congregations of groups from throughout the region, and the mountain of Pachatusan is part of an important pilgrimage from the Cusco Basin to the sanctuary of Wanka in the Sacred Valley.[5] Lower peaks without permanent snow cover (e.g., Pachatusan, Huanacaure) were also venerated regionally as sacred places (*wak'akuna*).[6]

Areas of glaciated *cordillera* are found to the west of Cusco, as well as to the north of the Sacred Valley, although there are many other areas of high elevation, as seen in figure 3.1. The *cordillera* and upper *puna* surround relatively small valley areas where agriculture and herding can sustain large, dense populations. In Inca times the highest peaks were

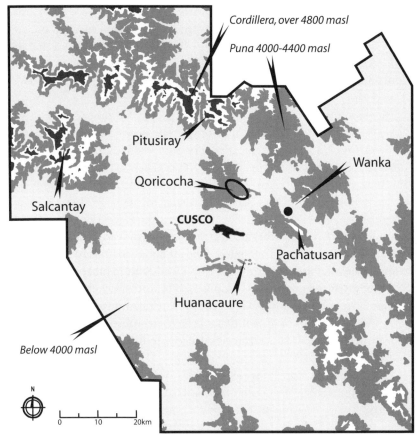

Fig. 3.1. Areas of high-elevation grassland (*puna*) and *cordillera* in the Inca heartland

used to delimit territorial boundaries (*saywa*) and were revered as the most important shrines in local and regional ritual life.

Puna

The *puna* zone in the Cusco region is not nearly as extensive as in the Titicaca Basin or Junín regions, but it did represent an important economic area in pre-Hispanic times. In the Cusco region, the upper *puna* (particularly elevations above 4200 meters) tends to consist of small spring-fed valleys and rolling high plains that would have provided excellent pasture for camelid herds, as well as habitat for wild vicuñas and deer species.[7] These areas are not productive agricultural zones, and many modern Andean herders living at such elevations make exchanges with agricultural communities at lower elevations. The viability of small family herds is maintained through social relationships that reduce risks of predation, theft, and herd disease.[8]

The lower *puna* is used for grazing, as well as for tuber horticulture, with a wide variety of potato and other root crops (including oca, *ullucu, mashua,* and *maca*) typically cultivated in small, dispersed plots.[9] Above 4000 meters, only the hardiest, most frost-resistant crops thrive, and soils need long fallow periods between cultivations. Several researchers have noted the incredible diversity of tuber production in the Cusco region, often counting several dozen different varieties in a single community.[10] Andean tuber production is aimed at averaging out ecological risks over time and space. The practice of freeze-drying root crops (especially bitter potatoes) allows families to manage annual crop variations, while maintaining biodiversity and dispersed plots reduces the risk of total crop failure in a given year.[11] Ecological studies in the Department of Puno by Carol Goland have demonstrated that the efficacy of such risk reduction strategies declines as distance from the household increases.[12]

Puna grasslands are prevalent to the south of the Cusco Valley, as well as on both sides of the Sacred Valley. The Qoricocha area just north of Cusco is still an important herding area, and the chronicler Bernabé Cobo mentions that the Incas kept state herds there (fig. 3.2).[13] Lower *puna* lands are common throughout the Cusco region and represent important agricultural resources for the production of tubers.[14]

Suni

As with the lower *puna* elevations, lands in the upper *kichwa* (also known as *suni*) tend to be dry-farmed and are exploited in the same system of small, diversity-rich plots (fig. 3.3). *Suni* lands can often be used for more than one growing season but require an extended fallow period to recover. Within this zone, horticultural products include quinoa, *kañiwa,* amaranth, *tarwi, ñuñas* (popping beans), and many of the root crops mentioned in the preceding. Studies in the Cusco region indicate that European cultigens like wheat, barley, broad beans, and onions have replaced many of the Andean crops, which are hardy and nutritious but

Fig. 3.2. The Qoricocha *puna*, an area where Inca elites are known to have kept herds of llamas and alpacas.

Fig. 3.3. Modern dry-farming of upper *kichwa* plots. Beans, tubers, and other cultigens are intercropped in the same field.

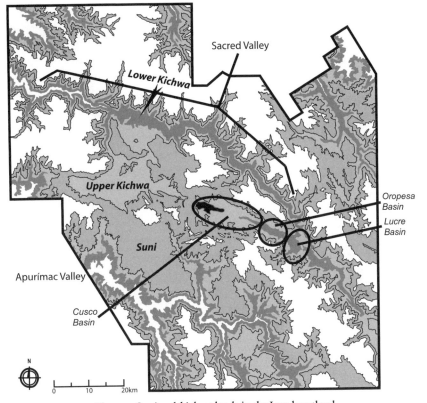

Fig. 3.4. *Suni* and *kichwa* lands in the Inca heartland

more difficult to process.[15] *Suni* lands dominate the sides of most valleys in the Cusco region, including much of the Anta-Maras-Chinchero area. Annual rainfall in the Cusco Basin and Anta-Maras-Chinchero area averages around 740 millimeters but is extremely variable from one year to another.[16]

Lower *Kichwa*

In distinction to the *suni* zone, Cusco's lower *kichwa* elevations are dominated by intensive maize agriculture, particularly between 2800 and 3200 meters (fig. 3.4). Improved maize lands are the most productive agricultural resource in the region but have very limited distribution. The floor of the Cusco Basin is used for maize production, as are parts of the Oropesa and Lucre basins. The most productive maize lands are found in the Vilcanota-Urubamba Valley, from below Quiquijana to around Ollantaytambo.[17] Below 3200 meters, the risk of frost is much lower, but these areas tend to receive much less rain than the upper *kichwa* lands around the Cusco Basin. Four towns in the prime maize-producing zone (Urubamba, Yucay, Calca, and Pisaq) receive an average of about 520 millimeters of annual precipitation, which is so variable that irrigation is necessary to ensure crop success.

Intensive maize can be grown most successfully near the valley bottoms throughout much of the Cusco region, and many narrow valleys like the Apurímac do not offer large areas for cultivation. Others have had to be improved to deal with seasonal flooding, meandering river beds, and steep valley sides (fig. 3.5). The early Inca state is thought to have executed much of this intensification.

Ceja de Montaña

In Cusco, *ceja de montaña* lands are restricted to the areas of Vilcabamba, Lares, and Paucartambo. Traveling to these areas from Cusco is difficult, as the Vilcanota Valley and some major areas of *cordillera* must be traversed. This zone is warmer and more humid than the *kichwa* and can be used for the cultivation of crops prized by highland groups, such as coca leaf and chile peppers (*uchu*). Some tropical fruits can be cultivated in this area as well, and some lowland varieties of maize flourish here.[18]

Montaña and Selva

The *montaña* and *selva* ecozones did not form an important part of the Inca heartland. Indeed, the Incas viewed the tropical lowlands as a culturally foreign place that was dangerous and unhealthy for long-term occupation.[19] In terms of agricultural products, these zones produce very different foods, including yuca, peanuts, and sweet potato. Natural and wild products like honey, feathers, and gold came from these areas, but the chronicles suggest that the Incas did not administer territory in the *montaña* and *selva* to the north and east of Cusco until the imperial period.

As with other parts of the Andean highlands, there is tremendous variability in climate, precipitation, and geology within the general elevation

M-27

Fig. 3.5. River canalization and terraces at Pisaq. (Negative no. 334763, Courtesy Dept. of Library Services, American Museum of Natural History.)

zones described.[20] As a region, Cusco has a diverse distribution of agro-pastoral resources, but its modern economic base is characterized by *kichwa* groups who coordinate the production of diverse resources. Contemporary communities near Cusco use a variety of means to exploit a wide range of ecological zones, including social relationships, archipelagic settlement patterns, and market exchange.[21]

Two Strategies of Agricultural Risk Management

Understanding the Inca state as a *kichwa*-based polity raises the issue of political economy and strategies for risk reduction. The simplest distinction to make in discussing this is between dry-farming and the pursuit of more intensive agricultural methods, namely irrigation, artificial fertilization, and improvement of farmland.[22] Dry-farming of a wide variety of crops is possible on most lands in the Cusco region, while intensive irrigation-based agriculture is much more restricted. The risk-reduction benefits of dry-farming can be realized with relatively low population densities, the maintenance of social relationships, and a relatively simple political economy. Intensive agriculture reduces risk through surplus production, storage, and improved techniques, permitting higher population densities but generally requiring more centralized or complex management. It is important to point out that these strategies are not mutually exclusive. State political economies might focus on intensive agriculture while subsistence farmers practice dry-farming, even though they might prefer more intensive methods.

The Sacred Valley study region is characterized by two main economic production areas. Improved valley-bottom lands represent a small percentage of agricultural lands, but they yield huge agricultural surpluses, almost exclusively maize. Many of these lands were developed by the Incas and have remained as private properties in the hands of Cusco's elite until the present. In the side valleys that drain into the Vilcanota-Urubamba River, some irrigation is possible at lower elevations, but most agricultural production consists of dry-farming multiple plots in upper *kichwa* and *suni* lands, where a diverse array of products is grown. Dry-farming is pursued on the vast majority of agricultural lands in the Cusco region, but such resources must be rotated and fallowed to ensure soil quality. Most dry-farmed lands are now held corporately by peasant communities who manage land use at the community level.

Dry-Farming as Subsistence Agriculture

Ideally, subsistence agriculture focuses on satisfizing rather than the production of surplus—that is, meeting household food needs with a minimum of labor input and risk.[23] Household production cannot simply track anticipated needs, however; it must also cope with possible fluctuations in productivity caused by climatic variation.[24] For small groups of sedentary farmers, this has traditionally involved a focus on crop diversity and maintenance of multiple small plots as a means of buffering the risks of crop failure and starvation.[25] Temperature, precipitation, and other climatic factors fluctuate widely throughout a given region, as well as from year to year, creating a patchy resource base that is unpredictable from one year to the next.[26] To minimize risk, Andean peasants intercrop multiple varieties and species in the same plot and maintain multiple plots in different locations.[27] Crop rotation and fallowing are necessary to maintain soil quality, and modern peasant communities manage such practices locally.

Farming multiple plots in a mountain environment means that in a given year at least *some* plots should be productive, but cultivating diversity also incurs travel costs, thereby reducing net caloric yield of a given crop.[28] Generally speaking, the proximity of land resources sets effective limits for diversity, and Andean peasants must balance risk management with potential declines in net caloric yield, rejecting the expansion of diet breadth when it would impose negative (or risky) net returns.[29]

Crop diversity, while an important risk-management strategy, is perceived by peasant farmers as the means to satisfying a "complete" diet breadth. Working in the Paucartambo Valley, Karl Zimmerer has shown how food is used to shape cultural identity and status, noting a recent trend among Andean peasants to value native cultigens over European ones.[30] It is clear that culinary values and considerations of secondary production costs (e.g., processing, requirements of fertilization, weeding, etc.) influence decisions of what to cultivate.[31] A complex set of criteria determines the *cultural* value of a given species or variety, and it has been observed that sometimes the cultivation of rare or low-yielding varieties is undertaken because of their high status as gifts.[32]

Based on settlement locations, many pre-Hispanic agricultural groups in the Cusco region probably relied primarily on agroecological diversity to reduce risk, cultivating several kinds of crops to maintain a complete diet (fig. 3.6). For groups engaged in both farming and herding, the principal settlements would tend to be located at the transitional elevations between production zones in order to maximize diversity while minimizing travel costs. Even after the introduction of intensive maize or tuber agriculture as a production strategy, diversity-rich farming has continued in one form or another until the present.[33] Principal carbohydrate sources for Andean farming groups include maize and root crops such as potatoes (*Solanum* spp.), oca (*Oxalis tuberosa*), *ullucu* (*Ullucus tuberosus*), *mashua* (or *añu*, *Tropaeolum tuberosum*), and possibly *maca* (*Lepidium meyenii*), many of which are still cultivated in the Cusco area.[34] While maize has a limited distribution in the Sacred Valley—typically in irrigated fields below 3500 meters—different varieties of tuber crops can be dry-farmed at elevations up to 4300 meters and are still grown today in an astonishing diversity. As Robert Rhoades and Virginia Nazarea observe:

> Farmers opt for an adaptive strategy of using biodiversity in such a way that it spreads production risk and labor scheduling across the landscape. In the Cusco Valley of Peru, for example, we found farmers who plant up to 50 varieties as well as several different species of potatoes at different time intervals in 20 to 30 scattered fields characterized by different altitude, soil types, and orientations to the sun. . . . This dispersion pattern reduces the risk that one disease outbreak or an unpredicted frost will devastate an entire crop. Simultaneously, by using different varieties a continuous flow of production through time and space can be realized so that different markets, household needs, or labor supplies can be accommodated. Interspecific and intraspecific variation is also used for agronomic control of weeds and pests, microclimatic variation through shading, as well as a buffer against climatic and pest damage. Andean potato farmers' strategies are based on a long-term, detailed knowledge of specific plant-environment interaction. Any variety is tested against several seasons of variable frosts and rainfall as well as performance in different soils.[35]

Studies in the Paucartambo Valley and our own field observations in the upper basins of the Sacred Valley confirm that diverse cropping of tubers constitutes a major food source for subsistence farmers.[36]

While European cultigens such as wheat, barley, and broad beans have largely replaced Andean equivalents in places like the Sacred Valley, quinoa (*Chenopodium quinoa*) and amaranth (*Amaranthus caudatus*) are still cultivated in many places.[37] *Kañiwa* (*Chenopodium pallidicaule*) might also have been an important crop in pre-Inca times, when populations shifted to high elevations and had to contend with colder

Fig. 3.6. Andean peasants sowing potatoes and oca. (Redrawn from Guaman Poma de Ayala 1980 [1615].)

temperatures and shortened growing seasons. These plants provide very high percentages of high-quality proteins, as well as significant amounts of carbohydrates and some fat.[38] The Andean grains are frost and drought resistant and are thus less risky to cultivate on more marginal lands, although they require more time to process for consumption.

Today, a common crop rotation pattern is tubers-quinoa-*tarwi*.[39] *Tarwi* (*Lupinus mutabilis*) has an extremely high protein content (averaging 46 percent), as well as oil and fat (about 20 percent), and as a nitrogen-fixing plant can be cultivated at the end of a rotation cycle, intercropped to protect other plants, or grown on extremely marginal lands to improve them for other crops.[40] *Tarwi* is still grown in the Cusco region and provides an important supplement of protein and fat for the subsistence farmer.

In describing the cultivation of diverse products as a risk-reduction strategy, we should recall that Cusco's agricultural groups were not strict satisfizers. The earliest sedentary villages reveal evidence of long-distance exchanges of goods not available locally, such as decorated pottery and obsidian. Exotic goods with utilitarian, status, and ritual uses could have been acquired through exchanges or by obtaining them directly by traveling to where they were produced or occurred naturally. Direct exploitation and exchange both would require some sort of surplus production, and local pre-Inca elites would have been involved in acquiring exotic goods, or at least in providing leadership and organization for the economic and social interactions necessary to acquire them. While still managing production systems in areas best suited for diverse dry-farming, some pre-Inca elites also mobilized local labor to build canals and small terrace systems. The formation of the Inca state shifted the focus of agricultural production from upper *kichwa* lands to new state lands in the lower *kichwa*, where intensive maize production would have radically altered local economies and diets.

Intensive Agriculture and the Inca Empire

Paul Halstead and John O'Shea have observed that in addition to diversification, human groups can also address resource fluctuations through mobility, storage, and exchange.[41] Rather than cultivate biodiversity, the Inca empire chose to move populations to resources (mobility) and construct storage facilities, while simultaneously intensifying agricultural production (fig. 3.7). The intensive agriculture favored by the Inca state

Fig. 3.7. Inca storehouses (*qollqa*). (Redrawn from Guaman Poma de Ayala 1980 [1615].)

used irrigated, well-drained, terraced lands and labor tribute to produce surpluses of a limited array of crops. As Zimmerer notes, this state agriculture was probably diversity-poor, focusing on a few varieties that would meet limited state functions.[42] The most important crop was maize, the cultivation of which was a central concern of the Inca religious calendar.[43] Several chroniclers attest to the central role of maize and its almost exclusive cultivation on irrigated and terraced lands.[44]

The Incas intensified local maize production, building irrigated terrace systems and scheduling planting, irrigation, harvest, and fertilization. While local lands were sometimes annexed for state use, the canalization of rivers, draining of swampy land, and introduction of a reliable water supply created agricultural resources that not only were less risky than dry-farmed fields but also did not require a long fallowing between plantings.[45] Fertilization with camelid dung, night soil, and guano from the coast raised the probability that these fields would yield large surpluses year after year.[46]

The state focus was on a few maize varieties, including one that would store well, such as *muruchhu sara,* a flinty maize said to have been preferred by the military.[47] In addition to addressing long-term storage concerns, the Incas developed high-yield varieties like Cusco Cristal Amarillo, which originated in the Sacred Valley and was introduced in Inca provinces to replace local strains.[48] Finally, the state required a few varieties (such as Cusco Cristal Amarillo and Chullpi) that had high sugar content, suitable for making maize beer (*aqha*).[49]

In places where maize was not the dominant staple crop (e.g., the Aymara-speaking Titicaca Basin), tuber production was reorganized by the Inca empire.[50] Of the estimated six thousand varieties of potato available in South America, the Incas selected a few for high yield, as well as for making *ch'uñu,* a freeze-dried product that could be stored for long periods of time and easily transported.[51] While Ludovico Bertonio's Aymara dictionary lists perhaps twenty varieties of potatoes and tubers, Diego González Holguin's Quechua dictionary provides limited vocabulary for tuber production, almost all of it *ch'uñu* related.[52] In the Cusco region, the Incas sowed early (*maway*) varieties of both maize and potatoes, crops that could be harvested several months before normal harvests would be ready.[53]

Inca surplus food production focused primarily on maize and *ch'uñu,* but these were not the only agricultural products grown on improved state lands. Archival documents and chronicle references indicate that coca leaf, chile pepper (*uchu*), cotton, and other crops were cultivated in lower-elevation state fields.[54] In some cases, terrace systems appear to have raised field temperatures sufficiently to raise exotic crops on state lands. These products represent the development of agricultural wealth and are discussed in greater detail in chapter 10.

Climatic Change in the Andean Highlands

Agricultural strategies of resource diversity or surplus production are intended to address interannual fluctuations in precipitation and temperature. Both strategies could survive periodic resource failure, but it is likely that sustained climatic shifts would require a revision of risk-management strategies. Although climate change should not be promoted as the prime mover in long-term culture change, it would have had varying effects on groups practicing different political economies.[55] Several indicators of prehistoric climate change have been measured for the Andean highlands, and some general trends can be noted for the past 1500 years or so. In the Cusco region, the Marcacocha lake core and Quelccaya ice core data provide comparable evidence for long-term climatic change that can be compared to other paleoclimate studies.[56]

The Marcacocha sequence shows a change in lake bed deposits around AD 100, interpreted as a cooler period from AD 100 to AD 1050.[57] An earlier stratum contained pollen possibly associated with the dry-farming of hardy crops such as quinoa, *kañiwa,* and *maca,* but this pollen decreases from AD 100 to AD 1050. The lake core evidence suggests the onset of variable climatic conditions after AD 900, with warmer and drier conditions than before.[58] The cultivation of quinoa and maize, and possibly tubers like potato and oca, would have been undertaken, and the construction of irrigation systems using melt water developed from AD 1100 to AD 1500.[59]

Ice core data from the Quelccaya glacier (located about 100 kilometers east of Cusco) indicate similar trends in temperature and precipitation from ca. AD 540 to AD 1984 (table 3.2).[60] The period from AD 540 to AD 760 was characterized by generally drier conditions, including marked dry periods from AD 540 to AD 560 and 650 to 730 and a severe drought from AD 570 to AD 610.[61] Only the period from AD 610 to AD 650 was wetter than average. This period of warm, dry conditions was followed by a prolonged cool period from AD 760 to AD 1040,

TABLE 3.2. Wet and Dry Periods in
Quelccaya Glacier Cores

Wetter Periods	Drier Periods
AD 1870–1984	1720–1860*
1500–1720*	1250–1310*
760–1040	650–730
610–650	570–610*
	540–560

Source: Thompson et al. 1985, 973.
*Extremes, in which precipitation deviates more
than 20 percent from the mean.

in which increased precipitation was common. Warm, dry conditions
prevailed from AD 1040 to AD 1490, with what L. G. Thompson and
colleagues call an "especially intense" dry period from AD 1250 to AD
1310.[62] Using data from the Nevado Huaytapallana glacier, Geoffrey
Seltzer and Christine Hastorf interpret glacial advances at this time as a
sign that temperatures at the end of the thirteenth century were cooler
than in preceding centuries.[63] They estimate that climatic zones would
have been depressed by as much as 150 meters, radically altering the
productive landscape in highland valleys. The onset of the Little Ice Age
around AD 1500 brought cooler and markedly wetter conditions that
would last until the eighteenth century.[64]

Settlement Patterns, Climate, and Political Economy

Paleoclimate data provide a means for approaching some of the issues
of settlement location and political economy. Major climatic shifts would
have altered the costs and benefits for certain settlement locations and
production strategies. Warmer temperatures would have raised the elevational limits for cultivating specific crops, while conditions of increased
aridity generally associated with such changes would have favored the
cultivation of hardy, drought- and frost-resistant plants such as potatoes,
oca, *ullucu*, quinoa, and *kañiwa*.[65] In times of drought, intensive valley-
bottom agriculture would continue to be a successful production strategy in locations with permanent streams, provided that intensification
did not outstrip reduced water resources.[66] Cooler conditions would
tend to favor shifts to lower-elevation settlement as the limits of ecolog-

ical zones were lowered. The concomitant increase in available water might encourage the expansion of intensive agriculture into more marginal environments, and such periods might be characterized by an increase in maize cultivation.

In purely environmental terms, diversity and intensive production both represent viable means of addressing interannual environmental fluctuations.[67] Major climatic shifts would affect these economies differently. A sudden shift from wet/cool to dry/warm conditions would have a negative impact on large systems of intensive agriculture, as has been argued for the Tiwanaku empire. Sudden climate change or catastrophic environmental perturbations such as earthquakes or El Niño Seasonal Oscillation (ENSO) events can have a devastating effect on centralized polities whose economies rely heavily on intensified agricultural resources.[68] Conversely, a shift from dry/warm conditions to wet/cool ones would affect high-elevation settlement systems relying on diverse cropping, as lowered elevational limits for crops (and too much precipitation) would impose greater travel costs and more frequent crop failure, reducing net returns from cultivation. Major climatic changes stress social systems by reducing food resources, but they also reduce confidence in the political and religious systems in which affected groups participate.

The settlement patterns in the Sacred Valley exhibit shifts in site location, only some of which can be accounted for using paleoclimate data. The first villages in the study region tend to be located in the *suni* zone, in areas where herding and dry-farming of diverse crops could be managed, probably organized at the level of the village or small polity. At around AD 400, the large, nucleated villages in the Sacred Valley study region were abandoned as population shifted to locations where simple irrigation systems could be exploited, possibly for an increased production of maize. These settlement patterns remained more or less stable for about 600 years until around AD 1000, when a second shift to nucleated high-elevation settlements occurred. This was followed by a gradual resettlement of population closer to the valley bottom beginning around AD 1300–1400. Many of these settlement shifts reflect changes in political or economic organization, and the following chapters consider how regional ecological changes influenced the formation of the Inca state.

CHAPTER FOUR

Wari Imperialism and Local Political Competition in Cusco

Some of the first Spaniards to traverse the Andean highlands described the ruins of impressive sites that had been built before the rise of the Inca empire.[1] Although the Incas insisted that they had been the first civilization to develop in the Andes, archaeologists now know of other, earlier, states and empires. Nearly a century ago, the archaeologist Max Uhle observed the need to link the Inca empire to these earlier polities using archaeological data. Some scholars look to the Wari empire as the inspiration for Inca statecraft.[2] This state flourished in the central Andean highlands and some coastal regions from around AD 600 to AD 900 or so and is known to have occupied and influenced the Cusco region, although consensus has not been reached regarding the degree to which Wari colonization influenced Inca state formation.

Some researchers suggest that the Incas inherited the Wari model of statecraft, preserved by the descendants of Wari colonists in the Cusco region in the centuries following the abandonment of Wari sites and leading up to Inca imperial expansion.[3] Although the Inca and Wari polities *did* share some structural similarities—for example, an urban capital, standardized state architecture, and the development of roads and intensive maize agriculture to facilitate state functions—they appear to have exercised different levels of intensity in provincial administration and the central direction of political economy. The development of regional settlement patterns now allows us to discuss the effects of Wari imperialism on political hierarchies and competition in the Cusco region. The available evidence suggests that a complex prestate polity already existed in the Cusco Basin when Wari colonies were established. This polity was not heavily impacted by the Wari presence, but centuries of contact with Wari colonists and administrators do appear to have transformed the nature of elite identity and group competition.

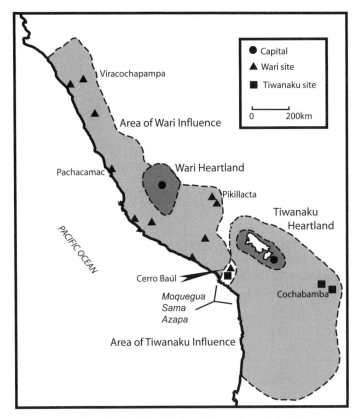

Fig. 4.1. Estimated territories of the Wari and Tiwanaku polities. These states did not exercise continuous control in the regions under their influence. Circles mark the locations of the two capitals, and triangles and squares identify important Wari and Tiwanaku sites, respectively.

Wari and Tiwanaku Integration of the Andean Region

The first Andean states formed on Peru's coast no later than AD 300, and succeeding cycles of state formation and regional balkanization extended the scope of state administration into highland regions.[4] Between about AD 500 and AD 700, the Wari and Tiwanaku polities united their respective highland core areas politically and began to establish colonies and provinces in many highland and coastal areas (fig. 4.1). The Cusco region has a marked presence of Wari colonial settlement that has been well studied, and the decline of Wari colonies there set the stage for Inca state formation and imperialism. Analysis of recently collected archaeological evidence from the Cusco region suggests that although the Wari colonial presence influenced Inca state formation, it was in less direct ways than some researchers have assumed.

Recent reviews of early Andean empires have pointed out that administrative control implemented outside of the Wari and Tiwanaku heartlands was territorially discontinuous and many "provincial" regions lack evidence of infrastructural investments consistent with the imposition of direct rule.[5] It is clear, however, that these polities achieved a degree of macroregional integration—particularly in the formal linking of coastal and highland regions—that was beyond that of early coastal polities like the Moche state. Both Wari and Tiwanaku polities had urban capitals surrounded by densely populated hinterlands.[6] Wari roads and rectangular architectural compounds have been identified widely throughout the Andean highlands, but the best evidence of resettlement and economic reorganization consistent with direct state administration is found within 100 kilometers or so of the capital.[7] The Tiwanaku capital administered a heartland of comparable size.[8] As observed in chapter 2, territories of 20,000 square kilometers or more are comparable to those observed archaeologically for many other early states.

Outside of its heartland, the Wari polity established its presence widely throughout the Andean highlands by establishing colonies in strategic locations.[9] The Wari appear to have had direct access to some coastal valleys that could provide a wide range of resources not available locally, including guano, seaweed, coca leaf, *Spondylus* shell, and fish.[10] In many regions colonized by Wari settlers, foreign influence was limited to a very small area around the colonies, with almost no evidence of direct interactions between local populations and the state heartland.[11]

The Tiwanaku polity intensified the agricultural resources of its heartland, constructing raised fields near the shores of Lake Titicaca at over 3800 meters. By draining large expanses of new agricultural land, Tiwanaku farmers were able to cultivate tubers intensively with lower risks of frost, providing food for hundreds of thousands of people living in and around the capital.[12] While surpluses of staple foods were produced abundantly, ceremonial crops like chile pepper and coca leaf could not be cultivated in the Titicaca Basin. Tiwanaku established formal colonies at lower elevations to the east and west of its heartland: in the piedmont lands of some Pacific Coast valleys (Moquegua, Sama, and

Azapa), as well as the Larecaja and Cochabamba regions in the Bolivian lowland valleys.[13] These colonies afforded direct access to maize, chile peppers, and coca leaf, as well as exotic goods acquired through contacts with groups living on the Pacific Coast and in the Amazonian Basin.[14]

Although the Wari and Tiwanaku polities might not have exercised direct control over all resources used in their political economies, they should still be considered to have been empires on the basis of having established colonies and administered ethnic groups living beyond their respective heartlands. The transition from colonization to provincial administration appears to have been a long-term goal of these polities, and formal provincial administration was either present or under development in some areas at the time that these polities declined.[15]

Local Political Organization in the Cusco Region, AD 400–600

Recent settlement surveys conducted in the Cusco region indicate that a complex polity already existed in the nearby Cusco Basin at the time that Wari colonists first began to settle in the Lucre Basin. Researchers have identified a local pottery style called Qotakalli that was produced prior to Wari imperial expansion.[16] Qotakalli pottery appears to have been produced in the Cusco Basin by about AD 400 and was distributed within that basin and in several neighboring regions.[17] This local style continued to be produced during the period of Wari colonization (after about AD 600), but a new local style called Araway—a local imitation of Wari imperial pottery made with a similar paste to that used for the Qotakalli style—came to be the more common decorated ware.[18] The distribution of Qotakalli pottery suggests the presence of a complex prestate polity in the Cusco region that might have controlled an area of up to 1000 square kilometers.

The Cusco Basin Polity

In the Cusco Basin, Brian Bauer has identified more than a dozen villages, many of which form distinct clusters on low ridges just above the valley floor (fig. 4.2).[19] Because of the extent of modern settlement in the valley and the more dispersed nature of Qotakalli Period settlement, it is difficult to identify a paramount center, although the argument could be made that the center of the Cusco polity comprised a cluster of villages

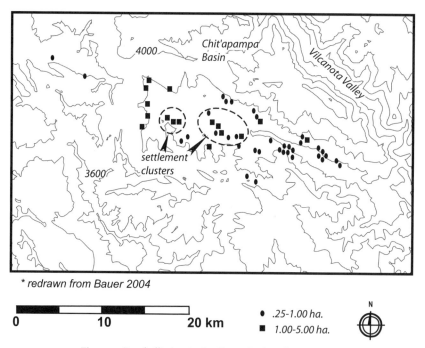

* *redrawn from Bauer 2004*

0   10   20 km

● .25-1.00 ha.
■ 1.00-5.00 ha.

N

Fig. 4.2. Qotakalli sites in the Cusco Basin (after AD 400)

located near the western end of the basin. Prior to the Wari occupation of the Lucre-Huaro area, the Cusco Basin was characterized by a two- or three-tier settlement hierarchy, with a few clusters of two or three small villages (1–5 hectares each) possibly indicating the most important settlement areas. In addition to these are single small villages, some of them surrounded by hamlets, as well as groups of hamlets. Most sites are located in places that are better suited to farming than community defense, and the distribution of Qotakalli pottery to the level of hamlets suggests a high degree of interaction between settlements within the Cusco Basin.[20]

Limits of Cusco Control in the Sacred Valley

Settlement patterns from the Sacred Valley Archaeological Project reveal a major settlement shift in the Chit'apampa Basin—located just over a low pass from the Cusco Basin—at around AD 400. For several hundred years prior to that time, settlement in this basin had been characterized

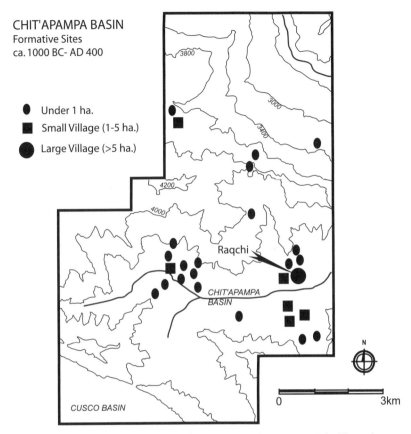

Fig. 4.3. Formative sites in the Chit'apampa Basin (ca. 1000 BC–AD 400)

by a three-tier settlement hierarchy, with the largest villages located about 15 kilometers from Cusco on lands where dry-farming could be pursued (fig. 4.3). This settlement pattern is consistent with a small chiefdom, an independent polity whose elite leaders probably had regular contacts with populations living in the Cusco Valley. The largest early villages of the Chit'apampa Basin cluster around Raqchi, a site built on a prominent ridge overlooking an important route from the Cusco Basin to the Sacred Valley (fig. 4.4). For the Formative Period, Bauer has identified another three-tier settlement system in the Cusco Basin, as well as thirty-one small sites in the Paruro region that may or may not have been organized hierarchically.[21]

At around AD 400, all large villages in the Chit'apampa Basin were

Fig. 4.4. Raqchi, a large ridgetop Formative village abandoned around AD 400

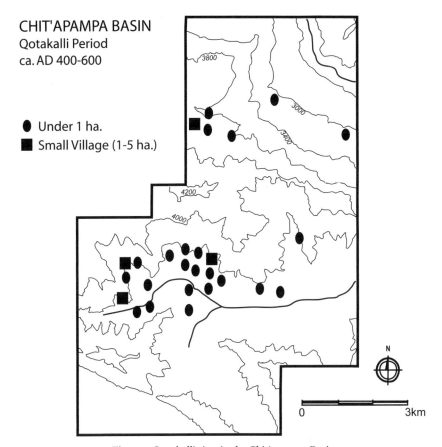

Fig. 4.5. Qotakalli sites in the Chit'apampa Basin

abandoned, and a new settlement pattern was established at the lowest elevations of that basin (about 3 500 meters) (fig. 4.5). In the Sacred Valley study region more than 70 percent of sites (thirty-eight of fifty-four) occupied from around 1000 BC–AD 400 have no evidence of continued settlement after AD 400. The new settlement pattern at that time is less hierarchical, and almost all decorated pottery found at the new Qotakalli Period villages in the Chit'apampa Basin was Qotakalli pottery from the Cusco Basin.

The distribution of the Qotakalli pottery style in the Sacred Valley study region was quite limited geographically (fig. 4.6). Almost all of the sites with high percentages of Qotakalli pottery on the surface relative

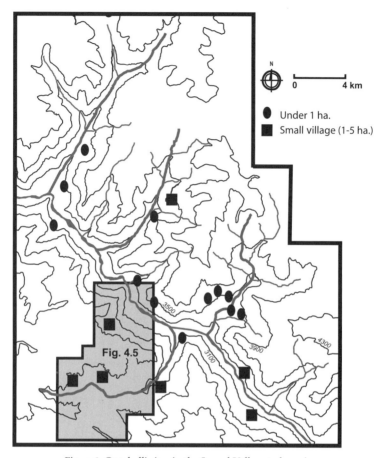

Fig. 4.6. Qotakalli sites in the Sacred Valley study region

to other contemporaneous pottery styles are found in the Chit'apampa
Basin. A cluster of twenty-three sites in the upper Chit'apampa Basin
represents over 6 hectares of occupational area, comprising half of all
sites in the Sacred Valley study region with this style present (fig. 4.7).
As with the Cusco Basin, most of these are small hamlets, but several
small villages of about a hectare in size (VS-082, VS-043, VS-055) were
also encountered. Because all of these sites were found in areas with substantial modern agriculture and settlement, the original size of these sites
was probably somewhat larger. Two other areas with substantial Qotakalli surface pottery can also be noted. Around modern Patabamba,

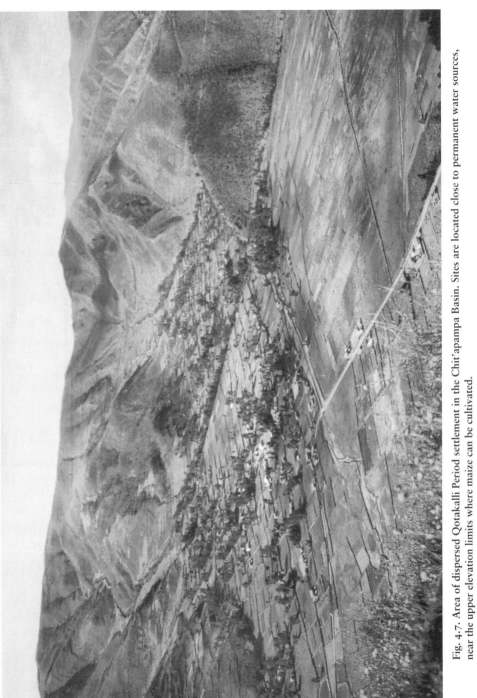

Fig. 4.7. Area of dispersed Qotakalli Period settlement in the Chit'apampa Basin. Sites are located close to permanent water sources, near the upper elevation limits where maize can be cultivated.

four sites (VS-378, VS-379, VS-380, VS-381) indicate the presence of a small village and some outlying hamlets, a total occupation area of around 3 hectares. The other important site, Willkarayan (VS-130), is located in the lower part of the Chit'apampa Basin. This site, built on a low prominence overlooking the principal route between the Sacred Valley and the Chit'apampa Basin, was about 1 hectare in area, surrounded by concentric terrace walls. This site, together with the sites in Patabamba, marks the limit of sites where the Qotakalli style constitutes a distinct majority of decorated shards. The distribution of Qotakalli pottery drops off sharply to the north of the Vilcanota River, as well as at sites in the valley proper.

Other sites with Qotakalli pottery are found in the Sacred Valley, as well as in its larger side valleys. The sites in the main valley tend to be quite small and are usually located 200 to 300 meters above the valley floor, in areas with natural defense that are close to small streams. Larger sites are found in the area of San Salvador around the Sanctuario de Huanca (Wanka), as well as in the Chongo Basin and around Calca. Qotakalli does not predominate at these sites, and the presence of local imitations of Qotakalli and Araway, as well as Wari Period styles (such as Wari and an unidentified style that may originate in the Paucartambo region), suggests that some of these sites continued to be occupied into the Wari Period. Regardless of the later occupation, it is clear that the Cusco styles comprise the majority of decorated surface shards only in areas within about a half day's walk of Cusco.

The distribution of the Qotakalli style in the study region reveals some important characteristics about the size and complexity of the Cusco Valley polity at this time. First, it is clear that Qotakalli dominates surface assemblages in areas close to the Cusco Basin, while the presence of the style drops off sharply to the north of the Vilcanota River. This comes as no surprise for a nonstate polity, whose leadership would have difficulties with the long-term administration of areas beyond about a half day's walk from Cusco. Clear Qotakalli settlement clusters were established around the modern communities of Huillcapata and Sequeracay in the Chit'apampa Basin and Patabamba in the upper elevations of the southern rim of the main valley. The site of Willkarayan marks the limit of Qotakalli stylistic dominance along a major route into the Sacred Valley but does not necessarily represent a site under the control of a Cusco Basin polity.

In the Chit'apampa Basin, the shift away from a pattern of nucleated settlements in upper *kichwa* lands (characteristic of the period from ca. 1000 BC to AD 400) to a more dispersed settlement pattern close to water sources is consistent with changes in local autonomy and economy. While it is difficult to say exactly how this area came to be dominated by groups living in the Cusco Basin, it is likely that interaction with these groups promoted new settlement patterns. In terms of defense, participation in a larger regional polity would reduce the dangers of raiding—and some of the need to live in nucleated settlements—while the leaders of the Cusco Basin polity would be expected to encourage movement away from sites affording protection from the paramount leadership. The shift toward water sources and agricultural lands may have been a response to tributary demands from Cusco, allowing locals to reduce travel time to agricultural plots in a safer political environment. Conversely, this may also be due in part to shifting production strategies, as higher-elevation lands were abandoned in favor of lands where simple irrigation systems could be developed. The cultivation of irrigated lands around 3500 meters may be indicative of an intensification of maize agriculture, although additional excavations are needed to confirm this. As mentioned before, the rise of political complexity in Cusco would have led to an increased participation in interregional exchange networks, and this may in turn have led to an increase in maize cultivation.

The regional settlement patterns of the three Cusco archaeological surveys indicate that a complex prestate polity had developed in the Cusco Valley by the latter half of the Formative Period, spreading its influence throughout the area within about a half-day's walk from a principal cluster of important villages located in the western end of the Cusco Basin. A general abandonment of Formative Period villages can be observed throughout the region, as well as the establishment of smaller settlements closer to valley-bottom agricultural resources. At this time, Cusco elites were probably in contact with emerging complex polities in other parts of the southern and central Andean highlands, and this may have led to the subordination of neighboring valleys, as well as a shift toward maize agriculture.

Cusco Influence in the Paruro Region

To the south of Cusco, Bauer has noted a similar geographical limit for Qotakalli pottery.[22] This style was identified at nineteen sites in Bauer's

Paruro survey area, sixteen of them located to the north of the Apurímac River. Almost all sites within 15–20 kilometers of the principal Qotakalli villages in the Cusco Basin had high percentages of Qotakalli pottery, and 79 percent of all sites (fifteen of nineteen) with the style present
were found within 25 kilometers of the principal Cusco Basin settlements. Bauer also identified a contemporaneous local style (Ccoipa) in
the Paruro region, present in very small amounts within about 10 kilometers of the main Cusco Basin sites but identified at thirty-five sites
in the Paruro survey region.[23] Sites with Ccoipa pottery were clustered in
the small valleys on both sides of the Apurímac River, with 74 percent
(twenty-six of thirty-five) found 20–40 kilometers from the principal
Qotakalli villages, beyond the administrative limits of a nonstate polity.
The distribution of Qotakalli pottery to the north and south of the Cusco
Basin may not be a good marker of political control, but it does suggest
marked differences in the rate of interaction and exchange between groups
as distances from the Cusco Basin increase.

Settlement patterns from the Sacred Valley and Paruro study regions
indicate that the polity in the Cusco Basin was capable of dominating
an area within about 20 kilometers of its principal settlements (fig. 4.8).
Groups living outside of that area interacted with the Cusco polity but
probably were not under its control. These included autonomous villages,
as well as other small complex polities. Given these territorial limits, it
appears that Wari established its colonies at the margins of the complex
Cusco Basin polity.[24] While Wari colonization left an indelible mark on
the Lucre Basin and Huaro area, it did not disrupt settlement in areas
where Qotakalli pottery was most prevalent.

Archaeological Manifestations of Wari Imperialism
in the Cusco Region

The Wari empire established colonies in the Cusco region during the
seventh century, at the time of its first major wave of expansion throughout the central Andes.[25] Archaeological research has identified two
major Wari installations and associated settlement clusters located about
25–45 kilometers to the southeast of modern Cusco, at Pikillacta in the
Lucre Basin, and at Batan Urqu located near modern Huaro.[26] Some
authors assert that religious patronage facilitated Wari colonization in
Cusco, stating that Wari immigrants settled on or near important local

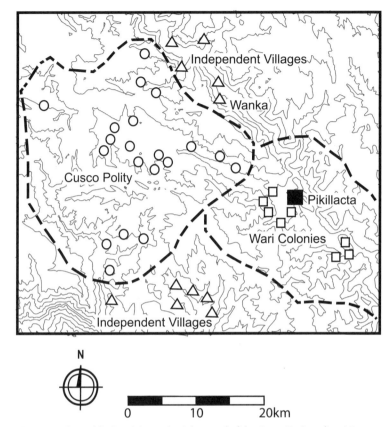

Fig. 4.8. Estimated limits of the territorial control of the Cusco Basin polity, AD 400–1000. Pottery distributions indicate that this polity was not organized as a centralized state.

shrines, co-opting sacred power and perhaps introducing the Wari state religion to local groups.[27] According to Julinho Zapata Rodríguez, Wari burials have been found at Batan Urqu, a site that had a pre-Wari religious complex, while Gordon McEwan suggests that the site of Mama Qolla in the Lucre Basin was an important shrine co-opted by Wari settlers.[28] The data for dating the establishment of Wari colonies in Cusco and assessing the regional importance of pre-Wari shrines have not been fully developed, so we must treat such hypotheses as preliminary.

The Wari colonies in the Cusco region were established in locations where it would have been easy to monitor caravan traffic throughout the region, particularly along the Vilcanota Valley and out of the Cusco Basin. It is possible that the Wari state was also interested in access to lowland areas northeast of Cusco, where coca leaf and gold could be found, and there is evidence that raw materials like obsidian and turquoise may have been worked in the Cusco region.[29] Wari colonists were probably able to attract local support through gifts of craft goods, obsidian, fancy pottery, and metal, which may have been given to reward labor service. Exotic goods available through Wari colonists would have presented co-operative local elites with the religious and economic means for ag-grandizing themselves, and exchanges with local groups may have helped Wari colonists to organize the labor that was invested in the ongoing construction of colonial infrastructure, including the site of Pikillacta.

Pikillacta and the Lucre Basin

Pikillacta is a massive installation comprising a 47-hectare rectangular enclosure (745 × 630 meters) and two areas of possible corrals in a total area estimated at nearly 2 square kilometers (fig. 4.9).[30] Construction of the principal compound began around AD 600 and continued in three discrete phases. Some parts of the site were occupied until AD 900 or later, although excavations have revealed that the site was still under con-struction at the time of its abandonment and was never fully occupied.[31] The main compounds at Pikillacta included open spaces for staging public feasts and more private ceremonies, as well as residential areas.[32] The presence of centralized storage is problematic at this site, and exca-vations in several structures in sector 4, a complex of 501 small rectan-gular buildings, yielded evidence of variable domestic use.[33] Although traditionally interpreted as a storage complex, the buildings in sector 4 might have served as temporary housing during periodic assemblies at the site in which labor tribute would be given by locals, feasts and rit-ual events performed, and exotic goods distributed by Wari elites. Even if these structures were *intended* for eventual use as storage facilities, the apparent lack of large-scale storage at Pikillacta suggests that any Wari attempt to convert the Cusco region into a centrally administered prov-ince was never realized. A lack of large-scale storage facilities at the site would contradict interpretations of centralized economic organization at the provincial level and would stand in marked contrast with Inca provincial administration practices.

McEwan has described the Wari transformation of the Lucre Basin

Fig. 4.9. Pikillacta, a Wari installation under construction from ca. AD 600 to AD 900. (Negative no. 334827, Courtesy Dept. of Library Services, American Museum of Natural History.)

from the seventh century onward.[34] In reconnaissance work, he identified Wari settlements at the sites of Minaspata, Qolque Haycuchina, and Waska Waskan, located a few kilometers to the south and southeast of Pikillacta. Surface pottery at these sites included Wari and local Wari Period styles, as well as waste flakes of turquoise and obsidian and broken marine shell. McEwan believes that these sites were occupied by Wari settlers perhaps living among local populations, and he suggests that craft production was important in the habitational sites.[35] Across the basin from Pikillacta, three small residential areas were identified close to the local shrine of Mama Qolla: Unca Puncu, Tukuwayku, and Morro de Arica. These sites show evidence of extensive local Wari Period pottery, with rare examples of the Wari style, leading McEwan to suggest that these were villages of local non-Wari populations.[36]

Finally, McEwan identifies four sites as controlling access into the Lucre Basin: Chokepukio, Muyurinapata, Rayallacta, and Mullimulliyoq. Some of these sites include Wari-style walled enclosures, but McEwan notes a presence of local and imitation Wari pottery at Rayallacta, among others. Such sites appear to have included a habitational element and appear to be associated with monitoring access into the Lucre Basin from the Vilcanota Valley and Cusco Basin. A system of roads and causeways connects several strategic Wari sites with each other and with Pikillacta, signifying a centralized administrative infrastructure in the basin.[37] Although McEwan's reconnaissance of the Lucre Basin was not conducted following a systematic survey methodology, his observations certainly demonstrate that Wari colonization had a profound effect on the Lucre Basin, sustaining a complex settlement hierarchy and probably a large population of colonists and subordinate locals.

Batan Urqu and the Huaro Area

Archaeological research is just beginning in the Huaro area, located about 15 kilometers southeast of Pikillacta, but it is important to note some similarities to the Wari occupation of the Lucre Basin.[38] Excavations at Batan Urqu have yielded large quantities of Wari pottery, as well as tombs indicating residence by elite individuals with access to large quantities of goods from the Wari imperial heartland.[39] Recent survey work by Mary Glowacki and colleagues has identified several habitation sites, some of them with Wari rectangular compounds.[40] Preliminary research suggests that Batan Urqu may have been established before the construction of Pikillacta was initiated, an occupation perhaps similar to that of Cerro Amaru in the Huamachuco region.[41] Sites in the Huaro area have low percentages of Qotakalli pottery from the Cusco Basin, with considerable amounts of pottery from the Wari heartland, including the Okros, Chakipampa, Viñaque, and Wamanga styles.[42] Wari imperial pottery is rare in other parts of the Cusco region, and the architectural remains at Huaro sites suggest nonlocal settlement of the area by groups with regular contacts with the Wari heartland. A well-established Wari colony in the Cusco region would provide the means for developing relationships with some local groups so that labor tribute could be coordinated for the construction of Pikillacta and other major colonial infrastructure. Additional research is needed to clarify the nature of the Wari occupation of Huaro, but it is clear that the area between the Lucre Basin and modern Urcos was heavily colonized during the Wari Period and that some local populations were full participants in the Wari colonial system.

Wari settlers may have been active in craft production for exchange with local populations or with the imperial heartland (or for acquiring goods not available locally). It is also possible that, like colonists from other early states, Wari settlers initially moved into the Cusco region in search of agricultural lands to sustain themselves. Given the severe climatic fluctuations of the seventh century, some Wari "imperialism" might constitute a diaspora movement that capitalized on new agricultural techniques, in particular the development of irrigation canals and agricultural terraces for intensive maize agriculture.[43] As the colonies grew and their administrative interests expanded, local populations probably provided labor to quarry stone and construct the architecture and road projects in the Lucre Basin. The segmented construction of walls at Pikillacta is consistent with rotational labor organized by local elites, possibly in rounds similar to modern *mit'a* (a system of rotating corvée labor).[44]

The Wari colonization of the Lucre Basin and Huaro area had an impact on the local landscape and its populations that many Wari researchers have interpreted as sustained and profound. The apparent lack of large-scale storage at Pikillacta raises the question of how directly local populations outside these areas were administered. If the Cusco region was an administered Wari province, the regional archaeology should indicate changes in political economy, revealed through settlement shifts and the intensification of agriculture. In addition, regional settlement should have become more hierarchical through the establishment of secondary administrative sites. Wari material culture should be visible throughout the region, particularly in areas with strong signs of imperial infrastructure. None of these indicators has been observed in systematically surveyed areas in the Cusco region.

The Scope of Wari Administration in Cusco

The establishment of Wari colonies did not have a major impact on preexisting settlement patterns outside of the Lucre-Huaro area. The settlement system in the Chit'apampa Basin does not show major changes from AD 600 to AD 1000 (fig. 4.10). In the Sacred Valley study region, twenty of the forty-six sites with Qotakalli pottery have no Araway pottery, although most of these were hamlets that were abandoned over time. At least one small village was established during the Wari Period, and one appears to have been abandoned. Most villages with Qotakalli pottery also have Wari Period Araway pottery, indicating that the most noteworthy development in about four hundred years of Wari colonization in the Cusco region was a general nucleation of settlement in some areas. This is especially true for areas closest to Cusco, while sites in the Sacred Valley proper demonstrate little change or Wari influence.

One site that highlights the lack of Wari administrative development in the Sacred Valley is Wanka, located approximately 15 kilometers from Pikillacta (fig. 4.11). The site is located within an easy three- to four-hour walk of Pikillacta, but it is probably too far from the Cusco Basin to have been administered by a prestate polity.[45] Situated at an elevation of about 3100 meters, Wanka is ideally situated for the development of maize agriculture because of permanent water sources and a frost-free valley-bottom climate. If Wari imperialism in Cusco were based on direct territorial administration and the intensification of maize agriculture, one would expect Wari influence to extend down the Sacred Valley at least to Wanka. This influence would be demonstrated by the presence of Wari-style pottery and architecture at this site and others located near prime agricultural lands in the Sacred Valley (and outside of the region interacting regularly with the Cusco Basin polity).

Surface collections from Wanka reveal an extensive Wari Period assemblage, but it is not characterized by a high percentage of Wari-style pottery. Surface pottery included Cusco styles (Qotakalli and Araway),

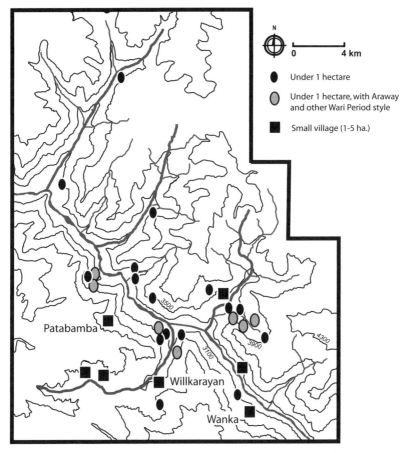

Fig. 4.10. Araway/Wari Period settlement in the Sacred Valley study region

local imitations of these styles, local Lucre Basin pottery, and several fragments of a style that may have been produced in the Paucartambo region to the north. Only a few Wari-style shards were collected at Wanka. The low frequency of Wari imperial pottery at Wanka is consistent with its distribution throughout the Sacred Valley study region. With the exception of a few isolated shards found at sites with large components of local Wari Period pottery, Wari-style pottery is almost completely absent.

This is largely true for the Paruro region as well, where Wari-style pottery was found in very low percentages at eight of nine identified

Fig. 4.11. Wanka, a local Wari Period site. Located near productive maize lands in the Sacred Valley, the site appears not to have been under the control of either the Cusco Basin polity or Wari colonists in the nearby Lucre Basin.

sites.[46] The exception to this pattern is the site of Muyu Roqo, a small (2500-square-meter) site located close to modern Paruro. Bauer conducted surface collections and test excavations at this site, encountering hundreds of fragments of Wari-style pottery and camelid bones.[47] The pottery included a high percentage of fancy bowls and drinking vessels, and one excavated bone yielded a calibrated date of AD 765–865, about two hundred years after the initial Wari occupation of the Lucre-Huaro area.[48]

The average distance of Paruro Wari sites from the principal settlements of the Cusco Basin was over 30 kilometers, with six of nine sites lying in a cluster of settlements around Paruro. By comparison, Pikillacta lies just 20 kilometers from Paruro, about a six- to eight-hour walk on well-established trails.[49] Bauer's data suggest that the Wari presence in Paruro did not constitute formal political administration but rather an indirect influence, possibly limited to feasts associated with the ceremonial maintenance of a local shrine.

The Wari appear to have exercised considerable influence within the Cusco Basin, although the evidence is lacking for political or economic reorganization of the local polity. The absence of major changes in settlement pattern and hierarchy contrasts with the intense Wari colonial presence in the Lucre-Huaro region, suggesting that formal provincial administration was never fully implemented. Within the Cusco Basin, Wari-style pottery from the Ayacucho region is rare and is never present as the dominant pottery style at any site. Instead, as has already been noted, a local imitation of Wari styles called Araway was produced in the Cusco Basin, using clay sources similar to those used in the production of Qotakalli pottery.[50] Araway pottery is found at nearly ninety sites in the Cusco Basin, as well as forty-two sites in the Sacred Valley study region and eight sites in the Paruro survey region.[51] Within the traditional sphere of Cusco political control, Araway pottery (and the occasional Wari vessel) appears to have been distributed through Cusco elites, who probably would have had direct ties to Wari colonists and may have helped to mobilize labor tribute at certain times of the year.

The stability of settlement systems and exchange networks for decorated pottery suggests that Wari administrators did not transform local economic production or bypass existing elite hierarchies to govern at the local level. Instead, Cusco Basin elites adopted Wari design motifs and distributed their local imitation of Wari pottery (Araway) throughout the area under their control. Wari elites had access to goods (craft items and metal) that were not available locally, and the Cusco polity probably came under Wari hegemony because local elites desired to obtain such goods and participate in Wari ceremonial life.

The Effects of Wari Imperialism on Inca State Formation

The Wari occupation of the Lucre Basin and Huaro area represents a major development of a peripheral region, but one of very limited geographic scope, similar to the Wari occupation of sites around Cerro Baúl.[52] The archaeological evidence indicates that Wari colonies were established in areas where they could have contact with several other regional polities. These colonies transformed their immediate environments, developing a complex administrative infrastructure. Existing patterns of interregional exchanges for goods like obsidian were interrupted,[53] and Wari officials appear to have co-opted ritual life in some places.

Still, settlement patterns from the Cusco region indicate that Wari's transformative effect was not felt locally in the Cusco Basin and areas under its influence. Local elites probably had close interactions with Wari colonists and may have helped to organize labor tribute for Wari projects. It appears that these elites used such interactions to their own advantage, redistributing Wari status goods throughout their political networks and even using established craft production systems to imitate Wari fancy pottery (fig. 4.12).

It is possible that the Wari polity attempted to formalize its hegemony as a means of developing more intensive tributary relationships with potential provinces. While the Wari collapse is poorly understood, the Cusco data may indicate local resistance to increased imperial administration. If so, local elites were undoubtedly involved in developing regional alternatives to the Wari system.[54]

The decline of the Wari empire stimulated the processes leading up to the formation of the early Inca state. Centuries of elite interaction during the Wari occupation must have had an effect on how elite status was communicated, even though Wari administrative control remained limited at the local level. The Wari influence on local sources of power was probably felt in political, economic, and religious/ideological ways. The practice of providing labor tribute for the construction of state facilities (including terraces, canals, and roads) probably increased the amount

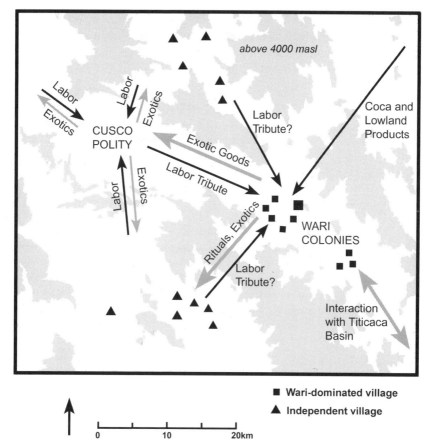

Fig. 4.12. A schematic of Wari influence in the Cusco region. Wari's control outside of the Lucre Basin and Urcos area appears to have been indirect.

of labor tribute that local elites could extract from their supporters. Economically, the intensification of agricultural production, devotion to maize agriculture, and improvement of agricultural lands created a reliable surplus in maize not witnessed in earlier local polities. Participation in Wari state religious rituals introduced local elites to more hierarchical and cosmologically overarching religious systems and imbued them with more authority than they might otherwise have had.

In short, Wari imperialism in Cusco had few local effects administratively, but far-reaching effects in the conceptualization of elite authority. The decline of the Wari was probably due in part to local elite

desertion of the existing tributary system. Future research should eluci-
date whether this was because the Wari were in decline and local elites
required a new expression of local authority or because of an active
challenge of imperial authority by local elites, including Wari provin-
cials. Either way, the abandonment of Wari's colonies created a political
vacuum in Cusco, with a large number of petty polities led by elite leaders anxious to dominate their rivals.

CHAPTER FIVE

Setting the Stage for Inca
State Formation (AD 1000–1200)

Wari colonies dominated the Cusco region for three hundred years or more, and their abandonment signals a major change in regional political organization. After AD 1000, settlement patterns and site hierarchies that had been relatively stable for centuries were transformed radically. In some areas, small valley-bottom villages were abandoned as new polities regrouped around defensible locations. For example, in the Sacred Valley study region, less than 20 percent (41/224) of the sites occupied between AD 1000 and 1400 (a period referred to as the Killke Period) have evidence of continuing settlement from the preceding period of Wari hegemony. Such changes are markedly different from the Cusco Basin, where most villages continued to be inhabited, growing larger as major Wari sites elsewhere in the region were abandoned. Settlement shifts in the Sacred Valley signal a new environment of political competition between several small complex polities, a situation culminating in the formation of the Inca state in the Cusco Basin. This chapter first considers the decline of the Wari and Tiwanaku empires, then looks at the transformation of settlement in the Cusco region, comparing settlement patterns in the Sacred Valley study region to those from the Cusco Basin, the Lucre Basin, and other parts of the region.

The Decline of the Wari and Tiwanaku Empires

Archaeological data from the Wari and Tiwanaku heartland and provincial regions reveal that both empires began to decline between about AD 900 and AD 1000, although processes of disintegration were not uniform throughout the Andes.[1] There is evidence suggesting that climatic stress played a role in political collapse, but some researchers believe that internal social competition led to rebellions that interrupted political integration.[2] In some provincial regions, imperial installations were abandoned at this time, and some of these were even burned.[3] Other areas saw the persistence of imperial colonies or enclaves, most of them now independent from administration by the capital.[4]

Processes of balkanization apparently characterized much of the Andean region from AD 1000 to AD 1200.[5] The Wari and Tiwanaku heartlands, incapable of integrating competing elite groups or funding centralized state governments, broke down into numerous petty polities. In the Titicaca Basin, several small Aymara polities (*señoríos*) emerged and competed for regional prominence.[6] Settlement in the Titicaca Basin after about AD 1100 became less hierarchical, characterized by a shift to clusters of small, undifferentiated hamlets and villages scattered around large ridgetop settlements that were surrounded by concentric walls.[7]

Decline of the Imperial Heartlands

By around AD 1100, settlement patterns in the Tiwanaku Valley indicate a population decline at higher-order administrative sites, with a growth in small sites dispersed throughout all environmental zones— evidence for localization of production and decline of centralized administration.[8] Marc Bermann has identified a return to single-family residence patterns and the possible disuse of administrative or public architecture at this time.[9] The state capital was abandoned by AD 1200.

Although extensive settlement data have not been published for the Ayacucho region, the Wari heartland appears to have undergone similar processes of decentralization at about the same time. The Wari capital may have been sacked around AD 1100, and the political unity of the Wari heartland gave way to the development of small petty polities organized around defensible settlements.[10] Areas just outside the imperial heartland, where clear Wari settlement patterns and infrastructure have been identified, also saw dramatic settlement shifts from low-elevation or valley-bottom sites to higher-elevation or ridgetop settlements.[11]

Both in the Titicaca Basin and the highlands around Ayacucho, small polities were organized to meet corporate defensive needs, and many new settlements were established on ridges or hilltops that provided protection, visibility, and access to more environmental zones that would permit self-sufficient local economies. Even in the absence of a centralized state government, elites in some of these petty polities might have retained some aspects of preexisting ideologies, social stratification, and the trappings of elite life—for example, political titles, the display of exotic goods, observation of sumptuary rules, and feasting.[12]

Processes of Balkanization and Secession in the Wari and Tiwanaku Provinces

Many areas with evidence of Wari settlement underwent political reorganization beginning in the tenth century.[13] In the highlands, these are typified by radical shifts in settlement and a simpler political organization. On the coast, the assertion of local autonomy actually led to the development of new complex polities, and challenges to Wari administration appear to have led some provincial or local elites to break away from the heartland. The establishment or urban growth of sites like Chan Chan, Marca Huamachuco, Túcume, Batán Grande, and possibly Cusco corresponds to the decline of Wari influence in these regions (AD 900–1100) and may represent cases where elites promoted local self-sufficiency as a viable administrative alternative to the Wari imperial system.[14]

The Wari presence along parts of the north and central coast gave way to the formation of new states between AD 1000 and AD 1200. The Sicán polity represents one case of secondary state formation, where a new centralized polity came to control parts of the north coast from AD 900 to AD 1100, when most of the Andean region was experiencing political breakdown.[15] In the Chincha Valley on the central coast, the decline of Wari influence led to a shift in settlement from control points along a valleywide irrigation system to locations closer to the coast. As the Chincha state developed, several large political and religious centers developed on the flood plain, linked by an intravalley road.[16]

Balkanized Polities of the Pacific Coastal Valleys

The Pacific coastal valleys of southern Peru and northern Chile provide some of the most detailed archaeological data on local Wari and Tiwanaku political balkanization after AD 1000. In the Moquegua Valley, the maize-producing elevations of the middle valley had been colonized by both Tiwanaku and Wari, and there appears to have been limited interaction between the outposts of the two empires until perhaps after AD 800.[17] Tiwanaku settlement was concentrated near the flood plain in the midvalley region, where large areas could be watered using simple canals. Tiwanaku influence in Moquegua appears to have stretched almost to the Pacific coast, and a foreign presence has been identified in the Azapa Valley of northern Chile, where Tiwanaku colonists coexisted with local groups.[18] The Wari occupation of Moquegua was concentrated around the sites of Cerro Baúl, Cerro Mejía, and Cerro Petroglifo, located above the midvalley Tiwanaku settlements in an area brought under cultivation through the construction of long irrigation canals and hillside terraces.[19]

The collapse of the Tiwanaku colonial system in Moquegua appears to have occurred by about AD 950 and resulted in the abandonment and deliberate burning of large provincial settlements and a migration of some groups to the coast or upper valley.[20] The Wari religious-administrative precinct at Cerro Baúl was burned and deserted a century or so later, although the excavators interpret this as an orderly abandonment.[21] From AD 1000 to 1200 the coastal valleys of the south-central Andes saw the development of a number of distinct local ceramic styles, including Chiribaya, Tumilaca, San Miguel, and Pocoma. Many of these are associated with distinctive architecture, mortuary style, and textile patterns.[22] It appears that several new ethnic and political groups developed at this time, some of them (like the Chiribaya and Tumilaca) probably including former Wari and Tiwanaku colonists, while others, like those living in the Azapa Valley of northern Chile, comprised indigenous populations.[23]

In the Moquegua Valley, Tumilaca sites continued to cluster around Cerro Baúl, but a series of new villages was established along the Tumilaca River, where agriculture would be less dependent on long-distance irrigation systems.[24] Settlement patterns from coastal surveys indicate clusters of relatively small polities. Burials from the Chiribaya culture of the lower Moquegua Valley reveal that local elites had access to precious metals and other exotic goods.[25] It is clear that highland and lowland regions maintained exchange relationships after Wari and Tiwanaku declined but that these were not based on administrative control or tributary obligations. There was considerable movement of exotic goods along the coast, as well as between coastal valleys and the highlands.

The Decline of Wari and Establishment of Local Polities in Cusco

According to Gordon McEwan, the site of Pikillacta was abandoned sometime after AD 900, a process that he describes as rapid yet orderly.[26]

The ongoing construction of the site was halted, and the occupants of Pikillacta sealed off some parts of the site as they systematically cleaned out rooms and subfloor offerings.[27] Much of the site was subsequently burned.[28]

The sudden abandonment of Pikillacta followed about three hundred years of stable settlement and coincided with processes of decline and abandonment at other Wari sites.[29] Given that the Wari heartland was itself in decline, it is unlikely that entire populations from distant, long-standing colonies would have relocated to the capital. Instead, the population movements observed in the Cusco region indicate that it is more likely that Wari colonial populations and the local groups under their control fragmented and dispersed throughout the region, setting up independent polities that competed with each other for regional domination.

The effects of the Wari collapse on the Lucre Basin have not been explored through systematic surveys, although researchers have conducted excavations at the post-Wari sites of Minaspata and Chokepukio (fig. 5.1).[30] Not all Wari Period sites in the Lucre Basin were abandoned when Pikillacta was depopulated, but the scale of emigration from the basin is unknown because we still lack data on the size of Pikillacta's permanent population.

Settlement patterns to the north and east of the Cusco Basin indicate that some major settlement shifts occurred as Pikillacta was abandoned (fig. 5.2). The small valley-bottom agricultural villages in the Oropesa Basin (located between the Cusco and Lucre basins) were abandoned, and that area was almost completely depopulated from about AD 1000 to AD 1400. Fertile valley-bottom maize lands ceased to be farmed, and the only Killke Period settlement was Pukara Tipón, a large, nucleated village located several hundred meters above the valley floor in an area where the village and its lands could be surrounded by a massive defensive wall.[31]

A similar buffer zone also can be observed in the Sacred Valley study region, as the small villages and hamlets of the Chit'apampa Basin were abandoned in favor of settlement of larger, nucleated villages in more defensible locations. The Sacred Valley saw a substantial influx of population after AD 1000, with the establishment of numerous large villages on high ridges. Given the modest number and sizes of earlier settlements, it appears that the decline of the Wari colonies was associated with major demographic and political restructuring in the Sacred Valley. After AD 1000, the Sacred Valley was home to several small complex polities. Some maintained regular contacts with the Cusco Basin, while others

Fig. 5.1. Chokepukio, located on a low rise across from Pikillacta (*foreground*) (Negative no. 334819, Courtesy Dept. of Library Services, American Museum of Natural History.)

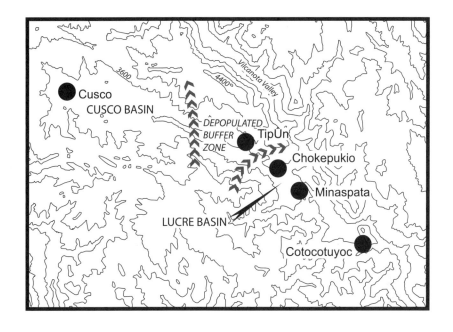

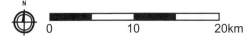

Fig. 5.2. Killke Period settlement in the Lucre Basin and Urcos area. Several large, nucleated villages or towns grew as the Wari colonies were abandoned around AD 1000.

developed distinct local architectural, mortuary, and pottery styles. Such distinctions in local material culture are indicative of differences in political or ethnic identity. Other archaeological research from the Cusco region indicates the formation of several small polities, organized around nucleated, often defensible, settlements. For example, reconnaissance by Kenneth Heffernan and Ann Kendall has identified such polities forming to the west of Cusco.[32] Evidence for Wari administration in these areas has not been reported to date, although much of the region remains to be surveyed intensively.

In contrast to the many small settlement systems clustered around defensively sited principal villages, most of the Cusco Basin after AD 1000 appears to have been integrated into a single settlement system in which site location was influenced more prominently by economic production

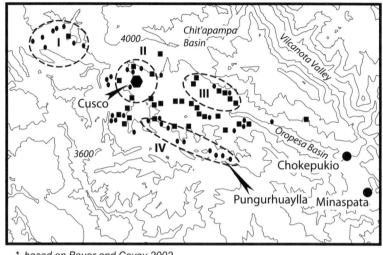

* based on Bauer and Covey 2002

I. Area of Sites with Burnt Daub on the Surface
II. Urban Cusco and Its Satellite Villages
III. Area of New Killke Period Terraces and Villages
IV. Area of Remote Killke Period Villages

Fig. 5.3. Killke Period settlement in the Cusco Basin. Survey work by Brian Bauer
has demonstrated a hierarchical settlement system with a high population density.

than defense.[33] Settlement patterns from the Cusco Basin indicate increasing settlement density after AD 1000 (fig. 5.3). The depopulation
of intermediate areas may partly account for the increased number and
size of villages in the basin, as groups living between rival polities cast
their lot with one or the other. Political complexity continued in the
Cusco Basin after AD 1000, with major increases in population that
were probably concomitant with increased competition between the
Cusco Basin polity and regional rivals.

The abandonment of Pikillacta was part of a massive transformation
of regional settlement resulting in the establishment of numerous com-

peting petty polities. Given the uncertainty regarding settlement at the
site of Cusco prior to about AD 1000, it would be problematic to posit
a direct link between the decline of Pikillacta and the rise of the early
Inca polity in Cusco. Settlement continuities in the Lucre Basin argue
against a complete relocation of Wari settlement into the Cusco Basin,
and it would seem reasonable that the development of Cusco as a paramount center was a local initiative, perhaps a reaction to the attempted
intensification of Wari administration in the region. The establishment
of a depopulated buffer zone between the Cusco Basin and Lucre Basin
would appear to indicate a lack of shared traditions between the two
areas, rather than a large-scale migration of post-Wari settlers to Cusco.
After AD 1000, the populations of the Cusco Basin and Sacred Valley
grew substantially, and the site of Cusco itself increased in size and population density.

Polity and Ethnicity in the Sacred Valley after AD 1000

Of all areas surveyed intensively, the Sacred Valley study region provides
the best systematic evidence for massive settlement shifts related to the
Wari decline. The timing of this shift appears to be at the very end of the
Wari Period, evidenced by the presence of a small component of Araway
pottery at thirteen Killke Period sites where no Qotakalli pottery was
present. Generally, there is little continuity between Cusco-dominated
Wari Period styles and Killke Period settlements, of which 83.5 percent
(183/224) have no occupation from AD 400 to AD 1000.

As the dispersed agricultural villages located on the lower slopes and
valley-bottom areas were abandoned, new nucleated villages were established on remote ridgetops and in locations with good visibility and
natural defenses. Twenty-one villages of 3 hectares or larger were identified in the Sacred Valley study region, located at an average elevation
of 3928 meters—almost 1000 meters above the floor of the Sacred Valley
(fig. 5.4). This movement represents a major change in site catchment,
implying a different political economy and new concerns for community
defense. Over two hundred small villages and hamlets were found at
lower elevations (3574 meters for sites under a hectare, 3589 meters for
sites 1–3 hectares), suggesting that, in many cases, large villages located
in *suni* or *puna* lands oversaw agricultural production at lower elevations.
This pattern of ridgetop settlements does not appear in Brian Bauer's

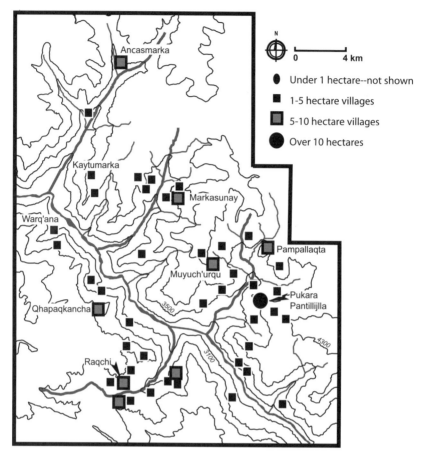

Fig. 5.4. Major Killke Period settlements of the Sacred Valley study region. The largest sites settled after AD 1000 are located at elevations of 4,000 meters or higher.

Paruro survey, but there is some evidence of remote or defensible settlements at high elevation in the southern part of the Cusco Basin.[34]

It is difficult at present to subdivide the pottery in use between about AD 1000 and AD 1400. A style called Killke was produced in the Cusco Basin at this time, but the process of collecting chronometric dates from stratified excavation deposits has not advanced sufficiently to permit archaeologists to identify a clear assemblage for the period from AD 1000 until the formation of the Inca state around AD 1200–1300.[35] The appearance of Inca-style pottery and architecture is also poorly understood chronologically and overlaps with Killke ceramic use in the fourteenth (and perhaps the fifteenth) century, making it difficult at this time to use pottery alone to establish calendar dates for the process of state formation.

Despite these limitations, it is clear that this period marks a radical change in the social organization and political economy of different groups in the Cusco region. Rank-size graphs for the Sacred Valley study region indicate a more hierarchical settlement pattern than was seen for preceding periods (fig. 5.5). The rank-size curve for the Sacred Valley for the period from AD 400 to AD 1000 is convex, consistent with conditions of upper-tier competition and a lack of central coordination.[36] From AD 1000 to AD 1400, the rank-size graph indicates a more linear distribution when excluding the city of Cusco and its secondary administrative center, established at Pukara Pantillijlla around AD 1300. Excluding Inca administrative sites, it appears that this region had a more complex and well-integrated settlement system.

Political Units in the Sacred Valley

Estimated territory sizes for the largest villages after AD 1000 are consistent with an administrative complexity below the state level, and it is possible to delimit the territories of several possible polities based on clusters of small and large villages. Site locations during this period are consistent with the exploitation of diverse animal and plant resources. Large villages like Qhapaqkancha, Kaytumarka, Markasunay, and Muyuch'urqu were situated at 4000 meters or higher, within easy reach of pasture lands for herding and agricultural lands for the production of tubers and Andean grains (fig. 5.6).

The largest villages in the Sacred Valley study region appear to have been the principal settlements of small complex polities. Local elites would have managed a mixed agricultural and herding economy and probably were involved in the organization of labor to construct irrigation canals—for example, the one bringing water to the site and fields of Kaytumarka—and defensive works, like the walls at Muyuch'urqu or the defensive ditch at Raqchi (fig. 5.7). Several of the largest settlements were located along important routes between *kichwa* valleys and the *montaña,* and local elites probably organized camelid caravans to obtain lowland agricultural products.

These small polities show evidence of a concern for community

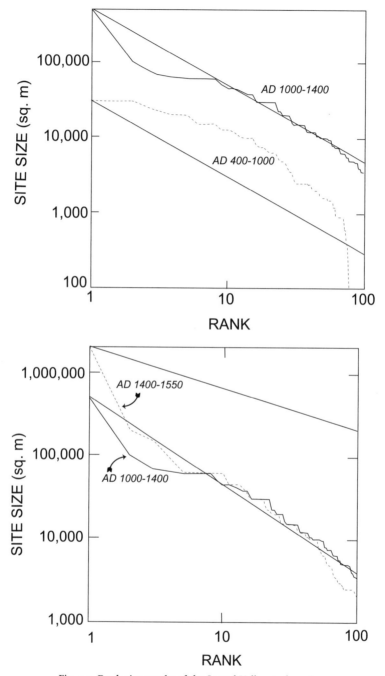

Fig. 5.5. Rank-size graphs of the Sacred Valley study region

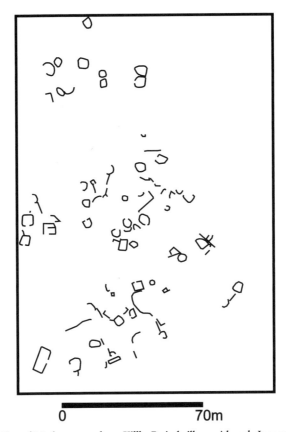

0   70m

Fig. 5.6. Plan of Markasunay, a large Killke Period village with early Inca architecture

protection against raiding and warfare. Not only were many large villages situated in inaccessible locations, but some of these also had walls or defensive ditches, indicating that community or polity labor was being invested in defense. In addition to inaccessible or defensive settlement locations, there are other possible indicators of conflict between groups. Burnt wall daub, evidence of conflagrations that might have been associated with raiding, is almost exclusively associated with Killke Period villages outside of the Cusco sphere of influence. Burnt daub is absent in the large valley-bottom villages of the Cusco Basin but was found at several sites around Poroy and Cachimayo to the west of Cusco. In the Sacred Valley study region, burnt daub was observed on the surface at twenty-eight sites, all of which had substantial components of

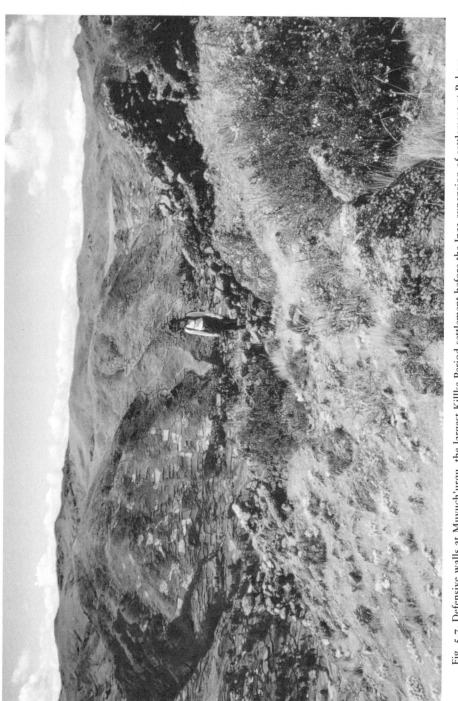

Fig. 5.7. Defensive walls at Muyuch'urqu, the largest Killke Period settlement before the Inca expansion of settlement at Pukara Pantillijlla.

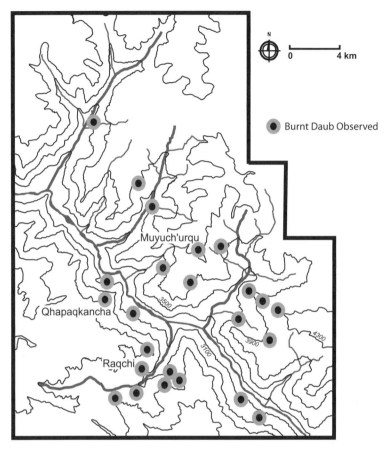

Fig. 5.8. Map of the location of burnt daub, possibly indicating the burning of settlements in warfare or raids after AD 1000

Killke Period pottery (fig. 5.8). A midden at Pukara Pantillijlla that dated to the thirteenth century contained sling balls and two stone axes, which might also serve as indirect evidence for conflict. Frequent raiding and warfare are common themes in many of the Inca chronicles for the prestate period, as discussed in greater detail in chapter 6.

A system of balkanized, warring petty polities has been described as the prevailing condition for the Andean highlands prior to the Inca conquest.[37] The chronicler Felipe Guaman Poma de Ayala conceptualizes the pre-Inca period in terms of decentralization, perpetual warfare, and irregular participation in regional ethnic confederations. The area surrounding the developing Inca state contained multiple political groups of varying organizational complexity, and the Incas would take advantage of ethnic and political variability to expand and consolidate their imperial heartland.

Ethnic Variation in the Cusco Region

In some cases "ethnic" distinctions were not based on differences in material culture or language, and there is reason to believe that many— but not all—of the small groups living around Cusco were Quechua speakers.[38] In contrast to their neighbors, Lucre Basin groups like the Muyna and Pinagua may have been more closely related to their Wari predecessors than to indigenous Cusco Basin groups. Variations in mortuary treatment and architectural style in the Sacred Valley allow us to distinguish between some populations.

In the upper side valleys to the north of the Vilcanota River, some local groups placed burials in small ovoidal mortuary structures, suggesting either an influx of nonlocal groups or the adoption of a new mortuary style by some groups in the region (fig. 5.9).[39] Groups in the Chit'apampa Basin, Pisaq area, and San Salvador area did not use such structures but buried their dead in simple cliff tombs. Cliff tombs below the site of Kaytumarka took the form of painted adobe boxes, while different styles of cliff burials were observed both in the Pisaq area and around Ancasmarca. Mortuary patterns indicate that groups living to the south of the Vilcanota River probably shared some cultural practices not observed among groups living to the north of the valley. The diversity of burial practices reveals that considerable cultural variation could be found within a very small region (fig. 5.10).

Similar variations can be seen in the domestic architecture and pottery of the Cusco region. Distinct pottery styles have been identified for the Chongo Basin, the Lucre Basin, the Chinchero area, and the area around Colcha, and it is likely that other subregions also produced their own pottery.[40] In areas where Killke Period architecture is well preserved, it is possible to observe variations in domestic architecture. Some sites are characterized by rectangular structures, others by ovoid or semicircular forms. Distinctive construction features like corbeled doorways, multistory construction, and interior wall niches have been identified at the site level.[41]

In the Sacred Valley study region, groups living to the south of the

Fig. 5.9. Mortuary structure, common to groups living to the north of the Vilcanota River after AD 1000.

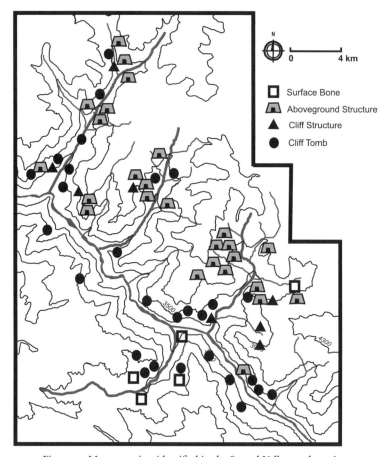

Fig. 5.10. Mortuary sites identified in the Sacred Valley study region

Vilcanota River appear to have been more closely related to the Incas, while some of the populations living to the north of the river appear to constitute one or more distinct ethnic groups. The prevalence of Killke Period pottery from the Cusco Basin is markedly different on the north and south sides of the Vilcanota River. Of the twelve wares identified from Killke Period excavations at Pukara Pantillijlla, four (designated numbers 9–12) are thought to have been produced in the Cusco Basin, based on similarities in paste, temper, and wall thickness. These wares made up the majority of the decorated pottery collected at sites in the Chit'apampa Basin and along the south rim of the Sacred Valley (78 and 66 percent, respectively). To the north of the Vilcanota Valley, these wares constituted far less of the decorated pottery collections, as low as 33 percent in the Qochoq Valley above Calca and 41 percent in the Chongo Basin. Along with differences in mortuary treatment and domestic architecture, it appears that the Vilcanota Valley represented a major cultural divide prior to Inca state formation.

Intensification and Diversity in Pre-Inca Political Economies

The establishment of a number of small polities after AD 1000 involved substantial changes in Cusco's regional political economies. From AD 600 to AD 1000 the Wari colonies had developed intensive maize agriculture in the Lucre Basin and Huaro areas and included some locals in the use of maize—both as a food and fermented alcoholic beverage—in feasting and ritual events of a scale beyond what local elites could arrange. The location and distribution of Wari settlement and cultural remains suggest a production system based on the intensive local exploitation of maize, supplemented by other crops. Herding may have been managed through Pikillacta, given the presence of large rectangular enclosures with no interior architecture that McEwan interprets as corrals.[42] Small storage facilities identified at Pikillacta would have held surpluses that could be mobilized to fete laborers and buffer Wari colonists against bad years, although province-level storage does not appear to have been in use at the site. The absence of evidence for large-scale production and storage of agricultural surpluses indicates that Pikillacta did not centrally manage provincial agricultural production and was not responsible for addressing resource fluctuations at the local level. It appears that Wari settlers relied on intensive maize production on improved lands but that they did not amplify production levels to the point that storage would be the primary risk-reduction strategy for the colonies and nearby local populations. It is possible that exchanges of exotic and craft goods would have provided another means for obtaining food and that the maintenance of caravans would have been an alternative to some staple production. This would require increased levels of agricultural production by local groups, who would then exchange agricultural surpluses for craft goods or exotic goods.

While populations in the Cusco Basin and Lucre Basin lived in close proximity to resources for intensive maize agriculture, a substantial component of the Cusco region's population met the challenges of a highly variable, and generally drier, climate by resettling in locations favoring more extensive production strategies. In the Sacred Valley study region, the largest sites before AD 1000 were located close to the valley bottom, where farmers had access to irrigated lands and productive dry-farming resources. After AD 1000, the largest villages in the study region were located on high ridges with an immediate catchment best suited to herding and tuber production.

Based on the shift of population to high-elevation sites, the local diet in the Sacred Valley at the time of Inca conquest probably focused on the production of a diverse array of tubers, as well as the rotation of quinoa, *kañiwa*, amaranth, and *tarwi*. Some maize was probably grown in plots close to the valley floor, but maize probably was the prerogative of the elite or reserved for ceremonial consumption.[43] While most agricultural production involved dry-farming on simple terraces, there is evidence for the development of pre-Inca irrigation works and terracing in some parts of the Cusco region.[44] Such projects are likely to have been developed through elite management of community labor.[45] This encourages us to consider how community or polity resources might have been allocated and managed prior to the Inca conquest.

Local Pre-Inca Elite Management of Ecological Complementarity

The discussion of crop diversity suggests that some risk-pooling strategies are beyond the administrative means of the household. The ethnohistoric and ethnographic literature indicates that organization of the labor and resources of extended families, lineage groups (*ayllukuna*), and polities provided access to a more extensive and reliable repertoire of food products. The Andean corollary to household risk reduction strategies is the concept of *verticality*, or ecological complementarity, in which suprahousehold risk management encourages direct procurement of the resources of multiple ecological zones.[46] This could be manifested in many ways, depending on the level of centralized management, as well as the patchiness of the resource environment and its vertical landscape.[47] As Craig Morris has suggested, decision-making processes involved with elite coordination of ecological complementarity may have encouraged the long-term formalization of centralized hierarchies.[48]

In many ways, the potential for centralized management of ecological complementarity is influenced by the distribution, patchiness, and phasing of resources. While resource distribution is seen as a factor in the foraging or collecting strategies of hunter-gatherers,[49] it also has a profound effect on how agricultural communities address risk and resource "completeness." The small pre-Inca polities to the north of the Vilcanota River were settled in a way that local leadership could have exploited the full range of agricultural diversity available locally. The largest villages at this time were located near lands that could be dry-farmed, as well as pastures where camelid herds could be kept. These settlements were often situated near important caravan routes, which might have allowed Sacred Valley elites to access *montaña* products directly through exchange relationships or small-scale colonization. Groups living to the south of the Vilcanota River may have lacked easy direct access to lowland products, which may have promoted their early dependency on the Inca state.

Between AD 1000 and AD 1400, most local agricultural economies in the Sacred Valley were probably not simple subsistence systems. The presence at Killke Period sites of defensive works and agricultural infrastructure indicates that community or polity labor resources were being directed into centrally managed projects that would require agricultural surpluses. Such projects may have benefited elite lineages and encouraged the development of ancestor veneration; Polo de Ondegardo observes that elite Inca mummies and their emblems were used by Cusco's descent groups in ceremonies and festivals to ensure sufficient water and good growing conditions.[50] Site locations in the Sacred Valley are consistent with the maintenance of complementarity between herders and cultivators, the cultivation of a wide range of agricultural products, and the limited acquisition of maize and crops grown at even lower elevations in the *montaña*. Although more archaeological data are needed, historical references to elites in the Cusco region at the time of Inca state formation mention many of these features.

John Murra has suggested that some pre-Inca local elites would have monitored local land tenure, organized redistribution of status foods (like meat, maize, and coca leaf), and undertaken the development of agricultural intensification.[51] In the Cusco region, local corvée could be applied to the construction of terraces and irrigation canals, creating a stratification of local resources between dry-farmed community lands and patches of highly productive improved lands that were disproportionately controlled by elites.[52] Apportioning community or polity labor to intensification strategies would require that local elites either divert labor from the maintenance of diversity or extract additional labor. In ecologically diverse areas like the Sacred Valley, groups would probably tend to be averse to such risks unless the perceived benefit far outweighed potential losses.[53] The management of regional resources would present a means for enforcing internal status differences and intensifying the kinds of interpolity competition ultimately leading to state formation.

Although difficult to quantify at present, it is likely that groups living in the Sacred Valley after AD 1000 used diet diversity to construct cultural and status identities. Elites probably enjoyed preferential access to higher-status foods, as well as a wider diet breadth.[54] Nonelites participated in a lower-risk production system and would have access to high-status foods in the feasting and food reciprocity that were part of their labor service (*mink'a*) for the local leader.[55] The linking of agricultural diversity to status would lend itself to local elite management and an internally consistent status hierarchy, but it would constrain the ability of such a system to adapt to new strategies of risk reduction. As discussed later, the production and consumption of diverse foodstuffs connoted lower status during the colonial periods and probably distinguished local diets from state food production in Inca times.

The Lucre Basin after AD 1000

The archaeological evidence from the Sacred Valley study region indicates a different political, economic, and cultural organization than existed before AD 1000. Such patterns may also hold for the upper Urubamba Valley, some areas to the west of Cusco, and the Apurímac Valley southwest of Cusco.[56] It is clear that the decline of the Wari colonies spurred the processes of political balkanization in these areas, but such processes appear to be less pronounced in the Lucre Basin. While systematic settlement data are lacking for this area, it is clear that the basin continued to be settled and that at least some sites near the valley floor continued to be occupied.

In the Lucre Basin, the sites of Chokepukio and Minaspata persisted after the decline of the Wari empire.[57] While these sites' sizes during the Killke Period occupation are unclear,[58] the presence of several large, nucleated towns to the east of the Cusco Basin sites represents a different kind of settlement system from many other parts of the Cusco region.

Mary Glowacki has reported that a large nucleated site called Cotoco-tuyoc was occupied after the Wari colonies around Huaro were abandoned, suggesting a similar pattern to that of the Lucre Basin.[59] The presence of at least four large sites (Tipón, Chokepukio, Minaspata, and Cotocotuyoc) without a higher order of settlement suggests that each site was the primate center of a small polity, and the Spanish chronicles refer to alliances between some of these groups at times of Inca aggression (fig. 5.11).

The general abandonment of sites located near fertile valley-bottom lands in the Oropesa Basin indicates that the territories of the two large, nucleated Lucre Basin sites may have been quite small, and it should be noted that Lucre-style pottery was not found to constitute a large component of the surface pottery at any sites in the Sacred Valley, Paruro, or Cusco Basin survey regions. It is likely that Chokepukio, Cotocotuyoc, and Minaspata were the paramount centers of small but hierarchically complex polities that focused on valley-bottom farming in a system based on resources initially developed by the Wari colonies.

The occupation of Chokepukio was established within and in proximity to large rectangular compounds built during the Wari occupation of the Lucre Basin, and radiocarbon dates indicate a continuous occupation through the fourteenth century.[60] Excavations at this site have uncovered numerous burials, as well as contexts identified by the excavators as shrines.[61] Large vessels excavated in these areas indicate that public feasting was used to integrate members of the polity and perhaps pilgrims visiting the site. Pottery from the Lucre Basin is stylistically distinct from that of the Cusco Basin, but its distribution is much more limited throughout the region compared to the Killke style.

After AD 1000, local groups in the Lucre Basin maintained and produced material culture and architectural styles distinct from those of other parts of the Cusco region. Discontinuities in settlement suggest that these groups were not allied with the Cusco polity, a condition that is corroborated by historical documents.[62] Edward Dwyer encountered evidence of massive burning at Minaspata, possibly the result of raiding or warfare, while Juha Hiltunen and Gordon McEwan report a major burning event at Chokepukio in the fourteenth century or first part of the fifteenth century.[63] Chokepukio, Minaspata, and Cotocotuyoc probably represent territorially restricted complex polities that retained or modified many Wari religious and politico-economic practices. While

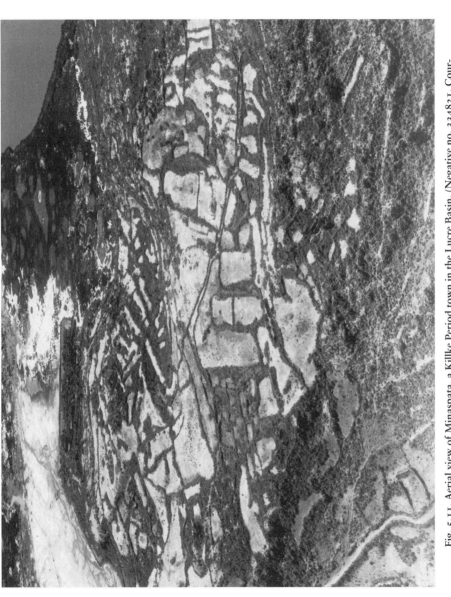

Fig. 5.11. Aerial view of Minaspata, a Killke Period town in the Lucre Basin. (Negative no. 334821, Courtesy Dept. of Library Services, American Museum of Natural History.)

allied with each other they were major competitors of the emerging Inca state, although there is clear evidence for the movement of material goods between the two areas, indicating that some nonmilitary contact was sustained. There may be evidence for elite interactions based on a shared regional religious ideology.

The Cusco Basin after AD 1000

While only some elements of the Wari settlement system persisted after the abandonment of Pikillacta, the Cusco polity appears to have survived the Wari collapse without itself experiencing substantial settlement relocation. Bauer's survey of the Cusco Basin has confirmed earlier impressions of a settlement system characterized by large, undefended villages located near the valley floor.[64] Many of the largest villages on the southern side of the Cusco Basin were established as early as the first millennium BC, and there is considerable settlement continuity from about AD 1000 through the Inca imperial period. The number and size of villages in the Cusco Basin indicate a complex polity that controlled a large population and productive resources within a relatively small territory.

The territory of the Cusco Basin polity may have been curtailed around the time that the Wari colonies were abandoned. The cluster of small villages and hamlets in the Chit'apampa Basin was abandoned around this time, leaving an unoccupied buffer zone between Cusco and the new small polities forming about 12–15 kilometers to the north. To the east of Cusco, the Oropesa Basin was depopulated, leaving fertile valley-bottom lands unoccupied for several hundred years.[65]

In the Paruro region, Bauer found no evidence of fortified settlement, suggesting that some of the small villages and polities of this area remained under the domination of Cusco or lacked the elite leadership to coordinate the construction of defensive works.[66] Within about 20 kilometers of Cusco to the south, Killke pottery predominates in surface assemblages, and there is strong continuity of occupation at these sites into the Inca Period. Beyond this limit, the Cusco-produced Killke pottery style is less common, and a contemporaneous local style called Colcha is found.[67] Bauer has demonstrated that the distribution of this style emanates from a group of sites located about 40 kilometers to the south of Cusco, about 10 kilometers from the modern town of Araypallpa.[68]

Excavations at the site of Tejahuasi yielded Killke and Colcha pottery, along with a radiocarbon date of AD 1010 ± 140, from the era before the Inca state had developed in Cusco.[69] Settlement patterns for this area indicate that the small groups living to the south of Cusco were not concerned enough with village defense to alter their settlement locations, and it appears that parts of this area continued to have regular contact with the Cusco Basin polity.

The Cusco Basin polity's control may not have been very direct at this time. Several sites in remote parts of the southern Cusco Basin were established on high ridges after AD 1000. Some of these settlements were located far from permanent water sources, and many were in areas with natural defenses. At least one of these, Pungurhuaylla, was walled (fig. 5.12). These sites were all established after the decline of the Wari and had little or no Inca pottery present, perhaps indicating a temporary— and unsuccessful—attempt by some groups in more distant and difficult-to-reach locations to remain independent of the Cusco Basin polity.

Summary

The decline of the Wari colonies resulted in the establishment of several distinct polities of varying sociopolitical complexity (fig. 5.13). Within the Lucre Basin, a few large primate centers continued to be occupied and may have preserved some of the features of Wari hierarchy and ceremonial life. These polities controlled small territories and were probably temporary allies in conflicts against other groups. To the west of the Lucre Basin, the Cusco polity also retained a substantial influence, probably continuing to dominate some small groups living to the south of the Cusco Basin. This control may have been centralized under a paramount leader, but it probably did not constitute a specialized administration. Some groups living close to Cusco may have chosen to resist incorporation into that polity.

The Sacred Valley and some areas to the west of Cusco witnessed a proliferation of small polities, which established themselves in locations that provided defense, as well as access to a wide range of agropastoral resources. Elites in these polities may have used their authority to underwrite small canal and terracing projects, as well as to develop defensive features for some settlements. After AD 1000, populations in the Cusco region maintained diverse ethnic identities, different levels of

Fig. 5.12. Pungurhuaylla, a walled Killke Period site to the south of the Cusco Basin.

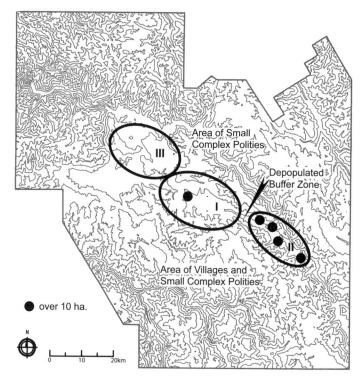

I. Territory of the Cusco Basin polity. Many villages to the south of the
Cusco Basin (within 15-20 km of Cusco) are thought to have been
dominated by this polity.
II. Area of large primate centers. These probably constitute multiple
polities, each with a principal town and small territory.
III. Possible location of a complex polity, known ethnohistorically as the
Ayarmaca.

Fig. 5.13. Schematic of political complexity in the Cusco region, AD 1000–1200

political complexity, and distinct systems of economic organization. Of
all groups in the region, the large, hierarchically-organized population
of the Cusco Basin possessed distinct advantages that allowed it to incorporate its neighbors through various expansion and administrative
strategies.

CHAPTER SIX

The Formation of the Inca State

Settlement patterns in the Cusco region after AD 1000 provide the critical link between the Wari Period occupation and the formation of the Inca state. The regional data have already demonstrated that the Wari had limited power over local people living more than a few kilometers away from their principal settlements in the Lucre Basin and Huaro. Although they transformed these areas profoundly, the Wari appear to have made no attempt to establish colonies or construct administrative compounds in the Cusco Basin. The regional data indicate that while Wari colonialism probably introduced new expressions of elite authority and stimulated competition between elite leaders throughout the region, there was no direct transfer of the tradition of Wari statecraft to the Cusco Basin when Pikillacta was abandoned.[1]

The Inca state was based on Andean principles of social organization and inspired by power relationships introduced hundreds of years earlier by Wari settlers, but Inca state formation must be viewed as a long-term local development rather than a direct borrowing. The archaeological evidence indicates that interpolity competition intensified with the decline of Wari's provincial network, leading to the emergence of the Inca state by the end of the thirteenth century. Inca state formation was a regional process involving many groups in the Cusco region and lasting for several generations. The description of this process draws on the many archaeological and historical indicators discussed in chapter 2. In this chapter, we first review the historical evidence for Inca state formation and then compare it with the archaeological data from the Cusco region.

The contraction of the area controlled by the Cusco Basin polity provides an opportunity for looking at historical references to the period leading up to Inca state formation.[2] Several of the most detailed chronicles describe a period in which Inca leaders maintained alliances with groups outside of the Cusco Basin, but promoted their interests through personal charisma rather than coercive power. For example, Miguel Cabello de Balboa states that the third Inca ruler (Lloque Yupanqui)

> governed his peoples kindly and peacefully, and with such commendable artifice that with the fame of his benevolence, discretion, and gentleness, he brought to his obedience and grace many Caciques . . . and of the first, the most noteworthy were Huaman Samo (Cacique and Lord of Huaro), Pachachulla Viracocha (a man of great discretion and prudence), and the Ayarmaca polities with their lords and regents—Tambocunca and Quilliscaches, and other neighboring lineages—who had heard word of his good government and conversation.[3]

This passage describes a Cusco Basin polity with a limited territorial range that is consistent with the settlement pattern evidence from after AD 1000.[4] Inca alliances with a limited number of neighboring groups depended on the personal interactions of elite individuals who acted on behalf of small groups like the people of Huaro, as well as larger ethnic confederations like the Ayarmacas (fig. 6.1).[5]

The limits of Inca control prior to state formation are indicated by elite marriage alliances, as well as descriptions of interactions within the Cusco Basin. Several colonial-period writers mention that before the Incas extended their political control beyond the Cusco Basin, they contracted marriage alliances with the elite of nearby towns such as Sañu, Oma, and Taucaray.[6] The chroniclers indicate that the Incas did not make lasting territorial expansions outside of the Cusco Basin and that some groups living in the basin had to be brought forcibly under Inca control as the state formed.

While the content of the Inca histories for this period is probably more myth than history—and certainly not chronologically reliable or appropriate for detailing the actions of historical personages—it does describe prestate political conditions that correspond to a certain degree with the archaeological evidence. Brian Bauer's work has demonstrated that some small groups living just to the south of the Cusco Basin continued to cultivate close contacts with the Cusco Basin, while other survey evidence indicates that the territorial extent of the Cusco polity after AD 1000 was somewhat circumscribed as depopulated buffer zones formed between Cusco and its regional rivals.[7] Competition between polities intensified with the abandonment of the Wari colonies, and the Cusco polity soon developed the characteristics of a centralized state.

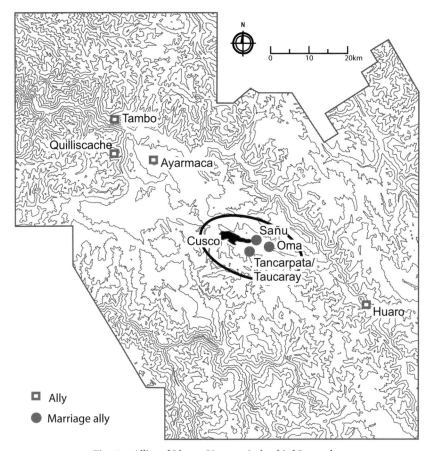

Fig. 6.1. Allies of Lloque Yupanqui, the third Inca ruler

The Ethnohistory of Early Inca State Formation

Archaeological survey research in the Cusco region has identified many of the places named in the Inca historical narratives, revealing that many colonial-period documents contain information pertaining to processes of Inca state formation prior to AD 1400.[8] As discussed in chapter 2, the kinds of changes indicating state formation in the oral histories of other states can be identified in the Inca histories, particularly in those chronicles that show an intimate toponymic knowledge of the Cusco region. The narratives of Miguel Cabello de Balboa, Pedro de Cieza de León, Pedro Sarmiento de Gamboa, and others provide important accounts of

how power in Cusco was transformed through military, economic, political, religious, and ideological developments to Inca culture.

Militarism and Territory

The chronicles refer to the earliest Inca rulers as controlling small territories, with little or no political control over neighboring groups. Beginning with the fourth ruler, Mayta Capac, the Incas are said to have
begun to consolidate their political control over the Cusco Basin, converting neighboring groups to subordinates and in some cases confiscating the lands and resources of these groups.[9] This ruler supposedly
appointed his sons to the leadership of other towns in the Cusco Basin.[10]
Such a strategy for political consolidation has been described for other
complex prestate polities, such as the Powhatan of Virginia.[11]

The chronicles describe a shift from raiding to conquest warfare from
the fourth Inca ruler onward, also revealing the development of a more
structured military hierarchy that enabled increasingly protracted campaigns. Figure 6.2 and table 6.1 indicate that Inca expansion outside the
Cusco Basin took place over several generations. After the territorial
consolidation of the Cusco Basin, the first military conquests appear to
have targeted important caravan routes that would give the Inca polity
direct access to lowland goods. For example, several sources describe a
campaign by Capac Yupanqui against the Cuyos as the first territorial
conquest outside the Cusco Basin. This expansion provided the Incas
with direct access to the Paucartambo lowlands, where coca leaf, bird
feathers, and other exotic goods could be acquired.[12] This has been observed for other developing states.[13] Military campaigns of greater scope
were possible because the Inca polity could manage the logistics of the
campaign while simultaneously protecting its own territorial interests.
References to delegated military authority and to multiple grades of military command suggest that Inca armies became more hierarchical at this
time.[14]

While the Incas merely raided some of their enemies, they reduced
other conquered territories to provinces, reallocating their lands and
resources. The chronicles are clear about the nature of conquest: after
raids or military defeats the Incas left strong enemies like those of the
Lucre Basin alone, but representatives of the Inca ruler established state
administration among less hierarchical groups in the Sacred Valley. In
some cases the Inca state implemented indirect rule using local elites, while

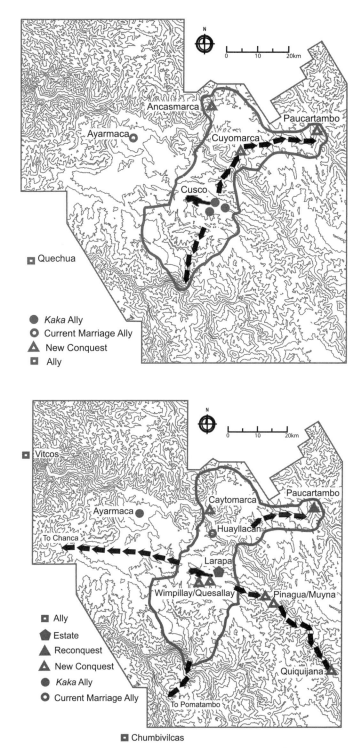

Fig. 6.2. Conquests of Capac Yupanqui (*top*) and Inca Rocca (*bottom*), the fifth and sixth Inca rulers. These indicate permanent territorial conquest to the north of the Vilcanota River and expansion along important caravan routes.

TABLE 6.1. Inca Conquests Outside of Cusco

Ruler	Cabello de Balboa [1586]	Cieza de León [1553]	Cobo [1653]	Murúa [1590]	Sarmiento de Gamboa [1572]
Capac Yupanqui Inca Inca Rocca	CUYO Wimpillay Quesallay MASCA MUYNA Caytomarca	Marca (Capacmarca?) To Pomatambo	CUYO MUYNA CHANCA Caytomarca Paucartambo	Antisuyu Wimpillay Quesallay Caytomarca Ocongate	Cuyomarca Ancasmarca MUYNA PINAGUA Caytomarca
Yahuar Huaccac					MUYNA PINAGUA HUAYLLACAN CAVINAS Mullaca Pillawara Choyca Yuco Chillincay Taucamarca

Viracocha Inca*				
Caytomarca	Calca	Calca	Calca	MUYNA
Calca	Caytomarca	Yucay	PINAGUA	PINAGUA
Huaypormarca	QANA	Maras	Caquia	AYARMACA
Maras	KANCHI	Xaquixaguana	Huaypormarca	PAPRE
Mullaca		QANA	Maras	Pacaycacha
		KANCHI	Mullaca	Casacancha
			QANA	Runtocancha
			LUCANA	Huaypormarca
				Mullaca
				Caytomarca
				Socma
				Chiraques
				Calca
				Caquia
				Collocte
				Camal
				Quiquijana

Sources: Cabello de Balboa 1951 (1586): bk. 3, chaps. 13–14; Cieza de León 1988 (ca. 1550): chaps. 34–44; Cobo 1964 (1653): bk. 12, chaps. 8–11; Murúa 1987 (1590): bk. 1, chaps. 11, 13, 15, 17, 19, 87; Sarmiento de Gamboa 1965 (1572): chaps. 18–25.

*Except for Viracocha Inca, conquests by a ruler's son during his lifetime are credited to that ruler. For Viracocha Inca, only the conquests of Inca Urcon are considered, while Pachacutic's victories are not.

it organized other areas under state administrators. Conquered areas appear to have lost much, but not all, of their autonomy; they were required to supply tribute, probably including labor service in the Cusco Basin. The Inca state did not have uniform territorial control over the Cusco region at this time, and there are even references to communities in the Cusco Basin requiring reconquest or reorganization as the state developed.[15]

Estates and the Intensification of the Inca Economy

As the Inca state formed, new relationships developed between rulers and intensive agricultural resources. The earliest Inca rulers are said to have occupied a single elite residence, the Qorikancha, which also served as the polity's principal temple.[16] Inca rulers would have received substantial labor tribute from villages under their control but probably had to contend with the diversion of some of this tribute by local elites. Marriage alliances with other elite lineages or ethnic groups would have brought additional labor tribute but would have required reciprocation. As the Inca polity began to consolidate its control over larger territories, it was necessary to bypass local elites and develop a more secure and direct form of labor tribute. The chronicles describe major projects of resource intensification and redistribution beginning during the reign of the sixth ruler, Inca Rocca.

This ruler is said to have used labor tribute to construct new agricultural terraces and irrigation canals throughout the Cusco Basin, although some of these projects are credited to his wife, Mama Micay, an elite woman from a semiautonomous neighboring polity who probably brought her own labor tribute from her natal community.[17] Inca Rocca is also said to have reorganized the elite lineages of Cusco, assigning new irrigation resources to the upper moiety, which comprised members of his lineage. A second project of irrigation canal and terrace construction was completed at Larapa, which became Inca Rocca's personal estate and was inherited by his descendants.[18] At this time, any resistant communities within the Cusco Basin seem to have been defeated, and their lands were supposedly divided between existing Inca lineages.[19] The reorganization of the royal lineage system and Cusco's agricultural lands may also have included the establishment of an estate for the lineages of Cusco's lower moiety. After the Spanish Conquest, descendants of the first five Incas were found living in villages on the south side of the Cusco

Basin, in and around the towns of Wimpillay, Cayaocache, and K'ayra, where the mummies or emblems of many, if not all, of their ancestors were discovered in colonial times.[20] Beginning with Inca Rocca, each ruler is said to have established one or more personal estates and built palaces.

The development of the estate system marks an economic transformation of Inca society. Local elite hierarchies were bypassed by developing new lands, establishing new villages on those lands, and attracting settlement away from large villages in the valley, where developed lands were probably in short supply for the growing population. Other productive areas were confiscated and reallocated by the state. The close link between Inca state formation and land development might help us to date these processes, as it is known that the Andean highlands experienced a severe drought between AD 1250 and AD 1310 (as described in chap. 3). Competition for improved land and reliable irrigation water and the intensification of agricultural resources certainly would have increased at a time when such resources were especially scarce. The extension of Inca political control into the Sacred Valley—where productive new lands could be developed—would be a logical decision for a polity seeking additional resources. As discussed in greater detail later, radiocarbon dates from Pukara Pantillijlla indicate that the Incas came to control at least some areas to the north of the Vilcanota River around this time.

The Development of Elite Life in Cusco

As administrative, political, and religious hierarchies developed in Cusco, the emerging Inca elite created new means for communicating its status, which involved ensuring access to and control over wealth objects. The chronicles suggest that early territorial conquests were made to establish direct access to exotic and wealth goods, including cloth, feathers, precious metals, and coca leaf.[21] A number of these references mention the reigns of Capac Yupanqui and Inca Rocca. For example, several writers indicate that the first Inca territorial conquests were made to gain access to coca-producing lands in the Andes, while Bernabé Cobo says that the conquest of the Cuyos was made because they refused to give exotic birds to the Inca ruler.[22]

Several chronicles also mention that Capac Yupanqui and Inca Rocca were given over to festivals, drinking, and leisurely living.[23] According to Cobo, the fifth Inca ruler planted shade trees in Cusco's main plaza and maintained a menagerie there for his personal enjoyment.[24] This same ruler gave fine cloth (*qompi*) and women to one of his governors, an act of generosity that is mentioned for subsequent rulers.[25] Elite ceremony was enhanced as the state formed, and elites were involved not only in public displays but also in developing private spaces where they could enjoy the perquisites of their status.

Changes in Religious Power

The chronicles describe how, as the Incas began to consolidate their control over the Cusco Basin and beyond, they transformed their religious system, embellishing the elite ancestor cult, organizing the worship of the sun as a state religion, and establishing relationships with important shrines throughout the Andean region. The development of a royal ancestor cult may have been linked to the organization of a royal estate system, but at least one author suggests that the creation of images (*ídolos*) developed along with the custom of burying the dead with their possessions, which then became a system of split inheritance.[26]

During the period of state formation, the veneration of the sun was promoted as the official state cult. Several different Inca rulers are credited with the institution of the sun cult and construction of the Qorikancha (Golden Enclosure), the principal temple in Cusco, including Capac Yupanqui, the fifth Inca ruler.[27] While the sources making this identification are not the most reliable chronicles for many kinds of information, it is interesting to note this agreement among multiple sources. Sarmiento de Gamboa states that while the early Inca rulers had established and rebuilt the Qorikancha, it served as both elite residence and temple until the reign of Inca Rocca, when it was turned over to the state sun cult for its exclusive use.[28] Cieza de León states that Capac Yupanqui began to take women from conquered territories to serve a new state religion involving veneration of the sun, and Sarmiento de Gamboa mentions that he also delegated religious authority by naming an older brother, Cunti Mayta, as high priest of the cult.[29]

The regional and multigenerational nature of these changes makes it clear that the evolution of the state cult was not the work of a single individual. One chronicle states that Inca Rocca completed the Qorikancha, then decreed that a complex of cloistered women associated with the state religion (*akllawasi*) be established in Inca-controlled towns.[30]

The complexes were involved in the production of fancy cloth (*qompi*) and maize beer (*aqha*) used in elite Inca festivals and gift-giving, so this development would be evidence for the development of religion, as well as the production of wealth goods controlled by the state.

The chronicles also mention important developments of religious cult under Viracocha Inca and Pachacutic Inca Yupanqui, the most important of which may be the establishment of the veneration of a creator deity (Viracocha) as the imperial cult.[31] Creator worship was already practiced in some parts of the Andes, and the development of a more esoteric religion would allow the Incas to impose their religious hierarchy on local systems with simpler religious forms.[32]

Other chroniclers mention Capac Yupanqui as a ruler who extended Inca religious interests to interact with important rival numina (*wak'akuna*) venerated throughout the region, as well as major pan-Andean pilgrimage centers. The Andean chronicler Joan de Santa Cruz Pachacuti Yamqui Salcamaygua describes an episode where this ruler visited the principal shrine (*wak'a*) of the Cuyos, subordinating it to the Inca state religion.[33] Martín de Murúa states that at this time Inca emissaries were sent to the coastal shrine of Pachacamac.[34]

The development of a state religion and its imposition on local populations appears to have begun as the Inca state formed. This may have begun as the promotion of an ancestral cult, but within a few generations a well-established religious hierarchy was developed, with the construction of a principal temple out of fine stone masonry and the emplacement of state religious infrastructure at the local level.

Ideological Developments

The Inca state emerged concomitant with the loss of autonomy of non-Inca groups and the reorganization of new areas under Inca control. Conquest and subsequent reorganization required the development of a state expansion ideology promoting Inca connections to ancestors and supernatual forces, which in turn necessitated the conquest of other groups and rulers who challenged this superiority.[35] Sarmiento de Gamboa describes an important change beginning in the time of the fourth Inca ruler:

> This Mayta Capac was brave, and he began to prevail by force of arms for the first time since Mama Huaco and Manco Capac [the founding

ancestors]. About this they tell about the bird *indi*, which Manco Capac had brought from Tambotoco, and whose successors would have
inherited it. And before Mayta Capac, they had all kept it shut in a
chest or box of straw, which they were not accustomed to open, such
was the fear that they had of it. Mayta Capac, braver than all and de-
sirous to see what this thing was that his forebears had guarded so
much, opened the chest and saw the bird *indi*, and it spoke with him;
and they say that it gave oracles. And from that collusion Mayta Capac remained very wise and knowledgeable in what he had to do and
of what would happen to him.[36]

While this story cannot be treated as historical fact, the connection
between the Inca ruler and the ancestors—*indi* is said to have been the
name of the image of Manco Capac—is interesting, particularly given
that other accounts of state formation sometimes include the discovery
of a talisman or adoption of a royal emblem.[37] During the imperial period, one name for the sun was *inti,* and the ninth Inca ruler added the
title *intip churin* (Son of the Sun) to the paramount (*qhapaq*) title.[38]

As a state sun cult developed in Cusco, Inca rulers emphasized their
peerless status, using it as a pretext for conquest. According to Cobo,
the fifth Inca ruler conquered groups living north of the Vilcanota River
after local elites refused to give him exotic birds, and Cabello de Balboa
states that the sixth Inca ruler conquered some towns simply because
they lay near Cusco and were autonomous.[39] Juan de Betanzos states
that the eighth Inca ruler named himself Viracocha after the creator god,
to distinguish himself from other regional elites who also used the title
of *qhapaq,* while Sarmiento de Gamboa says that this ruler took his
name after receiving a vision from the creator deity, in which he was inspired to conquer the remaining groups living around Cusco.[40] Cabello
de Balboa states that Viracocha Inca began this regional campaign on
territorial consolidation because "he was very inclined toward warfare,
and a great friend of subjecting nations, and thus he was disposed not to
leave in all the region around Cusco any nation outside of the yoke of
his command and obedience."[41]

Pachacutic, the ninth Inca ruler, was shown his future in a mirror by
Inti (in this case, the personification of the sun), and is said to have carried that mirror on his conquests.[42] Territorial conquest was a course of
action that the Inca ruler pursued on the basis of divine guidance and inspiration, necessitated by the insistence of neighboring elites in using

royal titles and resisting Inca overlordship. These ideological justifications continued during imperial expansion.[43]

The historical narratives of multiple independent chronicles describe multigenerational processes of Inca state formation taking place in the Cusco region prior to the reign of Pachacutic. While it would be misleading to credit a given ruler with the creation of the Inca state, we can identify a suite of qualitative, long-term changes in Inca social and political organization. If we compare descriptions of the Inca polity under an early ruler—under the third or fourth ruler, perhaps—with the conditions said to prevail during the reign of Pachacutic's father, the contrasts are difficult to deny.

As the Inca state formed, power was reconfigured in militaristic, economic, political, religious, and ideological ways. The Inca histories provide a valuable perspective on Inca state formation and can be independently evaluated using new archaeological data. While these sources cannot be expected to provide accurate chronological dates or fully to recount historical events involving real people, they can be used in coordination with archaeological data and anthropological theory to advance our process-based knowledge of Inca political origins.[44] When studied in tandem with the archaeology, the chronicles reveal elements of the strategies, practices, and motivations for Inca elites, something that is at best difficult to reconstruct using shards, regional settlement patterns, and architectural plans.

Archaeological Evidence for Internal Processes of Inca State Formation

As discussed in chapter 2, several archaeological indicators can be used to identify states in the archaeological record. These include (1) the emergence of a four-tier settlement hierarchy, (2) increasing centralization, evident in regional rank-size graphs, (3) the construction of palace and estates for the ruler, (4) the development of standardized and specialized religious and administrative architecture, and (5) evidence of lasting territorial control beyond a day's walk of the principal settlement. Using archaeological data, we can now attempt to identify the same qualitative changes already described in the Inca histories.

Evidence for the State in the Cusco Basin

From approximately AD 1000 to AD 1300, the city of Cusco grew rapidly, becoming the urban capital of the new Inca state. Although the modern city of Cusco sits atop the early Inca one (which was largely rebuilt in the imperial period), numerous excavations have confirmed the presence of this early Inca occupation at the site of Cusco, one that does not appear to have a substantial Wari Period precedent.[45] Early Inca (Killke) deposits have been found in excavations in the Qorikancha and close to the Haucaypata area, as well as in the areas of Collcampata, Lucrepata, and Cusipata.[46] Figure 6.3 shows that as the early Inca state developed, its capital grew rapidly, with a core area reaching 50 hectares or more. The area immediately surrounding the urban core was occupied by several other early Inca satellite towns (including Puquin, Killke, Qoripata, and Saqsaywaman), creating an urban capital whose metropolitan region may have been several square kilometers by the time of imperial expansion. By comparison, the paramount centers of the Lucre Basin and other important rival groups were probably somewhat smaller than Cusco at this time, while the principal settlements of other regional competitors were significantly smaller—less than 10 hectares in the Sacred Valley and Paruro region.

Settlement Continuities in the Southern Cusco Basin

Even if the largest Lucre Basin sites approached the size of early Cusco—the size of the occupations of these sites from AD 1000 to AD 1300 is still unclear—they apparently lacked the large and complex network of large and small villages and hamlets seen in Cusco. As discussed in chapter 4, few settlement shifts occurred within the Cusco Basin following the Wari collapse, although the number and size of settlements increased markedly between AD 1000 and AD 1300 (fig. 6.4). The southern side of the Cusco Basin continued to be settled by large agricultural villages, some of them reaching areas of 6–8 hectares. Even as defense became a primary concern for other groups in the Cusco region, population in the Cusco Basin increased in villages that were located on undefended low bluffs immediately above fertile valley-bottom lands, becoming more hierarchical after AD 1000. Irrigation canals were constructed in some areas, and the Huatanay River was probably canalized, improving valley-bottom lands.

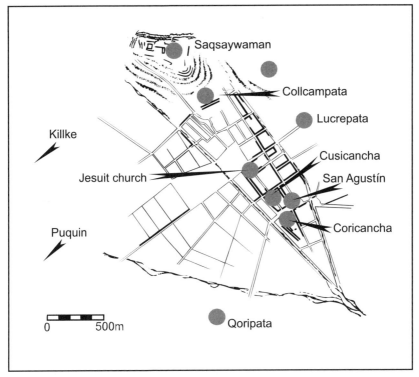

Fig. 6.3. Known Killke deposits under Cusco. Limited excavations have encountered evidence of Killke Period occupation under much of the Inca city and its satellite towns.

The huge increase in settlement from about AD 1000 to AD 1300 indicates population growth consistent with substantial immigration and surplus agricultural production. Some people probably moved into the Cusco Basin to seek safety from interpolity conflict, while others may have been attracted by productive agricultural lands that the Inca polity was developing using labor tribute.

New Villages and State Infrastructure in the Northern Cusco Basin

Sometime before AD 1300, the northern side of the Cusco Basin was dramatically transformed. This area consists of numerous narrow fingers of flat land separated by gullies, through which run a number of small,

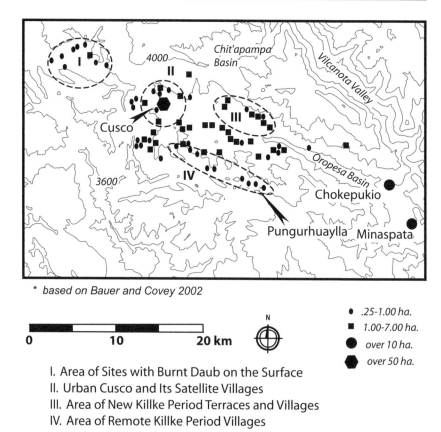

* based on Bauer and Covey 2002

0   10   20 km   N

● .25-1.00 ha.
■ 1.00-7.00 ha.
● over 10 ha.
⬢ over 50 ha.

I. Area of Sites with Burnt Daub on the Surface
II. Urban Cusco and Its Satellite Villages
III. Area of New Killke Period Terraces and Villages
IV. Area of Remote Killke Period Villages

Fig. 6.4. Cusco Basin settlement after AD 1000

deeply entrenched streams. The northern part of the Cusco Basin was almost completely depopulated until the Killke Period, perhaps because of the challenges in developing terracing and irrigation for reliable agriculture.[47] As the Inca state formed, a series of large villages was established on the lower northern valley slopes. These new settlements were built close to hundreds of hectares of newly constructed agricultural terraces, fed by irrigation canals that brought water from the nearby streams. The improvement of such lands would have been organized by Inca elites using labor tribute, but residence in the new villages probably would have been contingent on continued service to the emerging state elite. It is possible that some of these new settlements were established to meet the land needs of a growing Cusco Basin population or in reaction to the severe drought of AD 1250–1310. In either case, these lands represent a means whereby the state could undercut village elites—by attracting settlers and their labor tribute from existing villages—and establish a more bureaucratic rule over an increasingly dependent population.

As mentioned in the preceding, one of these new terrace systems was claimed as the personal estate of Inca Rocca, a ruler credited with some state formation processes in the histories. The construction of large terrace and canal systems would have required the diversion of considerable amounts of labor from subsistence farming, and it is likely that Inca elites used a rotational corvée system (*mit'a*) to fund construction, a practice that may have been introduced to the region (or intensified) in Wari construction projects in the Lucre Basin.[48] Along with other lines of evidence, the organization and execution of such a large project indicates that the early Inca polity was operating as a state by this time.

Evidence for the State in the Sacred Valley

The archaeological evidence for state formation in the Cusco Basin indicates processes of urbanism at Cusco, the development of palaces and estates by rulers, and economic intensification. New survey data from the Sacred Valley complement this picture with other lines of archaeological evidence.

Settlement Patterns and Degrees of Centralization

The formation of an early Inca state is demonstrated by the development of a four-tier settlement hierarchy, dominated by an urban capital (Cusco) with established secondary administrative centers located more than a day's walk from the capital. As figure 6.5 demonstrates for the Sacred Valley survey region, the Killke Period (ca. AD 1000–1400) saw the development of a four-tier settlement hierarchy (with Cusco as the top tier), prior to the development of the Inca imperial ceramic style around AD 1300–1400. The preceding Wari Period settlement pattern in the Sacred Valley consists of small villages and hamlets, only some of them controlled by the prestate polity in the Cusco Basin.

The largest Killke Period site in the Sacred Valley study region is Pukara Pantillijlla, a site with an area of approximately 10 hectares and the remains of more than one hundred stone and mud-brick structures.

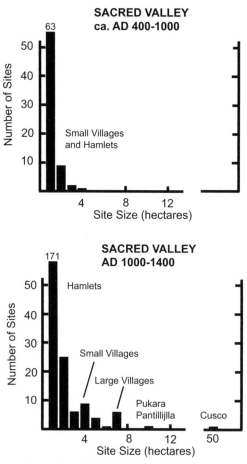

Fig. 6.5. Settlement hierarchy in the Sacred Valley study region. Settlement is much more hierarchical after AD 1000, and the integration of the valley under Cusco and its secondary center at Pukara Pantillijlla is consistent with a centralized state administration.

Architecture and artifacts encountered in controlled surface collections and excavations at this site reveal that an early Killke Period settlement was expanded by an intrusive early Inca presence indicative of the administrative reorganization of the surrounding Chongo Basin and the abandonment of important early Killke Period villages. The growth of Pukara Pantillijlla during the Killke Period represents the development of a secondary administrative site under the control of the early Inca state.

In addition to settlement hierarchy, rank-size graphs from the Sacred Valley study region indicate changes in the degree of centralized control over regional settlement. The rank-size graph of Sacred Valley settlement from AD 400 to AD 1000 displays a convex pattern, which some archaeologists would interpret as a lack of centralized integration of the region.[49] This convex pattern changes dramatically during the Killke Period, becoming a primate-dominated system consistent with regional integration by one large center. Comparison of the Killke Period and imperial Inca rank-size graphs reveals the continuity of centralized control, despite many changes to the regional settlement system. Settlement in the Sacred Valley became more hierarchical and centrally integrated well before imperial Inca expansion, indicating an extension of Inca state control over that region. This control clearly was not uniform throughout the Cusco region—the archaeological and ethnohistoric evidence from the Lucre Basin reveals that some groups living close to Cusco managed to resist incorporation into the Inca state until quite late.

Forts and Fortifications

As the Inca state annexed new territory outside the Cusco Basin, it appears to have developed a number of forts and fortifications to safeguard new conquests. Two sites in the Sacred Valley survey region may be early Inca forts. The site of Raqchi (VS-94) is located on a prominent ridge overlooking a principal route from Cusco to the Sacred Valley. A nucleated village was established there after AD 1000, probably to take advantage of the natural defenses offered by the steep slopes of the ridge. A prominent point at the end of the ridge was densely settled, and there are extensive architectural remains, completely collapsed and heavily looted. On the saddle below the promontory is a large enclosure that contains the remains of several large rectangular structures (fig. 6.6). The walls protecting the interior architecture are preserved to 3 meters or more, and a second set of defensive works can be seen in a dry moat dug to restrict access to the ridge. The fortified part of the site has almost exclusively Killke and transitional Inca pottery on the surface. This is in marked contrast to the village area on the promontory, where a wide range of Killke Period pottery styles was present, including pottery from the Cusco and Lucre basins.

Other sites that might represent early fortifications of the expanding Inca state include Warq'ana and Pumamarca.[50] Warq'ana is a densely

Fig. 6.6. Fortified enclosure at Raqchi (VS-94). This may be a fort built by the Incas after they conquered the Killke Period village located at the site.

nucleated settlement that occupies a prominence on the southern rim of the Sacred Valley. The rectangular structures at this site are better preserved than those at Raqchi, but some of the same enclosures appear to be present. Ann Kendall and colleagues report fortification walls associated with a defensive ditch restricting access to the ridge where the site is located.[51] The site has been interpreted as a pre-Inca nucleated village that was developed as a fortress when conquered by the Incas during the Killke Period.

Pumamarca is located in the transverse valley above Ollantaytambo, along a route to the lowlands. This site also has evidence of fortification walls and rectangular architecture (fig. 6.7). Excavations at the site indicate a similar occupational history to the other two sites. The three forts identified so far suggest that the Inca state was involved in the military conquest of autonomous groups and that it used defensible locations to develop forts in order to monitor traffic along important routes.

Palaces and Royal Estates

In addition to the archaeological evidence for an early estate at Larapa, a second estate has been identified at the site of Qhapaqkancha on the southern rim of the Sacred Valley (fig. 6.8), where a rectangular platform and Inca-style buildings were constructed. This compound was built within a large existing Killke Period village that appears to have been largely abandoned during the imperial period. Other royal estates have been identified in the Sacred Valley based on historic documents and the presence of Inca architecture and ceramics. The royal estates at Calca, Caquia Xaquixaguana (today called Juchuy Coscco), and Pisaq are associated with Killke Period settlements, although they clearly flourished as state settlements in Inca imperial times (fig. 6.9).[52]

Temples and Administrative Architecture

Possible Killke Period administrative architecture and temples are identifiable in the Sacred Valley at sites such as Qhapaqkancha, Markasunay, and Pukara Pantillijlla. As mentioned in the preceding, Qhapaqkancha has an architectural compound indicative of public or administrative functions. This compound is an intrusive construction within a large Killke Period village and comprises three rectangular structures attached to a 2700-square-meter platform. The two flanking structures face the

Fig. 6.7. The fortified site of Pumamarca. (Negative no. 334772, Courtesy Dept. of Library Services, American Museum of Natural History.)

Fig. 6.8. Qhapaqkancha, part of the estate of Yahuar Huaccac, the seventh Inca ruler.

Fig. 6.9. The Q'allaq'asa complex at Pisaq. Killke Period settlement has been encountered here. (Negative no. 334764, Courtesy Dept. of Library Services, American Museum of Natural History.)

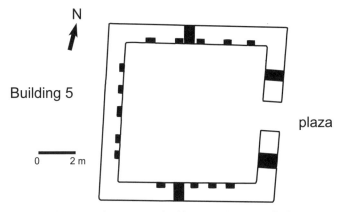

Fig. 6.10. Administrative building at Pukara Pantillijlla

village, while the central one faces onto the platform. Based on surface ceramics and architectural style, this platform was built toward the end of the Killke Period, and it represents an open space that would have been used for public events that could have involved an entire subject polity.[53] A plaza of similar size is present at Juchuy Coscco (called Caquia Xaquixaguana in the chronicles), a royal estate said to have been developed prior to the first major campaigns of Inca territorial expansion.[54]

The open spaces and architectural complexes at the administrative site of Pukara Pantillijlla are much smaller than those just described. Two buildings at this site (designated *building 5* and *building* 15) may have been used for administrative or ritual activities (fig. 6.10). Building 5 is a large square structure that faces a small plaza area. This building has thick stone walls that are preserved to approximately 3 meters and has four windows and fourteen internal niches. Test excavations in this structure revealed the remains of a cobblestone floor, something not seen in residential structures excavated at the site. A higher percentage of plates and bowls (61.8 percent) was present in this structure than was seen in the site as a whole (46.4 percent), with a lower incidence of cooking vessels. It is possible that this building and associated plaza were used for activities involving local elites, Inca administrators, and the consumption of food and beverages prepared elsewhere at the site. A radiocarbon date of grass temper from wall plasters in an interior niche in building 5 yielded a calibrated two-sigma date of AD 1300–1370 (48 percent probability) or AD 1380–1440 (47.4 percent probability), suggesting that this building was built well before the traditional date for Inca expansion.[55]

Building 15 was built later in the site's occupation, probably in the fifteenth century. This structure has a similarly high proportion of plates and bowls, with fewer cooking vessels. It is possible that these structures had nonresidential functions, while the semicircular structures at the site were used as residences of local elites. In addition to these buildings, a compound of four rectangular structures (buildings 10–13) was built during the expansion of the site occupation under Inca rule. These buildings were not excavated, but their layout suggests both residential and nonresidential functions, perhaps including storage.

More excavation is needed throughout the Cusco region in order to clarify the question of when and where special administrative and religious architecture developed, but the available evidence suggests that some small-scale examples began to be built during the Killke Period Inca state expansion into the Sacred Valley.

Territorial Control

In terms of administered territory, it is difficult to assess the total area administered by the early Inca state, although it is clear that the polity in the Cusco Basin had surpassed the operational boundaries for prestate social organization. To the north of Cusco, the Vilcanota River presented a natural limit to the kind of face-to-face administration seen in complex polities where power and authority were not specialized or widely delegated. For example, round-trip travel from Cusco to the important prestate village of Muyuch'urqu presents a difficult journey of over 40 kilometers, with a total elevation change of more than 5000 meters. By comparison, the site of Qhapaqkancha, on the southern rim of the Sacred Valley, could be reached in several hours' walk from Cusco. The development of the secondary administrative site at Pukara Pantillijlla indicates that the early Inca state had extended its control over some areas to the north of the Vilcanota River, requiring a permanent administrative presence and reorganization of local politics and economies.

Bauer has presented a second measure of the extent of Inca influence, based on the distribution of the preimperial Killke pottery style.[56] While local pre-Inca styles are distributed in an area within roughly 20 kilometers of the production site, Killke pottery is found well beyond such limits, up to 50 kilometers or more in some places. This figure may be an exaggerated indicator of political control, but it does suggest a qualitative difference in how the early Inca style was distributed throughout the Cusco region. Killke pottery is the most common style at sites located south of the Vilcanota River, but it is also common at sites as far away as Ancasmarca, the farthest point from Cusco in the Sacred Valley study region.[57]

Early Inca Expansion to the South of Cusco

The settlement patterns and distribution of Killke pottery described for the Sacred Valley study region can be compared with the ethnohistory and settlement archaeology from Bauer's Paruro fieldwork. Historical documents mention the Chillque, Masca, Tambo, Queguar, Papre, Aco, Yanahuara, and Quechua ethnic groups as living to the south of Cusco. Archaeological surveys have been conducted in the historic territories of the Chillque, Masca, and Tambo; these are among the smaller groups, the largest probably consisting of no more than a few thousand individuals.[58] The center of the Chillque ethnic territory is the modern town of Araypallpa, the area of densest distribution of the Colcha ceramic style at the time the Inca state was forming.[59] The center of Masca territory was modern Yaurisque, while the Tambos lived around modern Pacariqtambo, both areas lying about 20–25 kilometers from Cusco.[60]

Bauer's survey research indicates that the regional moiety system described in the sixteenth century probably dates to AD 1200.[61] As discussed in the preceding, the Cusco polity after AD 1000 appears to have exercised influence over Masca and Tambo territory, with regular interactions with the Chillques around Araypallpa. Bauer notes that settlement for these areas remains stable over time, with no indication of defensive settlements from AD 1000 to AD 1300.[62] Instead, these groups lived in small villages and hamlets scattered throughout *kichwa*-zone lands. Their incorporation into the Inca state appears to have occurred early on, and without substantial reorganization of settlement or local economy. According to Bauer, all major sites occupied during the period of early Inca state formation continued to be occupied into the imperial period.

The archaeological evidence does not suggest that the Incas resorted to military conquest to incorporate groups living immediately to the south of the Cusco Basin,[63] and it is possible that these small groups chose to ally themselves with, and ultimately subordinate themselves to, the Inca state because of (1) a tradition of long-standing political association, (2) a desire to participate in Inca economic networks and religious systems, and (3) a need for protection against would-be enemies, perhaps including the Muyna and Pinagua polities of the Lucre Basin.

Groups living at a greater distance from Cusco apparently did not seek the protection of the Inca state. Although the archaeological data are lacking for most areas, the chronicles suggest that many groups living farther to the south of Cusco—for example, the Papres, Yanahuaras, and Chumbivilcas—were incorporated during regional military campaigns several generations after the first territorial expansion began (see table 6.1). Groups like the Quechuas are said to have contracted alliances with the Inca state but were not subordinates to the extent that they could claim Inca military protection.[64] By the time of Inca imperial expansion, all of these groups were under the control of the Inca state and were closely tied to Cusco by shared ethnic ties, politics, and ideology. Resistance at this time by groups like the Acos led to their resettlement in new imperial provinces.[65]

Summary

After AD 1000 the Wari polity's colonial influence in the Cusco region had declined, giving way to conditions of widespread political competition between a number of small polities. Conflict led to the depopulation of productive lands between the Inca polity and neighboring groups, leading some populations to resettle in the Cusco Basin. High rates of population growth in the Cusco Basin would have presented the Inca polity with administrative challenges, particularly in addressing resource fluctuations and political competition. The state formed as Inca elites reorganized the Cusco Basin, simultaneously reducing some neighboring groups to subordinates and instituting state administration over territory that had never previously been dominated by Cusco. Internally, Inca rulers promoted the reorganization of Cusco's descent groups and developed new agricultural resources as part of an estate system. They appointed relatives to religious, administrative, and military positions to meet the governmental requirements of the rapidly growing population of the Cusco Basin. Rulers prominently consumed and redistributed exotic goods, and Inca elites used feasting and gifts of cloth, coca leaf, and precious metals to reciprocate the services of their subjects. The state made direct access to these goods a priority in its expansion strategy.

Inca rulers began to construct their own palaces and estates and develop a ceremonial life that legitimated the Inca conquest of neighboring groups. This included control over local agricultural rituals and shrines, the development of a religious hierarchy, and the construction of temples.[66] The state took control of economic and religious aspects of the calendar, elaborating and reorganizing ritual life. The calendar provided a means for controlling economic production, and the developing state created new agricultural lands and used centralized management to amplify agropastoral yields.

Feeding an urban population would have been a central concern for the state, which began to intensify agricultural production and develop storage facilities that could buffer against lean years. A prolonged drought in the second half of the thirteenth century probably intensified the development of and competition for agricultural resources.[67] Storage of foodstuffs and wealth goods helped to maintain Cusco's political economy and ceremonial life, as well as to fund state expansion projects. The developing state began to resettle some depopulated buffer zones and extend territorial conquests along caravan routes to ensure direct acquisition of nonlocal resources like coca leaf and chile pepper. The lion's share of plunder from military campaigns would have benefited Inca elites, but some was probably distributed to reward soldiers. Conquered groups came to be governed by state administrators who often retained local elites to enact state policies locally. These new subordinates provided the labor for the continued extension and intensification of maize agriculture in the Cusco Basin and Sacred Valley. Not all groups were reduced to subordination during the initial territorial expansion. Some alliances were maintained, while hostile groups were attacked and raided periodically for decades before being conquered.

The Inca state expanded its territory through increasingly protracted military campaigns, conquering resistant groups and developing fortifications in strategic locations. Local resistance or rebellions led to the territorial consolidation of increasingly large parts of the Inca heartland, while long-distance diplomatic contacts (e.g., with shrines like Pachacamac or with polities in the Titicaca Basin) became more sustained or formalized. Inca imperial expansion began in earnest with sustained campaigns outside of the Inca heartland, against groups that were culturally distinct from those of the Cusco region. These were soon followed by final territorial consolidation of the Cusco region.

CHAPTER SEVEN

Elite Interaction and Local
Responses to Inca Expansion

In the last chapter we saw that the archaeological evidence and historical accounts of colonial-period Inca elites describe both processes of Inca
state formation and territorial expansion throughout the Cusco region.
Because the conquest or subordination of neighboring polities was an
important feature in oral histories describing state formation processes,
we should also attempt to consider the reactions of neighboring groups
to the development and expansion of the Inca state. An appreciation
of how cooperation or resistance by local elites affected the nature and
tempo of Inca expansion and political consolidation is critical for understanding how Inca imperial strategies developed. This chapter first describes patterns of elite interaction in the Cusco region, then presents
case studies that illustrate local responses to Inca expansion.

Neighbors of the Inca State

Many of the internal processes involved in Inca state formation have
already been discussed, and the early subordination of some groups
outside the Cusco Basin is identifiable in the archaeological evidence.
The expansion of the Inca state throughout the Cusco region involved a
number of groups that maintained more autonomy than the ethnic groups
of the Paruro region, discussed in the previous chapter. As the Inca state
extended its territory to the north and south of Cusco, it also interacted
with complex polities and numerous ethnic groups lying to the east and
west of the Cusco Basin. Systematic survey data are not yet available in
the latter areas, but it is possible to describe the groups living around the
Cusco Basin and describe their interactions with the Inca state over time
(fig. 7.1).

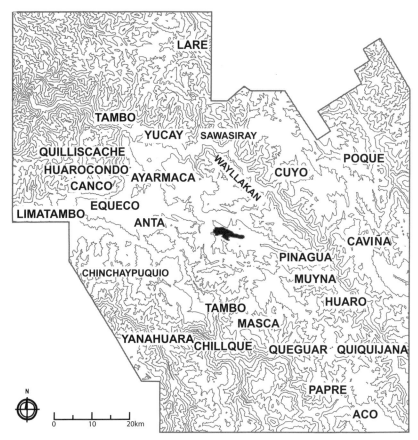

Fig. 7.1. Political and ethnic groups of the Cusco region

Areas West and Northwest of Cusco

The region to the west of Cusco was occupied by a large number of different groups, including the Limatambo, Quilliscache, Mayo, Equeco, Sanco, Huarocondo, and Anta. The location of these groups and their sacred places (*wak'akuna*) indicates that most represent small polities, in some cases occupying only a single village and its surrounding territory.[1] Ethnically, some of these groups might not have been closely related to the Incas; a sixteenth-century administrative visit (*relación geográfica*) states that they spoke their own languages (*lenguas particulares*) in addition to Quechua.[2]

Few references are made regarding these groups in the Inca histories (except for the Antas, discussed in greater detail in this chapter), although survey work now underway in the region west of Cusco will soon provide archaeological data for addressing the level of local political complexity and cultural integration. Reconnaissance work in the Limatambo area indicates a similar settlement stability to that observed for the Paruro area to the south of Cusco.[3] Documentary references and archaeological observations from the Quilliscache territory note the presence of defensive ridgetop sites, probably indicative of local resistance to Inca control until the end of the regional consolidation process.[4]

Ann Kendall, working in the Cusichaca area about 70 kilometers northwest of Cusco (an area at the margins of the Inca heartland), has reported settlement patterns that reflect a concern with defense, as well as local evidence for the construction of some small canal and terrace systems prior to Inca incorporation.[5] Site locations for the small groups between Limatambo and Cusco appear to be consistent with an early incorporation into the Inca state, a proposition that will be considered by archaeological research currently in progress.

The area to the north of the Anta-Limatambo area was occupied by one of the largest and most complex groups of the Cusco region, the Ayarmacas. This group occupied the Maras and Chinchero area and may have controlled some parts of the Sacred Valley around Urubamba.[6] The Spanish chronicles describe the Ayarmacas as a complex polity with a paramount ruler (Tocay Ccapac) who had political alliances throughout the region and dominated many of the small neighboring groups. The Incas made marriage alliances with this group during the period of state formation but also warred with them on occasion before finally bringing the polity under territorial administration around the time of initial imperial expansion.[7]

To date, the limited reconnaissance and excavations conducted to the west and northwest of Cusco do not permit the systematic evaluation of the historical accounts, although regional survey data are being collected that will provide an independent means for describing the Ayarmaca polity and its relation to the Inca state.[8] The available data indicate that a distinct pottery style was produced in this region and distributed in parts of the Sacred Valley. Some sites are located on prominent hills or ridges, possibly to provide defense against raiding, and the principal Ayarmaca settlements appear to have been large valley-bottom villages located close to maize lands near modern Maras.[9]

The Lucre Basin

The political climate of the Lucre Basin in AD 1000 has already been described. The archaeological and documentary evidence indicates that the basin was occupied by the Muyna and Pinagua polities and that these groups were not allies of the Inca state, but rather should be considered among its most important rivals.[10] The depopulation of the area between the Cusco and Lucre basins persisted until the Incas conquered the region and established labor colonists in new settlements.[11] The only substantial Killke Period settlement within this buffer zone was Pukara Tipón, a nucleated village whose settlement and agricultural lands were surrounded by a massive defensive wall constructed of rough fieldstones and mud mortar that stands approximately 5 meters high. Areas not protected by the wall had sheer cliffs blocking access to the site. Together, the wall and cliffs created a defensive perimeter of more than 6 kilometers, one whose construction would have involved considerable investment of local labor. The group that built Tipón must have considered security to be more important than ecological risk or the intensification of the local political economy.

Within the Lucre Basin, the local polities produced a distinct pottery style, one that has limited distribution at sites in the Cusco Basin and in the Sacred Valley. It is unclear how the Muyna and Pinagua defended their principal sites (Chokepukio and Minaspata), and it is possible that they relied on the size of these settlements to discourage raids. Still, the Spanish chronicles refer to repeated Inca incursions against these polities, which occurred over several generations before the Lucre Basin was reorganized politically under direct Inca administration.[12]

Even though Cusco did not annex the Lucre Basin polities until late in its program of regional consolidation, there is documentary evidence that Cusco maintained diplomatic and political relations with polities to the east of the Lucre Basin. The Huaro area is mentioned as an early ally of the Cusco polity, and its mention as an affinal group (*kaka*) by the chronicler Guaman Poma suggests that political alliances were maintained through elite marriages.[13] The chronicler Pedro Sarmiento de Gamboa describes a military campaign that conquered sites in the Vilcanota Valley above Pisaq, thereby allowing the Inca state to bypass the Lucre Basin and surround the holdout Muyna and Pinagua polities.[14] Several authors mention Inca military conquests beyond the Lucre Basin well before the reduction of these polities was complete.[15]

Although archaeological data from areas to the east of Cusco are still being developed, the Spanish chronicles suggest that early Inca state expansion was stymied by the complex polities of the Lucre Basin. The Inca state cultivated alliances with groups beyond this area and bypassed the Muynas and Pinaguas while extending their territorial control up the Vilcanota Valley. By the time of imperial expansion, Inca rulers were developing personal lands in the area of Quiquijana and beyond,[16] and they supposedly were able to draw military support from the Qanas and Kanchis, although these groups were not considered to share Inca ethnicity and lived outside of the Inca heartland.[17] Survey and excavation work in the Vilcanota Valley between Huaro and Sicuani should clarify the limits of the Inca heartland and the dates for Inca expansion beyond the heartland region.

Elite Interaction: Alliance, Warfare, and Defense

The proliferation of local elites in Cusco's small post-Wari polities led to the development of new kinds of elite interactions, predicated on shared language, ethnicity, economy, and political organization. The Spanish chronicles indicate that as the early Inca state formed in the Cusco Basin, elite hierarchies were becoming increasingly complex throughout the region.

Elaboration of Elite Hierarchies

The documentary and archaeological evidence suggests that elite hierarchies did not remain unchanged following the decline of the Wari empire. Although elite *authority* had been elaborated through the Wari colonization of the Lucre Basin and Urcos area, state administrative and religious institutions did not persist after the abandonment of Pikillacta. The Inca histories describe early rulers as being the paramounts of unspecialized governments of a limited size and complexity, rather than inheriting a tradition of statecraft directly.[18] For example, chronicle references to the third Inca ruler, Lloque Yupanqui, describe an Inca polity where the paramount interacted with other local leaders as primus inter pares but was not appreciably more powerful than his allies and rivals. Several writers state that Lloque Yupanqui was able to attract the leaders of many nearby towns to his service but that this was due to his personal charisma rather than any coercive power that the Cusco polity could exert outside of the Cusco Basin.[19] Interestingly, the leaders of these ethnic groups, towns, and polities are mentioned in the chronicles as individuals without political titles indicative of a regional political hierarchy.[20] These references provide a point of comparison for the use of political titles during the period of Inca state formation.

The chronicles indicate a multigenerational process of developments within the Cusco Basin that was followed by territorial expansion that incorporated the once-autonomous groups living throughout the Cusco region. This period of Inca state formation, territorial expansion, and regional consolidation also corresponds to a vertical and horizontal diversification of regional elite hierarchies and political competition. Chroniclers like Pedro Sarmiento de Gamboa and Miguel Cabello de Balboa mention several non-Inca elites as they describe the beginnings of Inca territorial expansion in the region.

Elite interaction can be understood better by looking at the Quechua vocabulary for elite status. Significantly, terms like *kuraka, llaqtakamayuq,* or *tukrikuq* that were used to describe imperial Inca positions are absent from this vocabulary.[21] Instead, a separate set of titles may be found in the names of rivals to the early Inca rulers.

Chronicle references to local elite titles are all but absent until the time that state formation began in the Cusco Basin, when the Inca ruler is first described as being named *qhapaq,* a paramount office that the colonial Quechua dictionaries gloss as "king."[22] The office of *qhapaq* was not the only level of noble in the Cusco region, and the documents refer to secondary elites as *apu,* a title meaning "great lord" or "judge" and implying a secondary elite status that could be organized in pairs— perhaps the paramount leadership of a moiety within a complex polity.[23] The first Inca ruler mentioned by Sarmiento de Gamboa as using the title *qhapaq* had several sons and nephews named *apu,* to whom new governorships, priesthoods, and military commands were delegated.[24] Early elite vocabulary also includes the term *thupa,* which means "lord," often lordship over a town or region that was conquered.[25] The term *inka* itself is an honorific, implying membership in the nobility.[26] Finally, *ylla* suggests wealth and prosperity.[27]

Analysis of elite titles associated with early Inca expansion indicates how important elite interaction was in developing alliances and justifying military action (fig. 7.2). The strongest rivals to the Incas are named *qhapaq,* including the paramount leaders of the Ayarmaca (Tocay

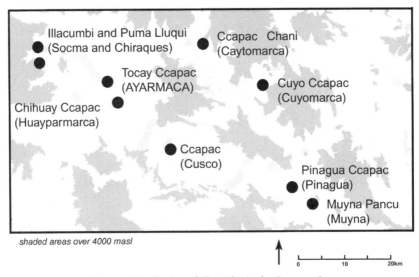

Illacumbi and Puma Lluqui
(Socma and Chiraques)

Ccapac Chani
(Caytomarca)

Tocay Ccapac
(AYARMACA)

Chihuay Ccapac
(Huayparmarca)

Cuyo Ccapac
(Cuyomarca)

Ccapac
(Cusco)

Pinagua Ccapac
(Pinagua)

Muyna Pancu
(Muyna)

shaded areas over 4000 masl

0   10   20km

Fig. 7.2. Distribution of elite titles in the Cusco region

Ccapac), Pinagua (Pinagua Ccapac), and Cuyo (Cuyo Ccapac) groups. These leaders may have shared similar political hierarchies and economic organization.[28] It is unclear whether multiple *qhapaq* offices refer to a diarchy or conditions of alliance, but some rulers employing the *qhapaq* title appear to have been united with another paramount leader. At any rate, these elites may have dominated small confederations that included pairs of secondary lords who were called *thupa, ylla,* and *apu*.[29] In addition to the most powerful regional competitors, pairs of village or moiety leaders are also mentioned for some areas, indicating a wide range of political complexity. In referring to leaders of *qhapaq* status, Cabello de Balboa also makes reference to the conquest of "other lords of lesser title."[30]

Inca imperial expansion is explained by some chroniclers as occurring because Inca rulers were not content that other paramount rulers should pretend to use titles like *qhapaq*.[31] The Incas referred to rulers like Qolla Ccapac and Chimú Ccapac as one-time equivalents of the Inca ruler, and Juan de Betanzos mentions that Viracocha Inca elevated his title to that of a deity to distinguish himself from other *qhapaq* title users.[32] By the imperial period, the Inca ruler had a well-established series of titles emphasizing uniqueness and divine descent (*sapa inka,*

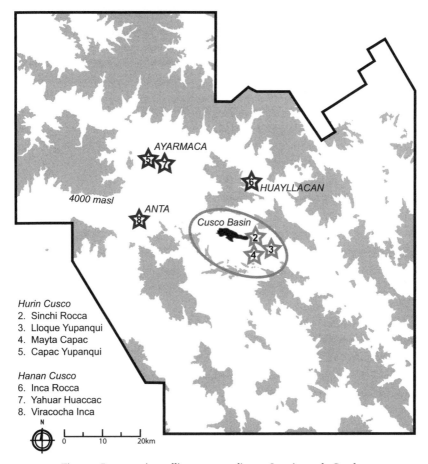

Fig. 7.3. Inca marriage alliances, according to Sarmiento de Gamboa

intip churin, etc.), and new administrative and bureaucratic titles also came into use.

Marriage Alliances

Marriage alliances helped to determine status in Cusco's elite hierarchies, as well as the kinds of relationships that competing polities had with each other (fig. 7.3). As has been observed, some groups (e.g., the Pinaguas) maintained no marriage alliances with the Incas, while others were described as *kaka,* or affinal male relatives.[33] In his early Quechua dictionary, Domingo de Santo Tomás demonstrates a link between marriage and affinal labor service, equating the mother's kin with the presentation of tribute or service.[34] The duties of kinship made elite marriage alliances a means for creating social obligations that lasted for several generations.

Prior to the imperial period, Inca elites used marriage alliances to create asymmetries with other elite lineages and polities, in part by taking advantage of the practices of virilocal residence patterns, bilateral descent, and polygyny.[35] Wife-giving polities appear to have been subordinate to wife-taking polities as the Inca state formed, and the offspring of these unions inherited labor tribute and resources in their mothers' communities.[36] At the time of state formation, dominant rulers throughout the Cusco region also took multiple secondary wives from neighboring polities as a means of increasing political control. Not only would the subordinate communities have to provide labor service to their elite women, but the male relatives of these women also would have certain social obligations to these women's children.

The importance of female elites in these processes should be emphasized. The chronicles state clearly that the women who became principal wives of the Inca rulers at the time of state formation were daughters of local lords, and one is described as being a female ruler (*cacica*).[37] In some cases, these women are said to have actively sought out political alliances between their relatives and the Inca state. Mama Micay, wife of Inca Rocca, the sixth Inca ruler, is credited with developing new agricultural infrastructure, evidence of using personal labor tribute to the benefit of the royal lineage.[38] Elite Inca women continued to hold personal estates in the imperial period and were active in developing political factions and influencing imperial administration.[39]

The children of elite marriages had very real ties to their mothers' communities. Several colonial authors indicate that the obligations of the mother's kin among Andean societies included ritual actions, as well as labor service. Pablo Joseph de Arriaga states that when a child was four or five years old, he or she had a hair-cutting ceremony in which a new name was given, and for which the parents' kin—both the father's family (*masa*) and the mother's relatives (*kaka*)—gave the child "wool, maize, camelids, silver, and other things."[40] Felipe Guaman Poma de Ayala states that incest taboos and social obligations of *kaka* groups to *masa* groups persisted over several generations: "and these godparents [of haircutting and marriage rituals] helped with the work, with other necessities, and when they were sick, and in eating and drinking, and in the festivals, and in the field, and in mourning their death, and after death, and at all times while they were alive, and afterwards their children and descendants, grandchildren and great-grandchildren were served."[41] These statements help to reveal the long-term effects of intergroup marriages: herds and agricultural lands in the mother's community would be worked for her children, and labor might also be expected for other projects outside of that community. In return, the individuals receiving these resources and labor would be responsible for ceremonial reciprocation of service through feasting, bringing wife-giving groups into the ceremonial life of the wife-taking polity.[42] The case of the Huayllacans illustrates how marriage alliances influenced Inca state expansion.

The Huayllacans: Marriage Alliances and Political Competition

Chronicles and archival land documents locate Huayllacan territory in the communities of Patahuaillacan (identified as modern Patabamba), Micocancha, Paullu, and Paulopampa (fig. 7.4).[43] These sites are named in a land document pertaining to the area around modern Patabamba and Paullu, located on the southern rim of the Sacred Valley just over 15 kilometers from Cusco.[44] Huayllacan settlements were concentrated in an area of rich tuber production and dry-farming, but with easy access to both the high *puna* pastures in the Lake Qoricocha area, as well as the maize-producing *kichwa* lands near the floor of the Sacred Valley.

At the time that the Inca state began to expand throughout the Cusco region, the Huayllacans are described as being a small polity (probably of Quechua speakers) with hereditary leaders who had regular contact and strong marriage ties with Inca Cusco.[45] According to Pedro Sarmiento de Gamboa, the sixth Inca ruler, Inca Rocca, married Mama Micay of Patahuaillacan, who was the daughter of the leader of the Huayllacans, Soma Inca, and is herself described as a political leader.[46] This marriage marked a shift of Huayllacan elite marriage alliance—and, thus, political subordination—from the Ayarmacas to the Incas, although it is clear that Inca influence at the time was limited to hegemony rather than formal political administration.

Mama Micay had been promised as wife to Tocay Ccapac, the leader of the Ayarmacas, and this change in allegiance sparked a war between

Fig. 7.4. The Patabamba area, with Qhapaqkancha in the background. The principal Huayllacan villages were located in this area.

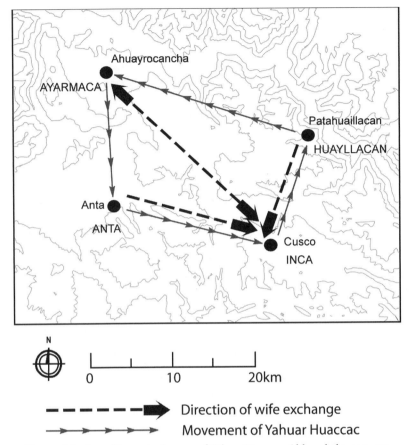

Fig. 7.5. Marriage alliances in the story of Yahuar Huaccac. Although the story cannot be considered a historical reality, it describes an important process whereby subordinate groups transferred their loyalty from the Ayarmacas to the Incas through marriage alliances.

the Ayarmacas and Huayllacans. That the Incas did not interfere in this conflict suggests that the Huayllacans did not enjoy their military protection and that the Huayllacans were free to contract external relations with other groups, both indications of continuing local political autonomy. When the Ayarmacas proved stronger in the conflict, they forced the people of Patahuaillacan to help them kidnap Titu Cusi Huallpa (known more commonly as Yahuar Huaccac), the son of Mama Micay and Inca Rocca (fig. 7.5).

To comply with the Ayarmaca demand, a Huayllacan chief named

Inca Paucar, who was a paternal uncle of Titu Cusi Huallpa, asked that he visit the community of Micocancha in order that he might come to know his relatives on his mother's side and claim resources in the community.[47] The boy was about eight years old, and different accounts state that the visit was to correspond with the inheritance of estates and camelid herds in the Huayllacan territory. The Huayllacans left the child in the village and went to their fields, allowing the Ayarmacas to enter the village and take the boy.[48] He was carried off to Ahuayrocancha, the principal settlement of the Ayarmacas, and was sent by Tocay Ccapac to live in difficult conditions among the herders of the Ayarmaca ruler. A secondary wife of Tocay Ccapac named Chimbo Urma helped to rescue Titu Cusi Huallpa and return him to Cusco. An elite woman from Anta, she convinced her male relatives to assist in the rescue and transfer their political allegiance to the Incas. To avoid a war, the Ayarmaca and Inca rulers made a reciprocal marriage exchange, whereby an Ayarmaca woman became the principal wife of the seventh Inca ruler, and an Inca woman married the succeeding Tocay Ccapac.

While this should not be considered an account of a historic sequence of events, the story of the kidnapping of Titu Cusi Huallpa reveals the likely significance of elite marriage alliances in the Cusco region as the Inca state began to expand territorially.[49] Inca elites intermarried with other groups, and kin ties were used to communicate subordinate status. This story describes how the Incas had become powerful enough to attract new subordinates, groups that had traditionally intermarried with and served the Ayarmacas. The chronicles mention that as the state formed, Inca rulers began to take multiple secondary wives, increasing the number of neighboring groups obliged to serve the Cusco elite in fulfillment of kinship obligations. Elite Inca polygyny would have helped to promote Cusco above other important settlements in the region, as a place where members of many groups would come to celebrate festive and ritual occasions, to serve rotations of labor tribute, but also to assert their own individual statuses through competitive displays of wealth, feasting, and dancing.

Long-term changes in Inca-Huayllacan relations are illustrated in a second episode between the Incas and the Huayllacans that occurred later in the reign of Yahuar Huaccac (Titu Cusi Huallpa). After the return of the Inca heir to Cusco, the Huayllacans were spared after humbling themselves before the Inca ruler. Still, they remained sufficiently involved in Inca politics to attempt to promote the succession of an illegitimate son of Yahuar Huaccac named Marca-yutu, to whom they were related.[50] Because this ruler's principal wife was the Ayarmaca daughter of Tocay Ccapac, Marca-yutu might have been the son of a secondary Huayllacan wife—otherwise he could not be both "illegitimate" in terms of succession and also more closely related to the Huayllacans than the legitimate heir. To advance their interests, the Huayllacans conspired to kill Pahuac Huallpa Mayta, the second-born son who had been named successor. They requested that Yahuar Huaccac send him to Paullu to visit his grandfather Soma Inca and then killed the boy and his guard of forty nobles. To avenge the assassination of his appointed heir, Yahuar Huaccac led his armies against the Huayllacans, killing some and banishing others from the region, then taking their lands as a personal estate. Centuries later, members of his descent group continued to live in the territory of the Huayllacans, and the mummy of Yahuar Huaccac was found by Polo de Ondegardo in Paullu.[51]

This second Huayllacan story indicates that as the Inca state grew stronger, it redefined its relationship with subordinate groups. The Huayllacans shifted their principal marriage alliance from the Ayarmacas to the Incas, presumably based on the assumption that this change would most effectively preserve local autonomy and promote local political interests. When an Ayarmaca woman became the Inca ruler's principal wife, the Huayllacans conspired to promote the succession of someone they considered their relative. The attempt to maintain the representation of their own interests in the Inca state ultimately led to the destruction of the Huayllacans as an autonomous political entity. Their conquest led to the transformation of Huayllacan territory into a royal Inca estate, one that emphasized Inca dominance rather than kin ties to the local people.[52] At the same time, this conquest is said to have been the prelude to a more sustained military campaign in which Inca armies conquered ten towns located in the Vilcanota Valley.[53]

Archaeological Evidence for the Huayllacan Polity

Archaeological data collected by the Sacred Valley Archaeological Project provide new perspectives on the Huayllacan polity. At around AD 1000, settlement in the Patabamba-Paullu area shifted away from unprotected locations near Patabamba to a large ridgetop site called Qhapaqkancha. Located above 4000 meters, the site comprises over 4 hectares of densely nucleated semicircular stone structures, many of which have been poorly preserved. The density of surface pottery was very high in some parts of the site, and identifiable shards were predominantly of a Killke-related variety, with less frequent examples of Killke pottery from the Cusco Basin and a few isolated fragments of Lucre Basin pottery.

The site size is somewhat misleading, as the flanks of the mountain below the zone of buildings and domestic terraces are covered with small irregular agricultural terraces that may have included some residences.[54] From approximately AD 1000 to AD 1300, Qhapaqkancha was a large village commanding a vista of the Sacred Valley between Pisaq and Lamay. The site was situated close to large numbers of *puna* corrals, a productive, well-watered area of tuber production, and lower-elevation fields where other crops could be grown.

About twenty small sites are associated with Qhapaqkancha, ranging from isolated hamlets to small villages that skirt the flanks of the main settlement on the lands of modern Paullu, Coya, and Macay (fig. 7.6). This area appears to have been an independent polity during the first part of the Killke Period. The paramount center was located in a defensible area with good views of the main valley, while about four small villages were situated below it, several hundred meters above the main valley floor.

That the site was incorporated into the Cusco polity later in the Killke Period is indicated by the presence at Qhapaqkancha of a large rectangular platform with three early Inca buildings on it (fig. 7.7). This complex is constructed on a prominent point at the northernmost tip of the ridge on which the site is located. All of the buildings are built of stone and have multiple entrances on a single side, as well as interior niches. The two flanking buildings face the main Qhapaqkancha village and may have been used for ordinary administrative activities. The central building faces away from the village onto the open platform that measures approximately 2700 square meters. The size of the platform and its relationship to the central structure suggests that this may have been a public space used by the state for political or ritual activities. When compared to other Inca architectural complexes, it is clear that this one lacks many of the characteristics of multiple open spaces and controlled access seen in imperial Inca palatial and residential architecture.

Rather than functioning as an elite residence, the Inca complex at Qhapaqkancha may signal the establishment of Inca administrators to govern the local populace, apparently sometime prior to AD 1400. Of a collection of more than fifty decorated shards collected from the surface,

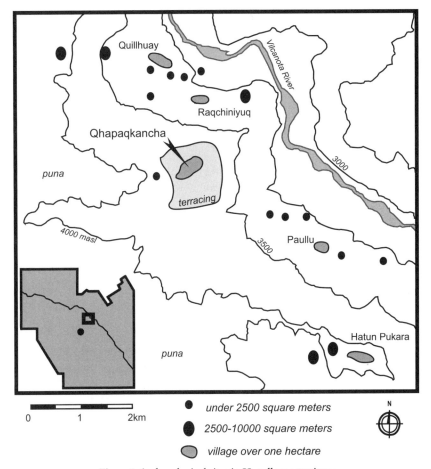

Fig. 7.6. Archaeological sites in Huayllacan territory

only eight transitional or local Inca fragments were encountered, and these were restricted to the area of the Inca platform. These were associated with some Killke pottery and local Killke Period styles. The platform group, built in what is identifiable as Inca style, appears to be a late intrusion on the site occupation and represents the only discernible rectangular architecture at the site.

The archaeological data from this area indicate that the Huayllacans were a small complex polity that was brought under Inca control prior to the period of Inca imperial expansion. The imposition of state administrative control may have been based on the establishment of a royal

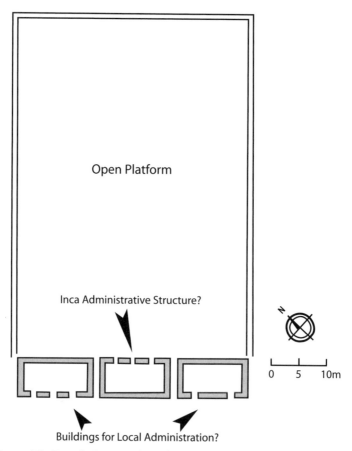

Fig. 7.7. The Inca platform at Qhapaqkancha. This may have been used by local elites for everyday administration and for gathering the entire polity on important occasions.

estate, but it was enacted through the creation of public spaces and administrative structures, also seen at Pukara Pantillijlla for the nearby Cuyo group. With the historical documents, it can be argued that, over several generations, direct control was extended over the Huayllacans—first through marriage, then through military intervention—and ultimately their resources were incorporated into a royal estate.

The integration of this group probably provided the Inca state with new camelid herds while simultaneously bringing large areas of *puna* pastureland under direct Inca control. Bernabé Cobo states that the eighth

Inca ruler, Viracocha Inca, was sent to Chit'apampa to manage Inca state herds, possibly referring to the Qoricocha *puna,* where numerous corral groups and colonial place names attest to pre-Hispanic herding.[55]

The historical and archaeological evidence reveals changes over time in the relationships between Inca elites and those of neighboring groups. At the time of state formation in the thirteenth century, the Inca polity became strong enough to attract alliances with groups that sought to preserve their own autonomy by becoming subordinates of the ascendant group in the region. Marriage alliances did not lead directly to political administration, and subordinate groups were left to make most local decisions relating to economy and defense. The continuing autonomy of these groups proved to be unsatisfactory for the state, particularly if marriage allies really did attempt to influence political succession patterns or factionalism in Cusco.

The Cuyos: Conquest and Consolidation

While marriage alliances promoted Inca hegemony over related groups, military conquest and political administration were also important means of expansion, as seen in the case of the Cuyos. The territory of the Cuyos is found in the Chongo Basin, a large side valley located above modern Pisaq, to the north of the Vilcanota River (fig. 7.8). Today, two towns in the Chongo Basin preserve the name (Cuyo Chico and Cuyo Grande), and some descent groups (*ayllukuna*) in nearby communities are named Hanan Cuyo and Hurin Cuyo.[56] Colonial documents place groups of Cuyos in higher elevations of the valley and in the *puna* between the Chongo Basin and the Paucartambo Valley, while Inca descendants of Pachacutic Inca Yupanqui lived near the valley bottom at Pisaq.[57]

The Cuyos lived only about 10 kilometers farther from Cusco than the Huayllacans, but their territory lay to the north of the Sacred Valley, a natural boundary for effective long-term administration by unspecialized polities in the Cusco Basin. Owing to this distance and an apparently greater political complexity, the Cuyos had a different political relationship with the early Inca state than the Huayllacans did. The chronicles mention that the earliest Inca territorial expansion extended into Cuyo lands, through which it was possible to access important caravan routes

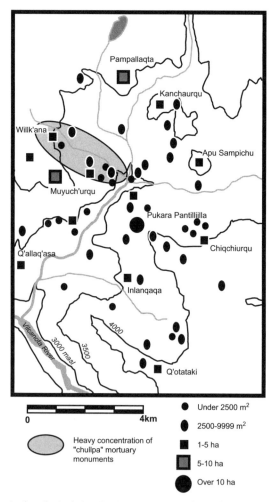

Fig. 7.8. Archaeological sites in Cuyo territory. The early Cuyo sites are located near a number of aboveground mortuary structures and have distinctive pottery on the surface.

to the Paucartambo Valley and lowland coca lands. According to Bernabé Cobo and others, the initial conquest took place under the fifth ruler, Capac Yupanqui, and represents the first external territorial expansion of the Inca state.[58] Sarmiento de Gamboa credits Yahuar Huaccac with the conquest of Paucartambo during the reign of his father, Inca Rocca, implying that Cuyo territory already had been encroached upon by this time.[59]

The Cuyo conquest is interesting because of an apparent administrative reorganization that accompanied it. Cobo states that Capac Yupanqui appointed a rival brother, Tarco Huaman, as governor over a new province, in part so that he would be removed from Cusco. Other chronicle accounts mention a province of Cuyosuyu, with a tributary organization of two *hunu* (twenty thousand households), organized into administrative halves (*saya*) that were ruled by lords named Apu Lalama and Yamque Lalama, who reported to Cuyo Ccapac—and presumably, to the Inca governor.[60] Population figures are almost certainly rounded off or exaggerated, but it is clear that the chronicles refer to a larger and more hierarchical group than the Huayllacans, evident by the use of the paramount title *qhapaq* and the establishment of pairs of *apu* under that leader. According to Martín de Murúa, one Cuyo lord was apparently of sufficient status to marry a daughter of the Inca ruler.[61]

After the multiple references to their initial conquest, the Cuyos seem to have remained under Inca hegemony until the reign of Pachacutic Inca Yupanqui, the ninth Inca ruler.[62] The chronicles relate that after defeating the Chancas, Pachacutic held a festival at which an attempt on his life was made. The Cuyos were blamed, although Miguel Cabello de Balboa claims that they were falsely accused. In either case, the Inca reaction was to campaign throughout Cuyo territory, destroying the principal settlement and killing many of its inhabitants. Estimates of the number killed vary, but there is general agreement that the Inca reprisal involved the destruction of Cuyo villages and widespread killing. Although some authors claim that the Cuyos were completely destroyed, they are mentioned in some colonial land documents and were possibly resettled in the Sacred Valley proper, in the *puna* above the valley, or in lowland coca-producing areas.[63]

The documentary record describes how the Inca state used military force to incorporate a complex polity near Cusco, possibly imposing some sort of administrative reorganization. The question of an assassination attempt is significant because of Cabello de Balboa's claim that the Cuyos were unfairly blamed. As John Murra notes, local rebellions during the imperial period provided a pretext for bloody reprisals and the confiscation and reallocation of local lands and resources.[64] After the decimation of the Cuyo population, at least part of the Cuyo territory was annexed by Pachacutic and developed as a personal estate centered at Pisaq, which would have administered new intensive agricultural infrastructure near the floor of the Sacred Valley.[65] When interviewed by

Francisco de Toledo, descendants of Pachacutic Inca Yupanqui living in Pisaq mentioned a group called the Chuyos, not as the autochthonous inhabitants of that area but as cannibalistic forest people living in the *montaña*.[66]

Archaeological Perspectives on the Cuyos

The archaeological evidence from the Cuyo area also seems to substantiate some of the information provided in the chronicles. Until AD 1000, the Chongo Basin had been home to small agricultural groups, living in small villages and hamlets but not organized hierarchically. Survey data collected by the Sacred Valley Archaeological Project indicate that in the first part of the Killke Period population increased dramatically as several large nucleated villages were established, most of them located on ridgetops at high elevation (at 4000–4300 meters). The largest of these was Muyuch'urqu, a 6-hectare village protected by cliffs and a series of defensive walls that are preserved to a height of 2 to 3 meters (fig. 7.9). Muyuch'urqu appears to have been the center of a complex polity surrounded by five or six smaller villages, positioned to control caravan traffic out of the Sacred Valley and probably overseeing a mosaic economy that included agricultural production and herding.

The Muyuch'urqu polity appears to have been culturally distinct from groups living in the Cusco Basin. While the Huayllacan sites show a strong presence of Killke ceramics from Cusco, these are almost completely absent at the early Cuyo sites. Besides distinct local pottery, this area has a different mortuary treatment, with dozens of aboveground mortuary structures erected close to the major villages. It appears that in the first part of the Killke Period the Chongo Basin was settled by an independent group that had little contact with the developing Inca state.

The distribution of late Killke Period sites (i.e., those with some Inca-style ceramics present) reveals a major settlement shift in the Chongo Basin, indicative of the imposition of administrative control by the Inca state. At this time, the principal settlement in the basin was Pukara Pantillijlla, a site located at about 3950 meters on a ridge across the basin from Muyuch'urqu (fig. 7.10). At Pukara Pantillijlla, Killke and Inca pottery are found commonly on the surface, and the site appears to have acted as a second-tier administrative center for the Inca state, which charged it with overseeing new villages established at lower elevations.

Fig. 7.9. The upper Chongo Basin. The principal settlement early in the Killke Period was Muyuch'urqu (on the ridge to the right); settlement shifted to Pukara Pantillijlla (on the ridge to the left) around AD 1300, after the Inca conquest of the Cuyos.

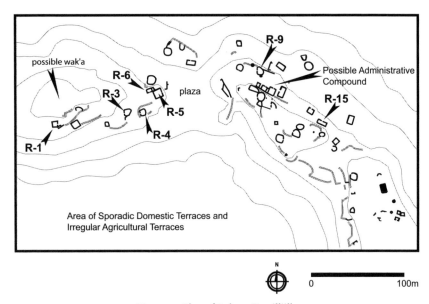

Fig. 7.10. Plan of Pukara Pantillijlla

Pukara Pantillijlla: A Local Center under Inca Control

Pukara Pantillijlla is located on a prominent ridge overlooking the upper
and lower parts of the Chongo Basin (fig. 7.10). At more than 10 hectares,
it is the largest Killke Period site in the Sacred Valley survey region and
is substantially larger than Muyuch'urqu. The remains of more than one
hundred stone structures are scattered along the ridge in areas where
modest domestic terraces could be constructed. Small agricultural terraces flank the hillside below the core habitation area. The establishment
of a large secondary administrative center to the north of the Sacred Valley changed the nature of the regional administrative hierarchy and
central control from the Cusco Basin.

    Pukara Pantillijlla is larger and architecturally distinct from the ear-
lier site of Muyuch'urqu.[67] There is a mix of mortuary, architectural,
and ceramic styles indicative of an increased interaction with the early Inca
state. Burials at the site include simple cliff interments, mud-plastered
mortuary boxes in rock outcrops, and some possible aboveground mortuary monuments. In addition, excavations by the Sacred Valley Archaeological Project uncovered four burials—an infant, a juvenile, and two
adults—inside public and domestic structures.

At least eight buildings at the site were constructed with square or rectangular plans, a distinct form from the other semicircular or irregular structures at the site. As mentioned in chapter 6, one of these, building 5, was built on a small plaza area and may have been used for religious or political functions (fig. 7.11). This building had a high, east-facing entrance that is much wider than doorways used for residential structures. The interior of the structure had fourteen square niches and four windows, and a sample of grass from the plaster of one niche returned a calibrated two-sigma AMS radiocarbon date of AD 1300–1370 (48 percent) or AD 1380–1440 (47.4 percent).[68] To the east of this structure lay a compound of four smaller rectangular structures, which might represent an elite residence or a complex of administrative buildings. This kind of architectural clustering is not common at other Killke Period sites in the area.[69] Finally, a single rectangular structure (building 15) was built on an artificial platform in front of and concealing a natural niche in a cliff that also made up the south part of the structure. The foundations of this structure were partially excavated out of bedrock, and its proximity to the hidden niche may indicate a ritual function.

The surface of Pukara Pantillijlla is covered with ceramic fragments that include the local pottery style, as well as substantial amounts of Killke and Inca pottery. Excavations indicate that only a small part of the site was occupied before AD 1250, during the time when Muyuch'urqu is thought to have dominated the upper Chongo Basin. This occupation has high percentages of local pottery, with a smaller proportion of Killke pottery than was found at sites to the south of the Vilcanota River. For example, a midden excavated near building 3 in the site core dated to the thirteenth century and had no pottery identified as Inca (out of 620 diagnostic shards).[70] By comparison, the complete excavation of a semicircular structure and a rectangular structure (buildings 9 and 15), both located in the eastern part of the site, yielded a much higher percentage of Inca pottery (12.71 percent, or 515/4051), with no evidence of previous settlement. Throughout the site, proveniences where Inca pottery was absent, and where Killke pottery constituted only a small percentage of diagnostic shards, were found in and around buildings 1, 3, 5, and 6, all of these located close to the site core. Buildings with substantial Inca components (buildings 4, 9, and 15) were built on newly constructed domestic terraces that do not appear to have had previous occupation. The site architecture and data from excavations and surface collection are consistent with Inca expansion into this zone.

Fig. 7.11. Building 5, a public building at Pukara Pantillijlla. (Photo C. Elson.)

As the Inca state expanded its territory north of the Sacred Valley, Pukara Pantillijlla grew considerably, with many older structures razed and new terraces and buildings constructed. The later occupation reveals much closer ties to the Inca state, with large amounts of Killke and Inca pottery present. Excavated midden contexts yielded the bones of camelids, deer, and guinea pigs, as well as carbonized potatoes and maize. Status markers like metal tools (axes) and ornaments (pins and pendants) were encountered, along with more mundane stone and bone tools that were used for weaving and other activities. The later occupation of this site appears to correspond to an elite residential site that included buildings used by Inca state administrators, some of whom might have lived at the site.

The abandonment of the site can be dated with new radiocarbon dates (table 7.1). The excavation evidence does not confirm that the site was burned at the end of its occupation, nor does it appear to have been completely deserted as imperial expansion began. Many buildings were abandoned, including large residences, and building 5 fell into disuse and was even used for human burial. Architecture and middens associated with the Inca occupation yield dates indicating that site abandonment probably began toward the end of the fourteenth century, but that some buildings were in use throughout much of the fifteenth century.

TABLE 7.1.   Architectural Dates from Buildings at Pukara Pantillijlla

Sample	Description	BP	95.4% probability
AA47651	Large irregular structure outside of Inca site core	642 ± 32	AD 1280–1400 (95.4%)
AA47655	Irregular structure in site core	546 ± 31	AD 1300–1360 (32.9%) or AD 1380–1440 (62.5%)
AA47656	Small rectangular structure with evidence of colonial reuse	443 ± 32	AD 1410–1500 (94.4%)
AA47657	Rectangular structure; part of administrative complex	519 ± 55	AD 1300–1370 (29.5%) or AD 1380–1480 (65.6%)]
AA47658	Large irregular structure in site core	590 ± 34	AD 1300–1420 (95.4%)
AA47659	Rectangular structure; possibly ceremonial function	382 ± 40	AD 1440–1530 (56.5%) or AD 1540–1640 (38.9%)
AA34946	Rectangular central structure; public building	555 ± 45	AD 1300–1370 (48%) or AD 1380–1400 (47.4%)

Note: Dates were calibrated using OxCal v3.5, and are calibrated to 95.4% probability. Values less than 10% probably are not listed. Sample AA34946 was processed as part of Brian Bauer's Cusco Valley Archaeological Project.

Few classic imperial Inca polychrome shards were found among the roughly fifty thousand shards analyzed from the excavations, and it appears that the use of the site as an Inca administrative center ended as the site of Pisaq was developed near the floor of the Sacred Valley (fig. 7.12). At that time, settlement of the Chongo Basin began to cluster near the bottom of the valley 900 meters below, where groups were governed by Inca elites living at Pisaq, a private estate of Pachacutic. Pisaq is even larger than Pukara Pantillijlla and also represents the expansion of an existing Killke Period settlement.[71] The architecture of Pisaq's most restricted complexes is of the classic Inca style, which is not present at Pukara Pantillijlla.

The continuity of settlement at Pukara Pantillijlla indicates that Inca stories of the Cuyo demise were greatly exaggerated. Rather than obliterating the Cuyos, the Incas appear to have marginalized them economically, and their early administrative site became redundant with the construction of Pisaq. Some Cuyos probably continued to live at Pukara Pantillijlla and in villages throughout the basin, but their local influence was greatly diminished as they lost their political autonomy.

New archaeological evidence from the Sacred Valley study region indicates that the Chongo Basin was occupied by an independent non-Inca group prior to the period of Inca state formation. Settlement was reorganized at Pukara Pantillijlla as this area came under the domination of the Inca state, and it is possible that people from Cusco resided there. Around the time of Inca imperial expansion, many Cuyo settlements were abandoned in a major settlement shift in which new sites were settled close to valley-bottom lands associated with maize production.

Elite Interaction and Inca State Expansion

As the Inca state formed, elites in the Cusco Basin sought to extend their territorial control and to subordinate or eliminate political rivals in the region surrounding their territory. Because of the political and ethnic diversity of the region, several strategies were necessary. Inca lords married elite women from subordinate groups that shared a compatible ethnic identity, and the children of these unions appear to have received labor tribute and owned camelid herds in the mother's community. The chronicles indicate that internal developments in the Cusco Basin were

Fig. 7.12. Pisaq, as seen from Pukara Pantillijlla.

accompanied by the shifting of marriage alliances from groups like the Ayarmacas to the Incas, as seen with elites from intermediate groups like the Antas and Huayllacans. It is clear that elite women had substantial political influence in their natal communities and were instrumental in determining alliance patterns and the hegemonic reach of the expanding Inca state.

While the Incas and Ayarmacas maintained diplomatic relations and occasional marriage alliances, no such mentions are made for other large groups like the Cuyos and Pinaguas. State expansion led the Inca ruler to take a principal wife and multiple secondary wives from a variety of ethnic subordinates. As the imperial pattern of sibling marriage developed, Inca rulers often arranged for their daughters to marry local elites, as discussed for the Cuyos and Chancas.

The Inca state took a more militaristic stance toward groups with whom it did not contract marriage alliances. Occasional raiding gave way to military conquest, which ultimately led to a shift from hegemony to territorial administration. In the case of the Cuyos, Inca conquest led to the establishment of an Inca governor over the region. The Cuyo paramount, Cuyo Ccapac, continued to function, but chronicle references to administrative units and the use of the *apu* title suggest state manipulation of local elite structures and tributary organization, a transformation that accompanies archaeologically observed settlement changes.

At some point in the Inca expansion sequence, the Inca ruler promoted himself from the office of *qhapaq* to that of *sapa inka* (or *sapay qhapaq*), a title implying absolute paramountcy rather than a dual or paired office. The time when imperial expansion began was characterized by a series of "rebellions" by the major *qhapaqkuna* of the Cusco region, whose continued local power impeded the full development of imperial infrastructure. As the Inca state developed direct control over the Cusco region, local elites were forced either to accept a subordinate, dependent role under an Inca-administered government, or to assert independence and attempt to use local power resources to maintain autonomy. In most cases where local elites chose to resist the state (e.g., the Cuyos and Pinaguas), their constituencies were not granted Inca ethnic status, and were marginalized in the imperial period. Conversely, cooperative groups—often weaker local groups where local identity would not sustain resistance—became "Incas-of-Privilege," a higher status within the empire, but one that often resulted in the loss of territory and massive resettlement throughout the empire.

CHAPTER EIGHT

State Expansion, Economic Intensification, and Local Resistance

The examples of the Huayllacan and Cuyo polities reveal a historical trajectory to the territorial expansion and administrative policies of the early Inca state. As the Incas extended their direct access to different kinds of resources, they also intensified their control over subordinate groups and polities. The state drew increasing amounts of labor and resources from local political systems, presenting local elites with new costs and benefits for resistance to or participation in the developing Inca system. Ultimately, there were fundamental conflicts between the strategies of Inca and local elites, and the final phase of Inca regional consolidation is characterized by increased militarism and the suppression of local autonomy.

Military Campaigns and Territorial Consolidation

As figure 8.1 indicates, increasingly sustained campaigns of military conquest characterized the period preceding imperial expansion, and the final consolidation of Inca territorial control in the Cusco region was still underway as the Inca state began to develop diplomatic ties with distant regions and engage the armies of rival polities and confederations such as the Qollas and Chancas. Inca rulers and their close kin led armies to greater distances from Cusco, engaging in the conquest of multiple towns in a single campaign. For example, the seventh Inca ruler is said to have fought the Huayllacans, then moved up the Sacred Valley to conquer five towns and the Caviña ethnic group.[1] The eighth ruler and his sons also engaged in sustained campaigns to the northeast and southwest of Cusco. According to Pedro de Cieza de León, these rulers were the first to organize campaigns to the Titicaca Basin, and the eighth Inca

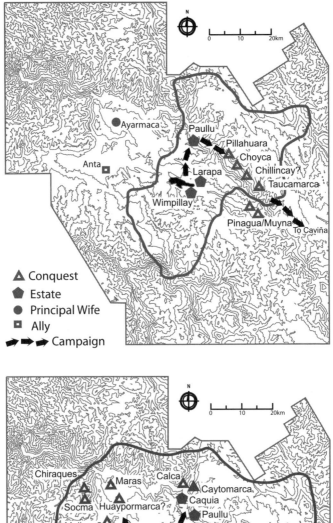

Fig. 8.1. Campaigns of Yahuar Huaccac (*top*) and Viracocha Inca (*bottom*), the seventh and eighth Inca rulers

ruler managed to extend Inca hegemony to that region while also subordinating the Qanas and Kanchis, two groups living outside the Inca heartland in the upper Vilcanota Valley.[2]

It is possible that chronicle references to earlier rulers "conquering" areas more than 100 kilometers from Cusco refer to raids or attempted invasions rather than to successful territorial conquest and administrative reorganization. Alternatively, Inca forces could have made such journeys not to fight but to intimidate local elites into forging alliances with the Inca ruler. Systematic archaeological data and well-provenienced radiocarbon dates from areas 50–150 kilometers from Cusco are almost completely lacking, and more research will be needed to assess the nature of Inca influence in the areas lying immediately beyond the imperial heartland.

The increasing ability of Inca armies to engage in more sustained campaigns near Cusco—and to impose provincial administration on conquered groups—probably indicates (1) advances in logistical capability, (2) numerical superiority of Inca armies, (3) conquest through siege or intimidation rather than pitched battles, and (4) the development of an ideology justifying permanent territorial conquest.[3] These developments are unlike the warfare conducted by nonstate societies in South America, where territorial conquest was not a goal or end result and where most conflict occurred within a day's walk of a village.[4] A large, well-provisioned Inca army would be able to avoid many direct conflicts through displays of overwhelming numerical superiority or by using siege tactics to conquer recalcitrant locals. These military strategies embody the fundamentals of Inca military tactics described in the Spanish chronicles for the period of imperial expansion.

Military campaigns throughout the Cusco region increasingly achieved the subjugation of new towns and polities, as well as the restructuring of local political systems. The intensification of warfare at this time might have been stimulated by competition over natural resources during a period when environmental conditions were fluctuating, but armed conflict was essential to the transition from Inca hegemony to direct territorial administration, as local elites attempted to throw off Inca rule and reestablish local autonomy. Inca state expansion and local resistance promoted the intensification of interpolity conflict until state administrative reorganization could be established locally.

Expansion of the Royal Estate System

As Inca armies made permanent military conquests, the royal estate system expanded outside of the Cusco Basin. As discussed in the preceding, the practice whereby rulers built sequential estates developed at the time of state formation, evidenced by the construction of new agricultural lands at Larapa that supported the lineage (*panaka*) of Inca Rocca. Other lands may have been allocated around Wimpillay to serve the lineages of earlier rulers. Starting with the seventh *sapa inka*, rulers are said to have developed their own estates in the Sacred Valley, using the resources of newly conquered groups. The seventh Inca (Yahuar Huaccac) established an estate around modern Paullu, confiscating the lands of the Huayllacans after they betrayed him. After conquering the people of Calca, the eighth ruler (Viracocha Inca)

> liberally authorized that they should continue to possess their lands
> . . . provided that at the appointed time and in accordance with the
> laws, they would give tribute to Cusco of that which was in their vil-
> lages, and that of those same ones that they should go immediately to
> the city and build him two palaces, one within it and the other in
> Caquia [Xaquixaguana] so that he could go out for his recreation . . .
> and so that they would understand what they had to do, and there
> would be no dissent among them, he ordered that a representative of
> his be left there with great powers, without depriving the local lord
> of his authority.[5]

In this case, defeat meant that labor tribute was levied on the local community and that an Inca governor was placed at the local level to organize and supervise it. The construction of Viracocha Inca's retreat at Caquia and its subsequent enlargement in the imperial period would have required a substantial amount of labor, which was reciprocated by feasts and exotic gifts from the Inca ruler (fig. 8.2).[6] Labor service on new agricultural fields associated with the estate sustained the ruler's *panaka* into the early colonial period.

The royal estate system proliferated throughout the region as the state expanded. Yahuar Huaccac had a single estate outside the Cusco Basin, but Viracocha Inca developed estates at Caquia, Calca, and Tipón, while Pachacutic is said to have had estates at Pisaq, Ollantaytambo, (Machu) Picchu, Amaybamba, and Alca.[7] The estate system created or improved thousands of hectares of agricultural land in the Cusco region,

Fig. 8.2. Caquia Xaquixaguana (today called Juchuy Cosco), the estate of Viracocha Inca. (Negative no. 334770, Courtesy Dept. of Library Services, American Museum of Natural History.)

sometimes expropriating existing natural resources and human labor from local systems. The development and maintenance of estates would have benefited Inca elites while forcing local groups to work harder or subsist on less, or both.

The Development of State Infrastructure

A shift to intensive valley-bottom agriculture in the Sacred Valley was an important means of producing surpluses to fund state projects and military campaigns. Throughout the Sacred Valley, local populations resettled as the Inca state developed new agricultural infrastructure in the valley for the production of maize. This involved draining swampy land, canalizing rivers, and constructing canals, agricultural terraces, and storage facilities in areas that had previously been only marginally productive.

Canalization, Terracing, and Irrigation

Prior to Inca conquest, small plots of valley-bottom maize lands in the Sacred Valley were probably maintained by local elites, but the distance of major ridgetop settlements from valley-bottom lands suggests that maize agriculture by nonstate polities was not a central component of the local political economy. Before the incorporation of the Sacred Valley under the Inca state, the construction of agricultural infrastructure near the valley bottom would have created a rich yet vulnerable crop in a location where it could not be protected from other groups. By bringing both sides of the Sacred Valley under its administration, the Inca state came to control a substantial, yet underdeveloped, resource that could be generate huge returns for the state through the investment of local labor tribute. During the imperial period, Inca rulers personally undertook the development of new valley-bottom lands in the Sacred Valley, creating resources that were held corporately by their descent groups (*panakakuna*) after the founders' death.[8] This process may have begun fairly early in the process of Inca state expansion—the first Inca ruler to establish a personal estate in the valley was the seventh Inca ruler, Yahuar Huaccac—and continued under every ruler until the time of Huascar.[9]

In the Sacred Valley, the development of maize lands involved four kinds of construction: draining swampy land, canalizing the Vilcanota-Urubamba River, constructing irrigation canals to channel water from permanent transverse streams and rivers, and developing agricultural terraces on the floor and lower slopes of the valley where reliable irrigation water was available. Ian Farrington has discussed river canalization in the Sacred Valley, which is also described in the documentary record, estimating that over 23 kilometers of the river were canalized in as many as six distinct projects.[10] By diverting the course of the river, it was possible to create new valley-bottom fields that would not be in danger of seasonal flooding, located at elevations where frosts are uncommon.[11] Farrington estimates that nearly 800 hectares of new lands were brought under cultivation through canalization, which could be used permanently to grow high-yield maize for the state.[12] Inge Bolin has demonstrated that much larger areas were improved with irrigation canals and new agricultural terraces.[13]

Because the Vilcanota River is too entrenched to provide irrigation water, valley-bottom lands were made more productive by diverting streams and rivers from side valleys though a series of new canals. In the Pisaq area, for example, at least four different canals were built to bring water from the Chit'apampa and Chongo basins, irrigating hundreds of hectares of new fields. The 65 hectares of terraces in and around the monumental complex alone could have fed nearly one thousand people throughout the year, if planted with maize.[14] During the Sacred Valley survey fieldwork, stream canalization projects were observed at San Salvador, Punabamba, Coya, Lamay, Patahuasi, and Calca, although dating these canals conclusively is not possible with present data. Other irrigation systems are recorded for the Sacred Valley below Calca.[15]

While the Sacred Valley shows the most obvious evidence for the development of agricultural lands, such projects were also undertaken in the Lucre and Oropesa basins, within the Cusco Basin, the Limatambo area, and other parts of the Cusco region.[16] Many of these date to the imperial period, but the presence of Killke pottery on new agricultural terraces or in close proximity to canals indicates that significant areas of new maize production had been developed prior to Inca imperial expansion. These lands augmented the resource base of the Inca state, allowing it to expand territorially while simultaneously transforming local economies.

Storage and Settlement under the State

New state lands developed in the Cusco region would have provided the Inca state with agricultural surpluses capable of feeding tens of thousands of people. These new surpluses were stored throughout the Cusco region in groups of *qollqa*, storage structures often located near state fields (fig. 8.3).[17] Figure 8.4 shows the locations of known storage facilities in the Cusco region, including the Sacred Valley study region, where several sites with storage facilities were observed. Such installations were widespread and were placed in visible locations as a means of communicating state control over the productive landscape. In the Sacred Valley below the study region, groups of storehouses have been identified around Yucay, Ollantaytambo, and other locations.[18] Storage buildings are present at Inca estates, an apparent shift in production and storage strategy, since large-scale, centralized storage is apparently absent in large pre-Inca villages. Settlement location and the distribution of Inca storage facilities indicate that the state relied on the storage of agricultural surpluses to buffer against shortfalls and environmental fluctuations.

While developing storage facilities around their new agricultural lands, the Incas also settled new villages close to these resources. Many new Inca villages were established close to the valley bottom, some just above new state canals. New settlements such as Paullu, Tancarpata, Tucsan, and Taray would have been dependent on Inca canals for their water and were established with much more concern for proximity to state fields than to the diverse agropastoral resources that were exploited by independent pre-Inca polities. Given their lack of defensive works and reliance on long irrigation canals, the new villages at or near the valley floor would have looked to the Inca state for defense. The shift to intensive maize agriculture would have lent itself to a more centralized and bureaucratic state administration, which would have restructured existing social hierarchies, greatly reducing the functions of local elites, as well as their ability to resist the state. As discussed in chapter 10, long-term resettlement processes would bring even more dependent retainer populations into the Sacred Valley and other parts of the Cusco region.

Roads and Way Stations

Another aspect of Inca state infrastructure that can be identified in the Cusco region is a system of roads and way stations (fig. 8.4). In the Sacred Valley study region, several probable Inca roads have been identified linking Cusco with Pisaq and Calca and ascending to the north of the Sacred Valley toward passes that lead to the lowland valleys of Lares and Paucartambo. Two possible way stations were identified during the

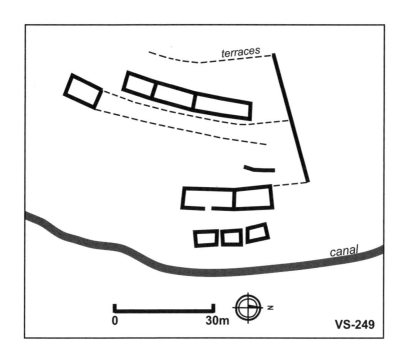

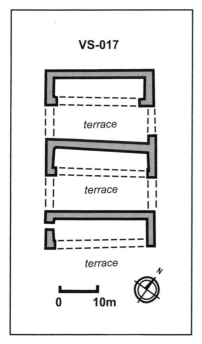

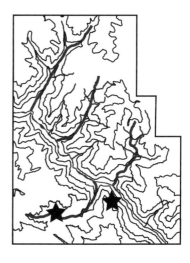

Fig. 8.3. Storage at two Sacred Valley sites. These facilities were probably constructed at the same time as nearby irrigation canals and agricultural terraces.

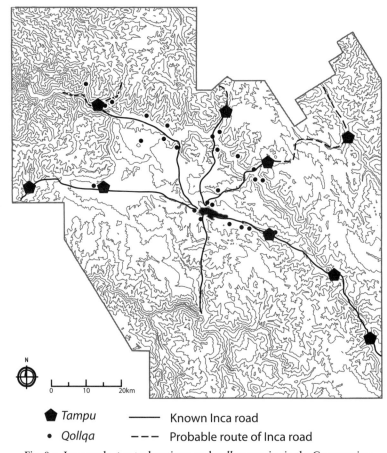

● *Tampu*   ———— Known Inca road

• *Qollqa*   – – – Probable route of Inca road

Fig. 8.4. Inca roads, *tampu* locations, and *qollqa* remains in the Cusco region

regional survey, one just below the site of Ancasmarca and the other in the
upper Chongo Basin. These both consist of rectangular Inca structures
without a significant scatter of shards inside or around the buildings.

The full development of the system of roads and way stations (*tampukuna*) described in colonial documents would have required territorial
administration over the entire Cusco region, a process that was probably completed just after the earliest campaigns of imperial expansion
began.[19] Killke Period sites in Paruro and the Sacred Valley are located
close to roads leading to Cusco, indicating that transportation infrastruc-

ture began to be developed in some locations well before the imperial period.[20] The process of organizing regular infrastructure for inter-regional travel led to the development of a more regular settlement lattice for the Cusco region, with large estates serving as secondary administrative sites.

Economic Specialization

Aside from chronicle references to state herds, the archaeological evidence provides some indication that the intensification of maize production at the valley bottom was accompanied by specialization in herding and cultivating economies.[21] The Sacred Valley study region does not include large areas of *puna,* but some large high-elevation sites were encountered that were occupied from the late Killke Period. One of these was Hatun Sayhua, a 3.75-hectare ridgetop site located at 4200 meters. Based on surface pottery, Hatun Sayhua was probably settled at the end of the Killke Period, when the important Killke Period site of Markasunay was largely abandoned. Settlement under the Inca state involved the occupation—or expansion of occupation—at Hatun Sayhua, as well as the construction of irrigation canals, terracing, and domestic and administrative architecture at the valley bottom near the modern town of Poques. The abandonment of Markasunay and Inca development of this area probably constituted an upward move of herders (from 3900 meters to 4200 meters) and concomitant downward resettlement of cultivators (to around 3600 meters). Such a division is probably indicative of increasing economic specialization, as is the late Killke Period expansion of other *puna* sites like Ancasmarca (figs. 8.5 and 8.6). These processes continued in the imperial period, as discussed further in chapter 10.

The archaeological evidence from the Sacred Valley study region reveals that the Inca state initiated major projects to intensify agricultural production and pastoralism, reduce local autonomy, and facilitate the flow of people, goods, and information throughout a centrally administered region. Such projects transformed the state's capacity to engage in sustained military campaigns, which by this time were justified by a developed conquest ideology. While state strategies are fairly easy to divine from the archaeology and history, it is also important to consider the consequences of economic intensification and resettlement on local populations.

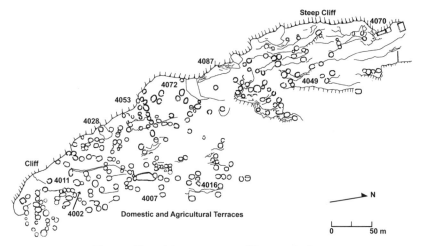

Fig. 8.5. Plan of Ancasmarca, a Killke Period village

State Strategies for Resettlement and Dependency

The proliferation of the Inca state maize economy had far-reaching local effects. As discussed in chapter 3, Inca state production strategies targeted a small number of species and varieties for intensive production. Inca risk-reduction policies were based on storage, as well as the ability to move people and resources as necessary. Inca maize agriculture in the Sacred Valley was conducted at elevations below the risk of frosts, in locations where reliable irrigation water was available. By the imperial period, guano and other natural fertilizers were used to increase yields in state fields, and selection of high-yield strains made state agriculture extremely productive.[22] The maintenance of these fields provided royal lineages and the state religion with large surpluses, but it required a more intensive labor input, initially from conquered local groups like the Huayllacans and Cuyos.

Inca control over local agriculture generally involved the use of local labor to create new agricultural resources that belonged to the state or the cult of the sun. Using local and imported labor, the state spread the intensive production of a limited number of varieties. An intensification strategy yielded surpluses on state fields in most years, which were used to fund territorial expansion and further intensification. State storage replaced diversity as a principal risk-reduction mechanism for yearly

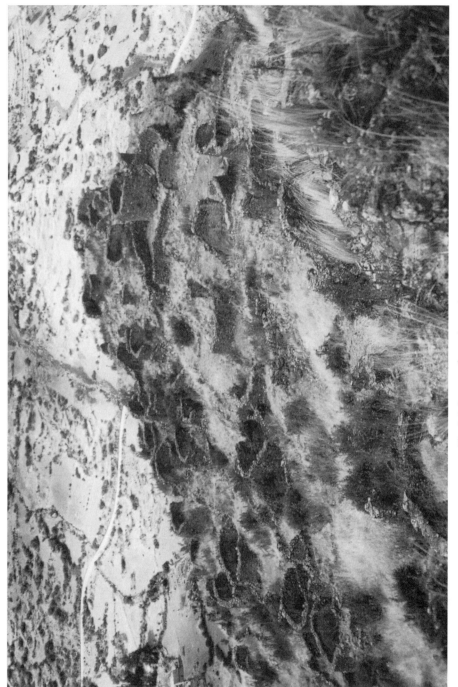

Fig. 8.6. Structural remains at Ancasmarca.

fluctuations, while an elaborate record-keeping system allowed the state to map provincial people onto available resources, thereby addressing regional variability.[23]

Although this reallocation of land, water, and labor resources increased state revenues and reduced risk at the polity level, it also affected local productive systems and the ways in which local status was constructed. Intensive maize production encouraged different settlement patterns, labor structures, and religious systems than those of independent local polities. State construction projects and storage systems created resources to which local groups had no reciprocal claims, and resource fluctuations would have increased local dependency on the state. Increasingly direct state administration would have made local elites redundant, and they were often replaced as state administration intensified. The differences between local economic systems in the Sacred Valley and those of the Inca state made a period of final rebellion and state consolidation almost inevitable.

Rebellion and Reconquest

Rebellion and reconquest represent internal and external expressions of the militaristic intensification of Inca state control. Pedro Sarmiento de Gamboa is clear about the nature of rebellion and reconquest among groups like the Muynas and Pinaguas:

> In seeing their goal, or upon the death of the Inca ruler who had vanquished them, [conquered polities] immediately sought to procure their freedom, and for that they took up arms and rebelled. And thus this is why we say repeatedly that a town was conquered by different Inca rulers, as was the case with Mohina and Pinagua, that although they were driven out and reduced to submission by Inca Rocca, they were also subdued by Yahuar Huaccac and then Viracocha Inca and his son Inca Yupanqui.[24]

This chronicler goes on to explain that even as the Incas were consolidating their political control over the Cusco region, several neighboring groups fought to maintain their autonomy, while others actually sought to extend their own influence in the event that the Incas should be defeated or weakened by constant warfare. This period of rebellion and reconquest marks the culmination of centuries of interpolity competition, a final political reorganization resulting in local subordination to the Inca state.[25] Simultaneously, it marks an increase in the tempo and intensity of Inca expansionism—the beginnings of imperial expansion outside of the heartland. Radiocarbon dates from such heartland sites as Chokepukio, Pukara Pantillijlla, and Huata indicate that the final phase of consolidation in the Cusco region probably occurred by the end of the fourteenth century, which corresponds to the earliest Inca dates in the Titicaca Basin, as well as chronicle references to military campaigns by the seventh and eighth Inca rulers.[26]

At Chokepukio, Gordon McEwan and colleagues report that ten radiocarbon samples from wood beams and grass temper in wall plasters date within a calibrated two-sigma range of AD 860–1410.[27] Although they do not provide more specific data, it appears that the Killke Period occupation of this Lucre Basin site ended by around AD 1400 as the last holdout groups were incorporated into the Inca state. Two samples of grass temper from structures at Huata were collected as part of the Sacred Valley Archaeological Project radiocarbon samples (AA47679 and AA47680) and yielded two-sigma calibrated dates similar to the date for the abandonment of the pre-Inca public building at Pukara Pantillijlla.[28] The architectural dates from Pukara Pantillijlla indicate that some irregular or semicircular structures were abandoned before the fifteenth century, while rectangular structures continued to be used during the imperial period. These three sites were all said to have rebelled against Pachacutic early in his reign, and each appears to have been in the process of being abandoned by the beginning of the fifteenth century.

As discussed earlier, local elites played a vital role in the management of systems of ecological complementarity and resource diversity and would have been influential in dictating the ultimate trajectory of the local system under the Inca state. The chronicles provide ample evidence that Inca imperial expansion strategies often involved co-opting local elites by offering them perquisites for cooperation while simultaneously threatening military force should this offer of "friendship" be rejected. As we have seen for the Cusco region, some groups appear to have been peacefully absorbed by the Inca state, although the renunciation of local autonomy was probably a response to the threat of military force from the Incas or their most powerful rivals. Groups submitting to Inca domination were usually afforded Inca ethnic status (as Quechua speakers) and were frequently used to fill low-level bureaucratic positions during the imperial period.

Conversely, many other groups had to be reconquered after they attempted to assert their local autonomy. What are described as rebellions in the Inca histories appear to have occurred at times when Inca rulership changed hands or when the Inca state was threatened by external pressures. Conflicts between local elites and the Inca state indicate competition in the intermediate levels of the state administrative hierarchy as the state sought to undercut local autonomy and reduce the Cusco region to a state-administered territory.[29] The fact that "rebellions" provided the Inca state with a pretext for bloody reprisals and local territorial reorganization should suggest that some accounts of local treachery were composed after the fact to justify state interference at the local level. Either way, it is clear that local elites and the consolidating Inca state had conflicting long-term interests that ultimately led to the restructuring of local economic and political systems under direct Inca administration. Local groups were not necessarily destroyed but were marginalized and appear to have had some of their resources confiscated by the Inca elite.

One potential source of conflict was the state program of resource intensification. The imposition of Inca rule over many areas led to the state-organized development of agricultural and pastoral resources, which undercut the role of the local elite in management of ecological complementarity. Provincial governors and bureaucrats would have allocated state lands, as well as assumed patronage of rituals associated with intensive maize production and resolved conflicts related to the management of state resources. Over time, the state was better able than local elites to reciprocate local labor tribute generously, and projects of the state diverted available local labor from those of the local elite. Subordination to the Inca polity probably would have curtailed the rights of local elites to raid or make war on their neighbors, thereby depriving local elites of one means of increasing their resource base externally. Local religious power was simultaneously eroded by the Inca promotion of state cults and sponsorship of local shrines, threatening local elite justifications for community support. While cooperation with the Inca state was perhaps appealing to local elites in the short term—for avoiding military conflict and increasing their access to exotic goods—several generations of Inca hegemony would have diminished their economic, political, military, and religious power and undermined their local authority.

In other words, where state production strategies were significantly different from those of local elites, rebellion was a logical consequence of hegemony, particularly at times when state legitimacy seemed weaker than local identity. While common, rebellions appear to have hastened the loss of local autonomy. John Murra has observed that rebellion or armed resistance during the imperial period was one of the few ways by which local people could be stripped of their traditional resource base.[30] Rebellion may be considered as an attempt by local elites to reestablish themselves as viable leaders of autonomous local polities, but it also offered the Inca state an excuse to accelerate the process of imposing administrative control. The consequences of an unsuccessful rebellion appear to have included widespread military reprisals followed by the transformation (less obvious in the documentary evidence) of local culture through alteration of agricultural cycle, diet, and religion.[31]

Of course, local elites of rebellious ethnicities persisted under the Inca state, although many of their privileges do appear to have been diminished. Some members of the Huayllacan, Cuyo, Pinagua, and Muyna groups continued to live in the Inca heartland, even as their traditional lands were increasingly encroached upon by royal Inca estates.[32] The Sacred Valley was transformed so that provincial retainers served Inca elites while indigenous ethnic groups became increasingly marginalized. This expansion process of hegemony-rebellion-direct administration also characterizes the Inca occupation of many of its provincial holdings, as discussed in the following chapter.

CHAPTER NINE

The Imperial Extrapolation of
Inca State Expansion Strategies

Inca State Expansion

Having looked at the developments in the Cusco region from AD 1000 to AD 1400, it is now possible to discuss how state formation enabled rapid Inca imperial expansion. The notion that the Inca empire was invented out of a tribal or chiefly tradition by a single charismatic ruler does not accord with the available evidence. The archaeological and documentary evidence indicates that processes leading to Inca state formation began with the decline of Wari colonies in the region. Inca interactions with neighboring groups over several hundred years led to the development of the strategies for territorial expansion and administration that were used and modified in the imperial period. This is not to say that some Wari notions of provincial government, religious ideology, or elite authority were not preserved or modified by the developing Inca state, but it is clear that the Incas did not simply borrow the idea of empire and implement a model that had lain dormant for some five hundred years.

As it came to dominate the Cusco region, the Inca state developed the political, military, economic, and ideological practices that enabled the rapid incorporation of unspecialized complex polities favoring *kichwa* production zones, as well as groups practicing dry-farming and herding. Early Inca expansion into the Paucartambo lowlands demonstrates an interest in controlling trade routes and achieving direct access to exotic goods not available locally. Patterns of territorial expansion and administrative consolidation in the thirteenth and fourteenth centuries reveal that many of the strategies employed in imperial expansion were developed locally during this time. In a general sense, these can be categorized as (1) *expedient expansion,* (2) *economic growth through indirect rule,* and (3) *long-term administrative intensification.*

Expedient Expansion

As discussed in Chapter 8, the early Inca state subordinated new groups by the most indirect means possible. While marriage alliances provided one means to ensure local support, they tended not to reduce local autonomy sufficiently, and most groups eventually had to be forcibly subjugated. Military campaigns often involved sending messengers to target polities, with offers of "friendship" and an invitation to come to Cusco.[1] The repudiation or alleged mistreatment of messengers gave the Inca ruler the ideological justification to retaliate, as his paramountcy was not recognized and his declarations of friendship were impugned. The *sapa inka* assembled a large military force and traveled to the offending polity in his litter, surrounded by a corps of bodyguards. The sight of such a large force was probably enough to dissuade some towns from further resistance, but direct assaults on their strongholds weakened any remaining resolve.

Even with groups that resisted militarily, the Inca ruler was said to be generous, offering marriage alliances and leaving local elites in positions of authority. This did not necessarily mean trusting local elites to organize labor tribute and serve the state faithfully, and the Inca ruler left his representatives in conquered territory to administer Inca interests. Labor tribute rounds were served locally in the construction of Inca estates and state infrastructure, as well as in Cusco itself.

Polities that were more centralized or resisted more strongly were bypassed during the initial stages of conquest, although it appears that groups like the Pinaguas and Muynas were attacked frequently. As it began to expand imperially, the Inca state already had a diplomatic protocol for justifying expansion, and it attempted to avoid costly set-piece battles with well-prepared enemies. By casting the conflict as a misunderstanding between elite leaders rather than a war between polities, the Incas often were able to find more cooperative local factions who wanted to avoid armed conflict or wished to increase their own local power by forging an alliance with the Inca ruler.

Economic Growth through Indirect Rule

The Inca state left local elites in their offices and tended not to expropriate large amounts of a polity's subsistence resources. In the Sacred Valley study region, the Incas allowed some conquered groups to occupy their ridgetop villages for a time, but the Incas applied labor tribute to the development of lands not currently in local use, focusing particular attention on valley-bottom maize lands. It appears that the state attempted to preserve the fiction of two parallel systems—an intensifying state economy and a more or less autonomous, unimproved local one—while extracting increasing returns from new territories. Many of the impositions of the early state at the local level were probably justified by state acts of generosity, such as feasts or elaborate religious rituals. The construction of administrative sites, roads, storage units, and agricultural infrastructure would have taken years, and the Inca state reduced administrative costs by avoiding unnecessary direct intervention at the local level.

Long-Term Administrative Intensification

Inca use of local labor tribute and establishment of state agents conflicted with the maintenance of long-term local elite authority, and rebellion or state-initiated administrative intensification was common as the state expanded. The conflict between two alternatives in the intermediate administrative hierarchy—local elites versus state officials—encouraged the state to replace or eliminate local elite leaders and impose more direct administrative forms. In the Cusco region, the estate system expanded to manage local production, and a permanent retainer class was developed that largely replaced autonomous local ethnic groups.

The full imposition of Inca state administration in many parts of the Cusco region required several generations as the state effected the transition from indirect to direct control. The same strategies developed during the process of state expansion and consolidation provided the basis for Inca imperial strategies, which were modified to meet local contingencies rather than inflexibly enforced. In early campaigns, complex but politically fragmented regions were targeted for incorporation through alliances, elite interaction, and warfare, and administrative intensity increased over time as opportunities arose to undermine local elite autonomy. As control over nonstate confederations and chiefdoms was being consolidated, the more complex states and empires were incorporated in the same manner, although they were administered differently. At the time of the Spanish Conquest, the Inca realm (called Tawantinsuyu in Quechua) was involved in provincial reorganization, particularly in areas that previously lacked local political complexity.[2]

The first campaigns of Inca imperial expansion involved the incorporation of highland valley systems, while lowland areas were bypassed and left for later conquest (fig. 9.1). The upper quarters (*suyukuna*) of the empire, Qollasuyu and Chinchaysuyu, were initially highland provinces, while the lower ones included territory along the Pacific coast (Cuntisuyu, to the west of the Andes) and in the Amazonian piedmont (Antisuyu, to the east of the Andes). Highland valleys made excellent targets for incorporation because they were often small and isolated, with local economies that could be intensified easily by the state without major disruption of local production. Local systems were self-sufficient in the production of staple resources, but new agricultural and pastoral resources could be created by the state and maintained by labor colonists. Road systems and administrative centers often were built in areas outside of the local productive system,[3] and state control of regional storage and state sponsorship of redistribution was intended to undercut staple autonomy at the local level. The Incas developed more direct control over the highland valley economies, exploiting local patterns of ecological complementarity to extend imperial control into lowland areas,[4] with the ultimate goal of achieving direct control over all resources used by the empire. Given the variability in local ecology and political organization, it is possible to appreciate the flexibility of Inca imperial strategies and to discern their development over time.

Inca Incorporation of Complex Nonstate Polities

Using well-established strategies for expansion and administration, the Incas began their imperial campaigns—permanent conquests beyond about 70 kilometers of Cusco—by moving against complex nonstate polities or confederations in the highlands. In some cases, Inca armies bypassed centralized states to campaign in highland regions with complex nonstate organization. The incorporation of such groups often took place in at least two stages, beginning with a period of alliance or hegemonic control, followed by the development of imperial infrastructure and administrative reorganization of the local system.[5]

Katharina Schreiber has argued that complex nonstate polities are ideal for incorporation into an empire because local hierarchies have

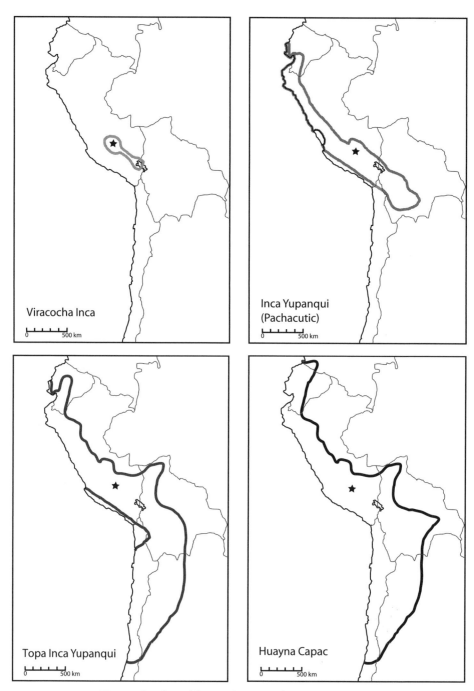

Viracocha Inca

0 500 km

Inca Yupanqui
(Pachacutic)

0 500 km

Topa Inca Yupanqui

0 500 km

Huayna Capac

0 500 km

Fig. 9.1. Inca imperial expansion. (Based on Pärssinen 1992.)

already been established, but not to a degree that extensive administrative restructuring is required to undercut local authority.[6] It is possible to impose additional levels of religious and administrative hierarchy on the local system and administer indirectly through local political structures. Indirect control initially benefits both the imperial system and some local elites, whose access to prestige items and local authority are increased. In the long run, however, administrative goals at the state and local level are generally incompatible.[7] Once an imperial province had been pacified, the Incas used local labor to develop more direct administrative systems and to increase and control state revenue, while local elites often rebelled in an attempt to maintain autonomy and reduce dependency on imperial structures and ideologies.[8] Local elites remained within the imperial system to the extent that it presented a better alternative to "going it alone,"[9] and provincial elites in Tawantinsuyu often found ways to exploit the imperial system to their own ends, using territorial control and tributary patterns to extract more resources for their own use. This situation was tolerated by the Incas in provinces where local elite cooperation was essential for maintaining order.

In complex polities with centralized (but unspecialized) political leadership, it was possible to incorporate large groups through elite interactions with a few self-interested individuals, and the exchange of gifts, marriage partners, and sacred objects (*wak'akuna*) was a common initial overture by Inca representatives, who offered friendship to local elites while simultaneously threatening war with vast armies assembled nearby. In such polities, the competitive nature of the political system made it likely that if one individual or faction proved disloyal or uncooperative, a replacement would be available. A relative of the *sapa inka,* accompanied by a large army and bearing a wide array of gifts and honors, could often incorporate a complex polity or undermine existing regional alliances without having to resort to warfare. Of course, the chronicles indicate that Inca armies were resisted on many occasions. Following the establishment of Inca rule, many provinces saw the development of imperial infrastructure, as well as local resistance to more extractive administrative demands. We can consider some of the better-documented cases.

Aymara Polities of the Titicaca Basin

The Incas appear to have begun processes of alliance building and conquest in the direction of the Titicaca Basin prior to the final consolidation

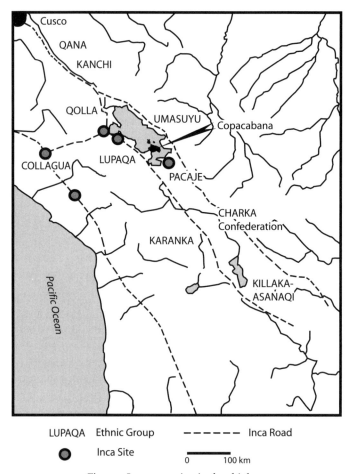

Fig. 9.2. Inca expansion in the altiplano

of the Cusco region.[10] The polities affected by this expansion initially included the Qanas, Kanchis, Qollas, and Lupaqas, and later expansion incorporated the Pacajes, Qarankas, Killaka-Asanaqi, and the Charka confederation (fig. 9.2). By the end of the fourteenth century, several polities in the Titicaca Basin and southern altiplano were in the process of organizing into large confederations or states. Archaeologically, it appears that these groups were organized regionally for defensive purposes and that their political organization, while not constituting strong centralized states, allowed a more direct influence in the upper valleys of the

Pacific coast, where maize could be cultivated.[11] Historical descriptions of these groups suggest that they were united at least nominally under hereditary leadership, but that political organization comprised multiple autonomous units that were not well integrated. Warfare was based more on raiding than conquest and administration.[12]

The Inca conquest of this region began by raising a massive army and marching it to the territory of target polities, then attempting to entice local elites to contract a subordinate alliance with the Inca ruler by offering gifts that included precious metals and fine cloth. Even where the combination of diplomacy and coercion was not successful in avoiding military conflict, the Incas often managed to manipulate local rivalries to keep a region from uniting in organized resistance. For example, while the Kanchis of the upper Vilcanota Valley fought the Inca army, neighboring Qanas withheld their support, then submitted to the victorious Incas in exchange for prestige gifts and a guarantee that their lands would not be looted.[13] Likewise, the rivalry between the Qollas and Lupaqas led to the two groups fighting each other, with the Incas forging an alliance with the winner.[14] In the case of the Lupaqas, a marriage alliance was proposed by Qari, the paramount ruler.[15] Some defeated Qolla elites were transported to the Inca heartland to work as retainers on Inca estates,[16] while cooperative Lupaqa and Killaka elites received honors from the Inca ruler, including fancy cloth, *Spondylus* shell, and the right to ride in a litter. These local leaders used their administrative positions to extend their own personal networks into the lowlands to the east and west of the altiplano.[17]

The establishment of indirect control through alliance building did not achieve a successful imperial administration over this region, and several chroniclers mention repeated rebellions that occurred for several decades.[18] This is probably because the effective administrative range of cooperative local elites was not sufficient to maintain order and because local patterns of ecological complementarity favored local elite autonomy and political instability.[19] Rebellions led by dissatisfied local elites occurred at the northern and southern edges of Lupaqa territory, particularly during the interregnum between Inca rulers or when Inca armies were occupied in other campaigns.[20]

The reconquest of rebellious areas ultimately led to the establishment of a more intensive imperial administration for the region. Huge Inca armies engaged in bloody campaigns to wipe out resistance, then resettled local populations and developed infrastructure throughout the Titicaca

Basin, including decimal organization within new imperial provinces.[21] The local road system was greatly expanded, and new Inca towns were built along it.[22]

At the same time an important imperial pilgrimage center was developed on the Copacabana Peninsula and islands of Coati and Titicaca in Lake Titicaca.[23] Following the military conquest of the Copacabana area, an Inca palace was constructed, and a provincial governor from the lineage of the eighth ruler was appointed to govern labor colonists from over forty different ethnic groups from throughout the empire.[24] This area had been part of an important regional shrine system in Tiwanaku times, and the Incas co-opted ideological and religious power by promoting a pilgrimage system commemorating a Titicaca version of the creation myth and establishing a royal estate at Tiwanaku.[25]

While local groups were organized under Inca administration and labor colonists were brought into the region from other parts of the empire, some local populations were also moved out of the Titicaca Basin and altiplano region. For example, the Incas developed an impressive state production enclave in the maize-producing lands of Cochabamba and Larecaja, using labor from numerous altiplano ethnic groups to produce agricultural surpluses to fund administration and military expansion.[26] The complex polities of the highlands served as the basis for colonizing and controlling areas from the Amazonian lowlands to the Pacific coast,[27] but direct control had to be developed to keep local elites from having sufficient autonomy to present a serious threat to Inca political stability.

Confederations of the Central Sierra

Inca reliance on local elites in the Titicaca Basin and Bolivian altiplano led to repeated rebellions as imperial infrastructure and administration were gradually implemented. There is evidence that this degree of local unrest was avoided as the Incas expanded their territory to the north of Cusco (fig. 9.3). Although local elite resistance is commonly mentioned in the histories, all evidence suggests that the development of imperial infrastructure in this area generally began at the initial period of conquest, leading to fewer long term problems than were experienced in the southern altiplano.

Having already defeated the Chancas in previous conflicts, the Incas began their expansion to the north of Cusco by making alliances with

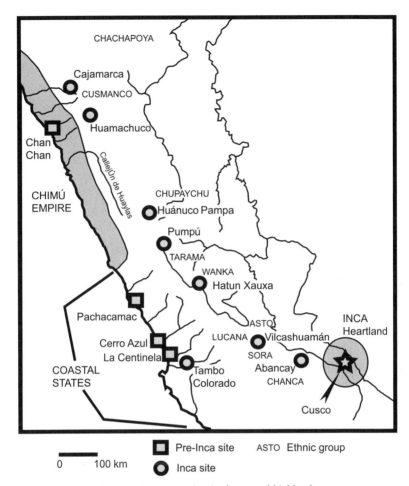

Fig. 9.3. Inca expansion in the central highlands

various Chanca elites, including at least one case of marriage exchange.[28] Miguel Cabello de Balboa states that in cases where fighting occurred, the Incas killed all local elites, replacing them with the local elites' children, who served under the supervision of Inca governors.[29] The next region targeted was that of the Soras and Lucanas, an area that appears to have been characterized by two- or three-tier settlement hierarchies and the existence of hereditary village leaders.[30] Linguistic heterogeneity and the absence of significant settlement hierarchy suggest that much of the region at the time of conquest was not consolidated under a single state or confederation. When attempts at peaceful incorporation of the Soras failed, the Incas defeated them in a fierce battle and then starved out the last resisters in an extended siege. At the same time, they made alliances with people in the Vilcas River region and began to construct administrative sites and reorganize local political and religious systems.[31]

A similar process took place among the Wankas, Taramas, and Chinchaycochas, and the establishment of Inca control led to immediate changes in local settlement and the construction of Inca administrative sites.[32] The northern Inca campaign successfully incorporated highland valleys as far as Huánuco, establishing a system of major administrative sites that reordered local economic and political organization under the decimal system in a way that used local elite networks and ethnic organizations to extract a variety of resources (fig. 9.4).[33] Inca tributary demands and the centralization of storage systems had an impact on local craft production and political economy.[34]

One result of these campaigns was the construction of a network of administrative sites along the imperial road system.[35] Local populations were reorganized under decimal administration, although local elites continued to hold low- and mid-level administrative positions, implementing imperial labor requirements.[36] Labor colonists, including members of many Inca-of-Privilege groups from the Cusco region, were also resettled into newly administered areas, including a major production enclave at Abancay.[37] Inca governors received their orders from Cusco but allowed local elites to manage administrative affairs through hereditary offices that could be passed to their eldest or most able sons. Inca administrators arranged local elite marriages and had control over the approval of new officials (*kurakakuna*). Archaeological evidence from sites like Huánuco Pampa indicates that the most important administrative relationship was between Inca administrators and a large number of local elites.[38] Inca cities were designed to reproduce Inca ideology and administrative structure, and many imperial rituals and ceremonies were practiced at the provincial level.[39]

The highlands northwest of Cusco remained closely integrated throughout much of the imperial period in part because local elites were tied closely to the empire through marriage and *wak'a* exchange and through obligatory inclusion in imperial rituals and administration. This integration was successful because Inca administrators were monitored through repeated provincial reviews by the *sapa inka* or trusted advisers. In this area, which had been the heart of the Wari empire, the presence

N

HUÁNUCO PAMPA

0 25 50 100 200
METERS

Fig. 9.4. Huánuco Pampa, an Inca administrative city. (Courtesy of Craig Morris.)

of roads or routes first established by the Wari and the legacy of more complex conceptualizations of elite authority may have aided the Incas in imposing stable provincial administration.[40]

The Inca Conquest of Ecuadorian Polities

By the time Inca armies had advanced northward into the lands of the Cañaris, Puruháes, Caranquis, Quitos, and other groups of the Ecuadorian highlands, Inca imperial strategies from earlier campaigns were already well established, and Frank Salomon has documented how imperial control was extended over time.[41] Inca armies appear to have targeted specifically those areas with more complex organization (e.g., the Caranquis), where local polities lived in large nucleated villages with monumental architecture and some agricultural intensification.[42] The incorporation of new groups in these areas led to the establishment of Inca fortifications to monitor the area and participate in exchange networks between the highlands and the lowlands, where *Spondylus* shell, cotton, gold, and coca leaf could be acquired.[43] Over time, colonists were brought in from other parts of the empire to farm in highland valleys, and a more permanent presence of Inca representatives was established in the lowlands, although the Incas had very limited direct control there.[44]

Like the Chachapoyas to the south, the Cañaris were massively resettled, particularly to Cusco, and at least six Cañari migrations took place during the reigns of Topa Inca Yupanqui, Huayna Capac, Huascar, and Atahuallpa.[45] These groups served full-time retainers (*yanakuna*) and messengers (*chaskikuna*), and John Murra has demonstrated that some members of these groups also became more or less permanent military specialists, evidence that the Incas were moving toward instituting a professional army and perhaps a more secular and militaristic administration of their empire.[46] The creation of a new retainer class with no ethnic affiliation and a direct obligation to the Inca elite was an important means by which the empire began to undermine traditional equations of kin-based reciprocity.[47]

Once new territory had come under Inca control, large state installations were developed at Tomebamba and Quito, constructed over preexisting settlements in what amounted to the development of new administrative capitals.[48] The evidence for Inca conquest in Ecuador suggests that Inca strategies for expansion and administration were modified to address local resistance and the changing needs of the empire.

Inca Incorporation of States and Empires

As the Incas developed infrastructure throughout many of their new provinces and continued campaigns of expansion against nonstate polities, they also began to incorporate centralized polities along the central and north coast. The coastal region had remained unconquered for a variety of reasons. The geographic emphasis on Inca conquest had been in areas with isolated complex groups whose agricultural and pastoral economies could be integrated and managed most effectively in the existing state political economy.[49] The establishment of Inca infrastructure increased production in areas whose full potential was previously untapped in the absence of centralized administration. While the Andean highlands could provide a wide range of productive capabilities, the Incas ultimately desired direct access to products available only from coastal valleys and the Amazonian lowlands.[50] These included both prestige items (e.g., *Spondylus* shell, precious metals, exotic bird feathers, and coca leaf) and more mundane products like honey, timber, fish, seaweed, and guano for fertilizing maize fields.[51]

Because the coastal polities already were organized into a number of centralized governments, the Incas may have had longstanding alliances to ensure access to some coastal products. Several chronicles mention marriage alliances and raiding along the coast prior to military incorporation, although there is no archaeological evidence of Inca control anywhere on the coast prior to AD 1400. Coastal polities were more difficult to incorporate because local economies and ideologies were already well developed and local elites often contested Inca hegemony.[52] In many cases, the Incas established complementary administrative and ideological systems without making radical internal changes to local systems.[53] Other systems had to be reconfigured hierarchically to impose imperial government.[54]

The Incorporation of the States of the Central and South Coast

As mentioned in the preceding, the south and central coastal regions were controlled by a number of small states. According to Pedro de Cieza de León, Inca conquest of these coastal polities began with an unsuccessful raid, which was then followed by peaceful overtures.[55] Some of the smaller polities such as those in the Nazca and Ica valleys appear to have been incorporated without a major fight, and areas that were previously not centrally organized saw the establishment of imperial administrative sites along a new coastal highway.[56] The Chincha polity was highly developed at the time of conquest, and continuities in settlement indicate that few changes were made at the local level following incorporation into Tawantinsuyu.[57] An early colonial visit to the Chincha Valley by Cristóbal de Castro and Diego de Ortega Morejón recounts the conquest of the Chincha polity as a peaceful one occurring around AD 1400 (fig. 9.5).[58] Other polities appear to have united in resistance to Inca expansion, raising armies or setting up defenses at fortified sites. For example, the Huarco and Lunahuaná polities refused to submit to the Incas, retreating to Ungará, a fortress in the Cañete Valley that protected the local irrigation system, and undergoing a protracted military siege by Inca armies before a final defeat.[59]

Coastal polities already had well-developed elite ideologies and hierarchies, specialized labor, and productive infrastructure (including road and irrigation systems), and the Inca administrative strategy appears to have been much less invasive than for nonstate polities.[60] In general, Inca administrators appear to have left many coastal areas under the leadership of local rulers, developing increasingly more intensive administration over midvalley coca and maize lands and intermontane herding areas that coastal polities had never controlled directly.[61] The Incas established administrators in imperial enclaves in capital areas and developed a regional system of roads and way stations (*tampukuna*), where the imperial presence is directly visible.[62] There is less evidence for the resettlement of labor colonists into or out of centralized coastal polities under the empire, and local material culture along the coast often has little evidence of Inca influence.[63]

While Inca administrators in many ways were set up as parallels to local elites—to look after imperial interests in these realms—Inca crafts and goods were distributed more pervasively along the central coast. Coastal elites used Inca pottery, cloth, and exotic goods, but they also produced Inca-influenced styles of their own and distributed them among their constituents.[64] As local elite hierarchies remained critical to the administration of the central coast, religion provided one means for extending imperial administration. Inca temples and *akllawasi* were constructed close to major regional shrines like Pachacamac and Chinchacamac, and the empire co-opted local cults and exchanged *wak'akuna* with local groups (fig. 9.6).[65] The distribution of Inca religious

Fig. 9.5. La Centinela, capital of the Chincha polity. An Inca palace was built within the main compound at the site. (Negative no. 334732, Courtesy Dept. of Library Services, American Museum of Natural History.)

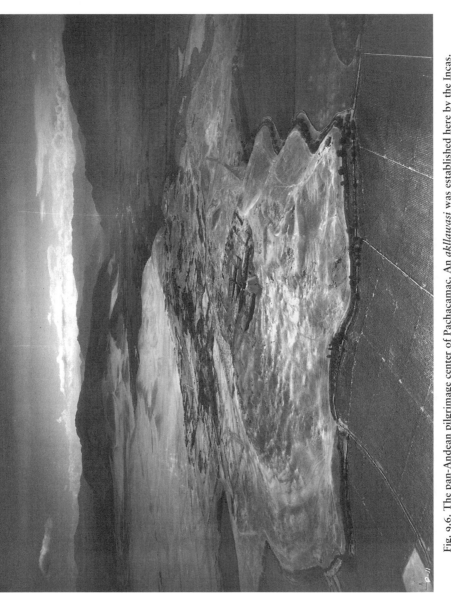

Fig. 9.6. The pan-Andean pilgrimage center of Pachacamac. An *akllawasi* was established here by the Incas. (Negative no. 334840, Courtesy Dept. of Library Services, American Museum of Natural History.)

architecture demonstrates that imperial investment was heaviest in the highlands of Chinchaysuyu, to the northwest of Cusco (fig. 9.7).

Even if long-term Inca strategies for the coast included undercutting local elite authority, individuals like the lord of Chincha continued to enjoy a degree of autonomy, receiving high honors for their loyalty up to the time of the Spanish Conquest.[66] The lack of Inca imperial pottery at the local or domestic level (contrasted with the prevalence of local decorative styles) indicates that powerful local elites retained their power and controlled regional distribution patterns.[67]

Inca Conquest of a Coastal Empire

The incorporation of the small coastal states supposedly began after the incorporation of the Chimú and Cusmanco polities to the north. The trajectory of Chimú imperial development had been similar to that of Tawantinsuyu—expansion within a heartland region, followed by north-south conquests of self-sufficient polities with like economies—if slightly earlier and more impressive in terms of its early material manifestations.[68] It is possible that the Incas chose first to develop an alliance relationship with the Chimú and their highland allies in the Cajamarca region, and Pedro Sarmiento de Gamboa mentions that these groups sent warriors to help Pachacutic Inca Yupanqui put down an early Inca rebellion in the Titicaca Basin.[69] This would be consistent with other accounts from other regions that describe Inca expansion as beginning with raiding or alliance building, followed by more direct incorporation.[70]

Inca administration involved the development of some imperial infrastructure and the partial reorganization of the Chimú imperial apparatus. According to Agustín de Zárate, the Chimú paramount title, Chimú Ccapac, persisted until the reign of Huayna Capac, when the Chimú elite rebelled against Inca rule.[71] While Chimú rulers became Inca puppets whose policy-making power was assumed by Inca administrators, local elites appear to have been affected in limited ways, and material culture shows only an ephemeral Inca presence outside of mortuary and elite administrative contexts.[72] The importance of local elites is underscored by their willingness to rebel against regional administrators during the Inca civil war and Spanish Conquest.[73] The Inca occupation of the north coast remains understudied, although several important projects have been conducted.[74]

It is possible that evidence of more direct Inca administration is to be

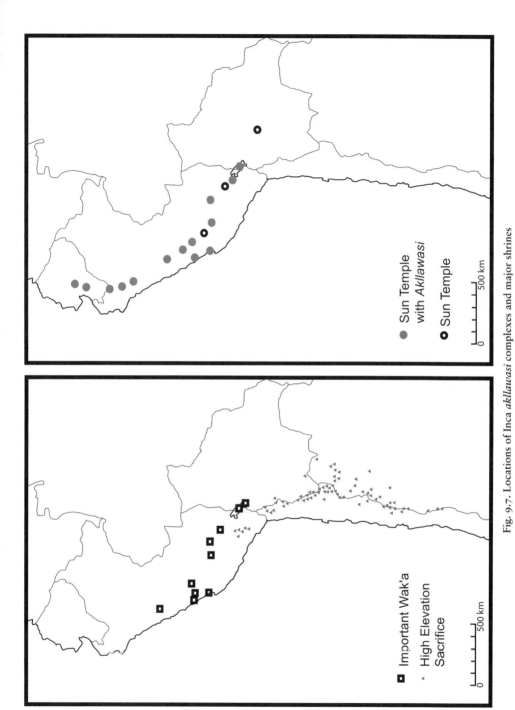

Fig. 9.7. Locations of Inca *akllawasi* complexes and major shrines

*information on high elevation sacrifices from D'Altroy 2002

Sun Temple
with *Akllawasi*

Sun Temple

500 km

0

Important Wak'a

High Elevation
Sacrifice

500 km

0

found in the highland regions that were formerly part of the Cusmanco polity. Documentary evidence from the Callejón de Huaylas and the Huamachuco and Cajamarca regions suggests that as the Incas extended their highland infrastructure, they may have placed the administration of upper coastal valleys under highland communities as the realignment of coastal infrastructure was underway.[75] It is unclear whether Inca administration was fully implemented on the coast, or whether processes of consolidation were underway at the time of the Spanish invasion.

Administrative Trajectories and the Formalization of Ecological Complementarity

Tawantinsuyu grew rapidly through the incorporation of complex polities, but as provincial control became more direct, the Incas attempted to occupy areas that lacked well-developed sociopolitical complexity. Initially, imperial order depended on local highland elites to organize the acquisition of nonlocal goods, and there is evidence that elite privilege and responsibility involved the supervision of hunting and herding in high-elevation grasslands, the exploitation of natural resources, and the acquisition of lowland resources.[76] In the case of Ecuadorian *mindaláes* and Chincha *mercaderes*, the Incas left specialized merchants and pre-existing exchange networks in place, perhaps because they were more effective in the short term than the direct reorganization of an ethnically complex region.[77] That is, given the short time span for Inca control in Ecuador, more direct strategies may not have been imposed. As the Incas moved northward through Ecuador, local networks were useful as a means of extending imperial hegemony as more direct control was implemented within established provincial regions.[78] Some of the areas requiring more administrative development included coastal and highland regions with sparse populations, as well as the lower *montaña* region, where many groups lacked hierarchical political organization.

One solution to areas with rich resources but sparse population was to send labor colonists (*mitmaqkuna*) to colonize the area and develop resources, with an ultimate goal of realizing a self-contained system of ecological complementarity. Colonization and administration were often based on extending existing patterns of ecological complementarity maintained by complex highland groups.[79] In the coastal valleys of southern Peru and northern Chile, Inca infrastructure developed in maize-producing regions but extended to the coast in some locations to exploit fish, guano, and other marine resources.[80] In high-elevation grasslands suitable for pastoralism, the imposition of an Inca imperial herd system transformed existing patterns of herd management and the social networks enabling them.[81] Control over the imperial roads and major caravan routes was essential for the maintenance of administrative control.[82] In many areas, local elites probably set the tempo for the imperial formalization of direct resource access, either by resisting or exploiting the system.

At the time of the Spanish Conquest, the Incas were successfully extracting exotic goods from lowland regions and redistributing them across the empire, often after their development as wealth items by craft specialists in Cusco and other administrative locations.[83] As Pedro Sancho de la Hoz observed, storage in the Inca capital included exotic bird feathers, precious metals, and pigments for decoration.[84] *Spondylus* shell came from Ecuadorian estuaries, and gold was found in the *montaña* to the east of the Andean highlands, while northern Chile and northwest Argentina provided copper and other resources.[85] Early in the Inca expansion, an effort was made to develop coca-producing lands to the east and west of the Andean sierra, and Inca infrastructure stretched into the *montaña* in areas around Cusco.[86]

To some degree, the Incas could regulate the production and distribution of wealth items within their polity and could actually increase wealth by restricting the flow of certain goods. Still, it is clear that the empire did not have complete control over some goods coming from lowland areas (e.g., *Spondylus* and bird feathers) and had to make concessions to local elites and lowland groups to gain access.[87] For example, tributary records from Huánuco and the Titicaca Basin indicate that highland administrators were responsible for acquiring some lowland materials directly (e.g., gold, silver, honey, coca leaf, and *uchu*) but only for the modification of others (e.g., the working, but not acquisition, of bird feathers).[88]

The direct incorporation of egalitarian lowland groups had rarely been made successfully by the time of the Spanish Conquest, but Inca imperial strategies increasingly targeted lowland areas, in part through the construction of networks of fortifications (fig. 9.8).[89] The Incas explained away their inability to incorporate such groups, saying that the lands lacked salt or worthwhile resources, the natives were cannibals, or that the climate was unhealthy. The major ecological differences between

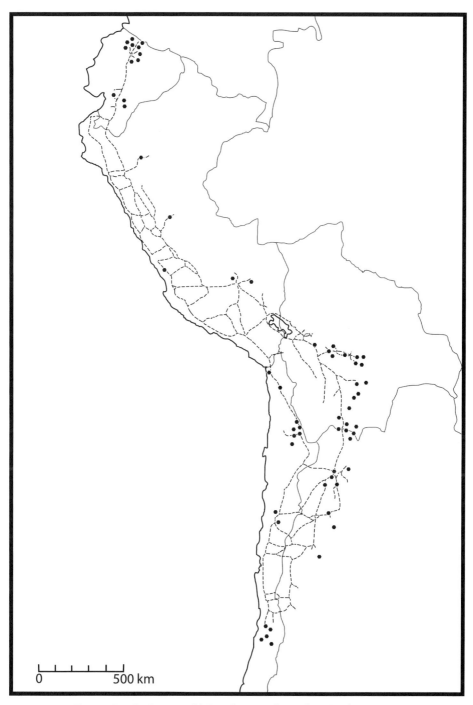

Fig. 9.8. Lowland areas, with Inca forts. (Redrawn from D'Altroy 2002.)

the highlands and the Amazonian lowlands may have created a boundary between language groups or kinds of political organization; at the very least, direct administration of the humid lowlands was a costly affair, and in most cases, it appears that the empire had to content itself with informal exchanges at the ecological interface between the two areas, probably in the coca-producing zone above 1500 meters.[90] The construction of roads down to the *montaña* and of systems of fortresses in some frontier areas suggests that the Incas would have continued to attempt to formalize their control, probably by depopulating lowland areas and bringing in settlers from the *montaña,* as was done near Cochabamba in Bolivia.[91] A gradual colonization of progressively lower ecological floors might have been the only way to introduce direct imperial control over such areas.

It is clear that in the southern reaches of the empire, where mineral wealth was considerable, but where local groups proved difficult to pacify, Inca control was less direct than in other areas.[92] Documentary descriptions of the southern boundaries of Tawantinsuyu exaggerate the southward spread of Inca material culture, and it appears that the degree of organized local resistance determined the limits of Inca expansion in this region and mitigated its intensity.[93]

It is likely that Tawantinsuyu would have continued its territorial expansion and administrative consolidation had the Spanish Conquest not occurred. Military investment at the time of the conquest was concentrated on northern Ecuador and southern Colombia, and it is possible that through long-distance exchange alliances the Incas would have eventually attempted to incorporate the large chiefdoms of the Popayan-Chibcha living in the Cauca and Magdalena valleys. In addition, there is evidence that eastward expansion toward the Amazonian lowlands was proceeding with limited success and that the Incas wished to incorporate additional territory in south-central Chile and northwestern Argentina. Clearly, while major rulership crises characterized the final years of the pre-Hispanic era, Inca administration was still in the process of being fully implemented in many provincial regions.

Summary

This brief discussion of Inca imperial expansion has demonstrated how many of the patterns of early Inca expansion in the Cusco region provided the basis for imperial expansion and administration. Elite inter-action, nonviolent incorporation of complex highland groups, and the gradual development of direct administration are all described for the Inca heartland during the process of state formation. Imperial conquest and administration led to the evolution of these strategies, which in turn changed the way that the imperial heartland was administered. As demonstrated in chapter 10, the Cusco region was transformed in the imperial period to meet new social and political demands as the Inca state grew into the largest empire in the Americas.

CHAPTER TEN

The Transformation of the Inca Heartland

Inca strategies for territorial expansion and the administration of subject populations developed over several hundred years as the Incas gradually established an advantage over neighboring groups, then incorporated them one by one as subordinates. As they contracted marriage alliances with the Ayarmacas, warred with the Cuyos and Pinaguas, and generously bestowed exotic gifts upon Anta elites, the Incas crafted the policies and strategies that guided them in their conquest of the Andean region. The incorporation of the Sacred Valley added a large subject population, but it also presented an untapped agricultural zone whose development was critical for imperial expansion. The transformation of valley-bottom maize lands enabled sustained long-term military campaigns outside of the Cusco region.

We have seen that Inca strategies and policies changed over time and were adapted for different regions, and the imperial period also saw a major change in the role played by the heartland region, particularly the Sacred Valley.

Ethnic and Ritual Definitions of the Inca Imperial Heartland

As the Incas expanded outside of their heartland, they developed continuous control over a region within about 50–80 kilometers of the capital. Most groups living in this area were granted Inca ethnic status and many were obliged to provide colonists to settle in provincial regions and implement imperial administration. The chronicles provide us with several ways of identifying the limits of the Inca heartland, including ethnic and ritual boundaries.

Inca Ethnic Boundaries

As discussed in chapters 6 and 7, numerous historically documented political and ethnic groups are known to have lived the Cusco region, including some (like the Huayllacans and Cuyos) that are not known to have been granted Inca status. Inca groups were allowed to pierce their ears, and their higher status in the imperial system is attested to by Spanish references to *orejones* (literally, "big ears") in positions of local prominence throughout the empire. The chroniclers Garcilaso de la Vega and Felipe Guaman Poma de Ayala provide some of the most detailed information on these groups, crediting their establishment to the Inca founding ancestor, Manco Capac.[1] Significantly, these and other gradualist chronicles take the boundaries of the Inca imperial heartland as a point of departure for imperial expansion, making them poor sources for evaluating how such a territory developed.

Lists of Inca-of-Privilege groups are found in multiple chronicles, although they often are contradictory or vague.[2] Thirteen groups are mentioned by multiple authors: Masca, Chillque, Papre, Tambo, Mayo, Sanco, Limatambo, Quilliscache, Quechua, Queguar, Huaro, Caviña, and Poque. In addition to these groups, another seven—Aco, Yanahuara, Anta, Lare, Huarocondo, Muyna, and Urco—are mentioned more than once by a given author. Finally, the Chinchaypuquio, Yucay, Xaquixaguana, Equeco, Ayarmaca, Quispicancha, and Chilpaca groups are mentioned once by a single author. Importantly, we also know from multiple sources that in addition to these groups were others, native to the Cusco region, who did not become Incas-of-Privilege, including the Cuyos, Pinaguas, and Huayllacans.

Some of the variation in groups named may be due to the use of geographic names to describe their occupants (e.g., Xaquixaguana [Qaqawana], Yucay, Quispicancha, Chinchaypuquio), but there is some confusion as to whether some groups living at the margins of this region—Yanahuara, Lare, and Aco—were in fact Incas-of-Privilege. Regardless, the region of Inca-of-Privilege groups represents the area that the Incas considered as their imperial core, a region within about 50–80 kilometers of Cusco that included dozens of groups that had to be integrated into the Inca polity.

Ritual Boundaries of the Inca Heartland

A second indicator of the imperial Inca conceptualization of its heartland emerges through the analysis of the Citua (also spelled *Çitua, Situa, Zithuwa*) ritual described by the priest Cristóbal de Molina.[3] This ritual was performed in the Inca month of Coyaraymi (August) and consisted of two parts: Cusco's descent groups ritually established the boundaries of the Inca heartland, and then provincial elites entered the region and proceeded to Cusco to give allegiance to the Inca ruler. As Molina describes the ceremony, runners gathered in Cusco's main plaza, one hundred from each imperial quarter (*suyu*) representing the royal and nonroyal Inca lineages. The Cusco representatives ran to about 15 kilometers from the city along the four principal highways, passing ceremonial weapons off to groups that Molina describes as *mitmaqkuna* (although they may have been Incas-of-Privilege). The secondary runners continued to four important confluences of major rivers (*tinkukuna*), where they cleansed their weapons in the water. Molina identifies the terminal points of this ritual as the Apurímac River below Limatambo and at the confluence with the Cusibamba River, as well as the Vilcanota River at Pisaq and at Quiquijana (fig. 10.1).

The Citua boundaries indicate an additional level of hierarchy to that described by the honorary Inca groups. The ritual marks the confluence of important transverse rivers into the Vilcanota and Apurímac rivers, probably staking a claim not only to the territory within the four points but to the drainages of the side valleys as well.[4] Simultaneously, the transfer of ceremonial authority along the route demarcated the ritual limits of the urban jurisdiction of Cusco, an area of about 500 square kilometers. The Citua ritual marked the boundary of the capital, as well as the limits of territory over which royal Inca lineages had traditional control.

Inca Towns in the Early Colonial Period

A third line of evidence for identifying the boundaries of the Inca heartland comes from a description of the 1571 celebration of the christening of Melchior Inca, the son of don Carlos Inca and great-grandson of the emperor Huayna Capac. Baltasar de Ocampo states that all Inca towns in the area were invited to the event and names thirty-four different *pre-reducción* towns from which all Inca people traveled for the event.[5] These

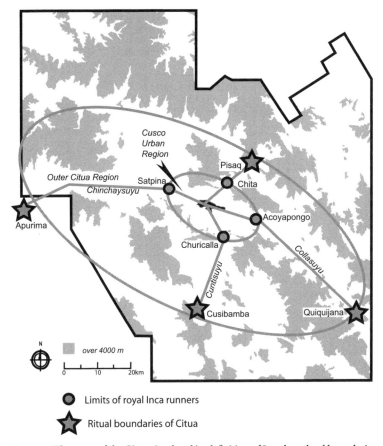

Fig. 10.1. The route of the Citua ritual and its definition of Inca heartland boundaries

towns are identified as Inca, in clear distinction to other invited groups, like the Qanas, Kanchis, and Qollas.[6] As figure 10.2 shows, these groups all came from within the limits—established by other measures—of the Inca heartland, and the list includes important boundary towns (Lima-tambo, Pisaq, and Quiquijana). The clustering of the towns suggests a similar heartland as defined by the Citua—that is, not including groups in the *ceja de montaña* like the Poques and Lares—but also one with a very strong ethnic connection to areas south and west of Cusco. The gaps in "Inca" towns in other areas are consistent with the territories of groups that were not considered Inca, such as the Pinaguas and Cuyos.

These three lines of evidence present an emic perspective on how the

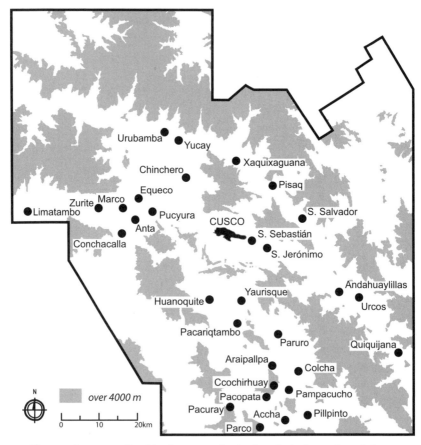

Fig. 10.2. Inca towns listed by Ocampo as having been invited to an Inca christening in 1571

Incas delimited their imperial core. The area that the Incas considered their ethnic and ritual heartland was perhaps somewhat smaller than their political and economic core. Ethnic identity was not distributed evenly but clustered in different ways based on a complex series of "Inca" identities. The imperial heartland was promoted above the four provincial regions, but the Inca elite was responsible for replicating provincial divisions ritually. As the capital of the empire, Cusco was elevated above the heartland itself. Such promotions underscore the transformative effect of Inca imperial expansion on the economy, politics, and religious life of the Cusco region.

Imperial Expansion and Cusco's Staple Finance Dilemma

Although the large-scale intensification of agricultural production in the Sacred Valley helped to enable imperial territorial expansion, agricultural resources would also have set effective limits for that expansion. Terence D'Altroy has observed that the logistical problems of moving staple goods increase with distance as the caloric requirements involved in transportation mount.[7] Effective transport limits could be extended in a number of ways, including the construction of roads for more rapid transit, the central management of large camelid caravans, and a focus on producing dried foodstuffs, including maize, *ch'uñu* (freeze-dried potatoes), and *ch'arki* (dried camelid meat). As it expanded, the Inca empire invested in road construction, herd management, and storage systems, extending the efficacy of Cusco-produced staple production. As conquests continued beyond these logistical limits, the Incas developed new production enclaves in provincial areas and used local production and storage to maintain imperial infrastructure.[8] Major state production centers were developed at Cochabamba, Abancay, and other locations, and the huge volume of provincial storage complexes bears witness to the integration of local staple production to sustain the empire.[9] Many state-directed projects to intensify local production were supported by relocating ethnic Inca groups from the heartland to other parts of the empire (table 10.1).

As staple goods from Cusco were no longer the most effective provision for many military campaigns, new provinces were also too distant for the Incas to use labor tribute to transport staple goods between heartland and provinces, although it is clear from the documentary record that the symbolic transport of staple crops to Cusco continued throughout

TABLE 10.1.   Colonization of Some Inca-of-Privilege

Ethnic Group	Area Colonized	Source
Aco	Ayacucho	Arnold 1993
Anta	Ayacucho	Stern 1982
Chillque	Arequipa	D. Julien 1993
Queguar	Angaraes	Relaciones Geográficas 1:201–204
Canco	Huamachuco	J. Topic and T. Topic 1993
Yanahuara	Arequipa	D. Julien 1993
"Orejones"	Huánuco	Grosboll 1993; Heffernan 1996
"Orejones"	Tumipampa	Heffernan 1996

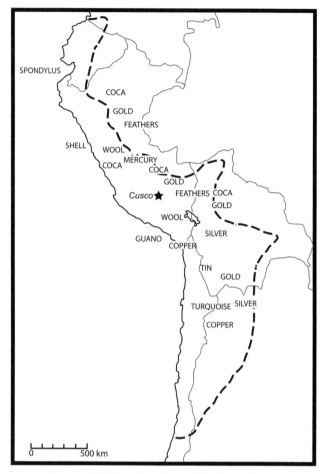

Fig. 10.3. Origins of wealth goods in Tawantinsuyu

imperial times. One solution to this increasing problem of long-distance transportation was the production of wealth goods—portable exotic items that were easily transferred between the capital and distant provincial regions.[10] These included *Spondylus* shell, precious metals, and fine cloth (fig. 10.3). Tawantinsuyu facilitated a trans-Andean movement of exotic goods, transforming ordinary sea shells from the Pacific Ocean into status objects merely by transporting them to areas like northwest Argentina where such things were not available locally.[11] While some wealth was created merely by transporting materials between regions, Inca administrative centers also produced wealth goods—tributary laborers and specialists produced imperial pottery designs for local distribution, wove cloth, and worked metals and raw materials into adornments and status markers.

The lion's share of the most precious and portable wealth goods would have been transported to Cusco, and eyewitnesses to the Spanish Conquest speak of temples plated with gold and silver, as well as of storage complexes with fancy cloth, exotic bird feathers, and other rarities.[12] Within Cusco, the display of wealth objects was a means of status validation for the Inca nobility.[13]

The transformation of provincial regions would have had a profound effect on the Sacred Valley. Economically, the intensive production of preserved staples not only became less critical for provisioning military campaigns but it presented a potential problem for the imperial economy. If the imperial heartland lagged behind the provinces in the production of wealth, it ran the risk of creating a centrifugal power drain as wealthier, better-developed provinces would seek to maximize their economies by encouraging local economic self-sufficiency (autarky) while also shedding the major economic burden of supporting a top-heavy capital nobility. Such processes might be inevitable in the long term, but the Inca needed to transform the heartland region to stave off more proximate crises.

New Strategies for Managing Staple and Wealth Production

One solution to this economic problem was to produce more wealth in the imperial heartland. This required a reallocation of productive resources, as well as an increase in available labor. While the Incas could not effectively bring their staples to the provinces, they *could* bring provincial populations to where the staples were being produced, and the Incas implemented massive resettlement programs that brought in labor from throughout the empire, particularly that of the Cañaris and Chachapoyas (fig. 10.4). While many of the new settlers in the Sacred Valley were *mitmaqkuna*—provincial labor colonists who worked for the state yet retained their ethnic identities—others were *yanakuna,* members of a retainer class permanently settled away from their natal communities and generally attached to the personal service of an Inca ruler and his descendants. Many of these provincial settlers were *kamayuqkuna,* specialists in such occupations as cloth production or stonework.

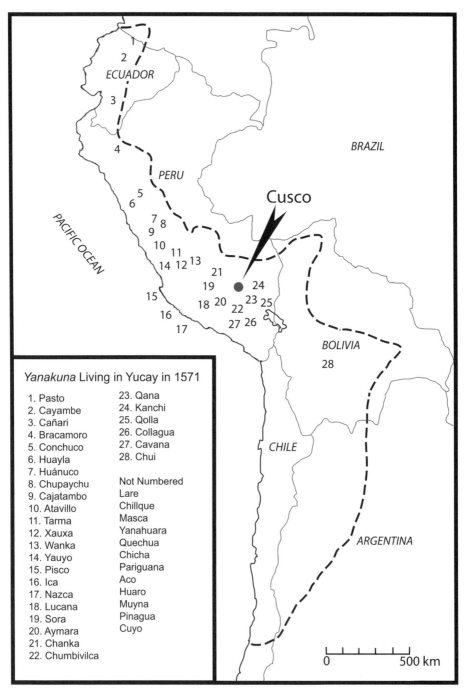

Fig. 10.4. *Yana* ethnicities in living in Yucay in 1571. Most of these individuals represent groups from the central highlands and Ecuador.

Settlement Patterns in the Sacred Valley

In the Sacred Valley study region, approximately 150 sites were identified with Inca imperial pottery on the surface. As figure 10.5 shows, the settlement pattern for the imperial period is markedly different from the period prior to the Inca conquest of the region. The largest towns, Pisaq and Calca, represent secondary administrative sites in the regional settlement lattice and were occupied by members of royal lineages. In early colonial times, members of the lineage of Pachacutic lived in Pisaq, descendants of Yahuar Huaccac lived in Paullu and Lamay, and the *panaka* of Huayna Capac was settled in Yucay.[14] The towns of Calca, Lamay, Coya, Pisaq, Urquillos (Urcos), Yucay, and Ollantaytambo are each known to have had a descent group named *Cusco ayllu* in colonial times (e.g., *ayllu Coya Cuzco*), possibly referring to groups resettling in the Sacred Valley from the Cusco Basin.[15] Other large villages like Poques and Caquia Xaquixaguana were found in productive lands a few hours' walk from the large towns, and the *panaka* of Viracocha Inca was settled in the latter community.[16] The majority of the valley's population in the Inca imperial period resided close to state maize lands located near the floor of the Sacred Valley.

This settlement pattern is strikingly different from the pre-Inca pattern. The focus of the more hierarchical imperial settlement system reflects a shift from high ridges to the valley bottom, where large towns and villages were strongly linked to state resources. It is important to note that many small villages in the area are located just above state fields, in areas where dry-farming is practiced today. Colonial documents pertaining to the Sacred Valley mention towns that would have been occupied by *yanakuna* and *mitmaqkuna,* as well as some that were populated by local ethnic groups. The communities of Patahuaillacan, Paulo Guayllacan, and Cuyo would have been settled by groups that did not become Incas-of-Privilege.[17] Descent groups and witnesses mentioned in colonial documents clearly identify permanent settlement in other villages by Qollas (around Pisaq and Vicchu), Wankas (around Lamay), and other provincial ethnic groups. The location of these villages suggests that while some groups in the valley lived in large Inca towns, others chose to live at the margins of the state system, where they could most easily work on state fields while still cultivating their own diverse crops. It is possible that retainers (*yanakuna*) occupied the royal estates and administrative centers, while local groups and ethnic settlers were given more flexibility in

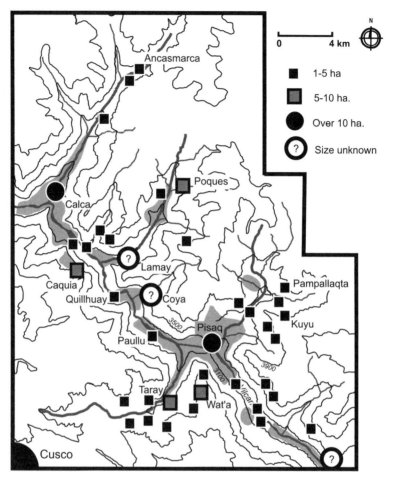

Fig. 10.5. Inca Period settlement in the Sacred Valley study region. The largest towns
are located at the valley bottom, close to state maize lands.

settlement. Archival documents from the valley suggest that local groups
were allowed to work lands that had not been improved by the state or
claimed for state herds or forests.[18]

The royal estates of the Sacred Valley continued to be occupied, and
new estates were developed in the imperial period. The descendants of
earlier Inca rulers like Yahuar Huaccac and Viracocha Inca lived in the
valley in early colonial times, while those of Pachacutic occupied Pisaq
and several other sites downstream from the Sacred Valley study region.[19]

Viracocha Inca's estate at Caquia Xaquixaguana was enlarged, probably during the reign of Huayna Capac or Huascar (fig. 10.6). Radiocarbon samples taken from wooden lintels and grass tempers in wall plasters indicate that major construction probably occurred around AD 1420–1530 (table 10.2). Huascar was in the process of developing lands around Calca and Coya when the Inca civil war broke out (fig. 10.7).[20] The references to estate development during the imperial period suggest that large numbers of provincial retainers would have traveled to the Inca heartland to live permanently.

Historical Evidence for Wealth Production

The presence of tens of thousands of provincial colonists and retainers had the effect of supporting intensive heartland staple production while also intensifying and centralizing the production of wealth finance goods. Permanent retainers had the added advantage of reducing the costs of travel time and teaching production skills.[21] Evidence of this kind of production can be seen in numerous historical documents from the Cusco region. For example, witness testimonies (*informaciones*) collected by the viceroy don Francisco de Toledo include a great deal of information on Inca resettlement policies in the heartland.[22] At least fifteen non-Inca ethnicities are represented in the *informaciones* for the Cusco area, many of whom had parents or grandparents who were brought to Cusco to supervise *mitmaqkuna* or *yanakuna* for different Inca rulers and their wives. The earliest references to resettlement are for Qanas, Qollas, and Soras, who claimed to have been brought to Cusco by Pachacutic Inca Yupanqui.[23]

A second list of ethnic groups can be assembled by looking at some of the land documents pertaining to the Sacred Valley in particular. In 1571, men from at least forty ethnic groups were found to be living in the Yucay Valley in what was formerly the estate of Huayna Capac, the eleventh Inca ruler (fig. 10.4).[24] These groups included honorary Inca ethnicities (e.g., Aco, Chillque, Huaro, Lare, Masca), conquered local ethnic groups (Cuyo, Muyna, Pinagua), and approximately thirty provincial Inca groups from across the empire. While some of these groups are known to have migrated to the Yucay Valley after the Spanish Conquest, men from more than twenty ethnic groups were living in the valley before the European invasion—a considerable ethnic diversity.

The documents suggest a variety of activities for individuals who

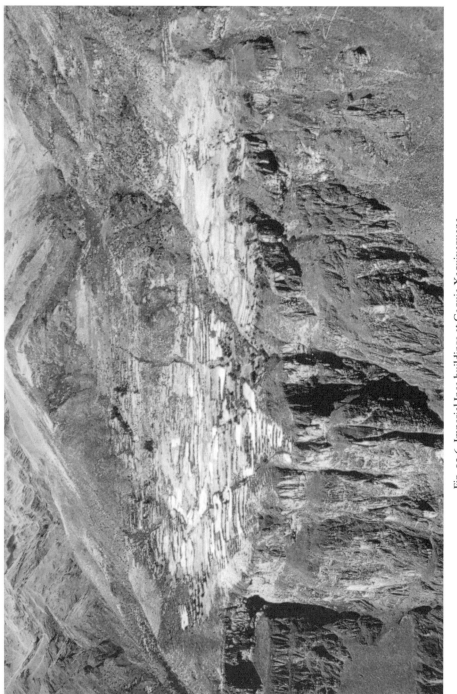

Fig. 10.6. Imperial Inca buildings at Caquia Xaquixaguana.

were permanently resettled to the imperial heartland by the Incas. Most of the provincial workers (*suyurunakuna*) probably worked state fields, and some of Toledo's witnesses supervised their labor, like the father of the Chupaychu Juan Condor Capcha.[25] Some specialists, like the father of Marcos de Cayogualpa, were involved in the construction and maintenance of agricultural terraces (*chakrakamayuq*),[26] while others worked stone and constructed buildings in and around the capital, like the grandfather of the Chupaychu Juan Guanaco, as well as Pedro Cayo Cuxi's parents.[27] Martín Capta's forebears were involved in the exploitation of salt (*kachikamayuq*),[28] and the parents of Pedro Yaure supervised groups of people who apparently trapped or kept birds (*aveadores*).[29]

Cloth Production

The most common designation for labor specialists in Toledo's *informaciones* was cloth production (*qompikamayuq*). The father of Juan Tarumaguia, a Lurinwanka, supervised cloth production for Huayna Capac, as did Alonso Conchay's father, Cusi Auca.[30] Documents in the Betancur Collection also mention cloth production, while a 1587 land document from the San Salvador area states that Qolla herders and cloth specialists were brought to the Sacred Valley, probably by Pachacutic Inca Yupanqui.[31] The intensification of cloth production would have

TABLE 10.2.   Architectural Dates from Inca Buildings

Sample	Site	Context	BP	95.4% probability
AA47660	Warq'ana	Grass sample from plaster of a window lintel	479 ± 39	AD 1390–1490 (93.9%)
AA47661	Caquia Xaquixaguana	Grass sample from a door lintel	411 ± 39	AD 1420–1530 (75.2%) or AD 1560–1630 (20.2%)
AA47662	Caquia Xaquixaguana	Grass sample from plaster of a window lintel	383 ± 40	AD 1430–1530 (57.0%) or AD 1540–1640 (38.4%)
AA47663	Caquia Xaquixaguana	Grass sample from plaster of a niche lintel	416 ± 28	AD 1430–1520 (89.9%)
AA47684	Caquia Xaquixaguana	Grass sample from wall daub	417 ± 30	AD 1420–1520 (88.6%)
AA47665	Urcon	Grass sample from a window lintel	400 ± 33	AD 1430–1530 (74.1%) or AD 1560–1630 (21.3%)

Note: Dates were calibrated using OxCal v3.5, and are calibrated to 95.4% probabilty. Values less than 10% probability are not listed.

Fig. 10.7. Modern Calca.

required special management of large state herds, apparently belonging to the estate of each Inca ruler, as well as to the state religious cult.[32] Pedro Ychoc testified in Toledo's *informaciones* that his ancestors were brought from Huánuco by Topa Inca Yupanqui to help supervise the herders of Inca Yupanqui (Pachacutic), while the Atavillo Santiago Tacuri stated that his grandparents were brought by the same Inca to manage his own herds.[33] Diego Cusi Condor's father was a herder for Huayna Capac.[34]

Cloth production by female specialists was also an important part of the royal estates, although it is less visible in colonial administrative texts. Several chroniclers make reference to the assignment of *mamakuna*—women with formal training in the production of fine cloth and the preparation of ceremonial foods and beverages—to the principal wives of Inca rulers, as well as the mummy cults of deceased rulers and some honored lords. Juan de Betanzos notes that Mama Anahuarque (sister-wife of Pachacutic) was given one hundred *mamakuna* at the time of her marriage and that she received another fifty from a priest representing the sun.[35] After the death of Viracocha Inca, Pachacutic assigned *mamakuna* and *yanakuna* to support his father's mummy cult by working fields and performing the life history of the dead ruler.[36] Pedro Sarmiento de Gamboa describes the complete destruction of the house of Topa Inca Yupanqui by Atahuallpa's soldiers following their victory in the Inca civil war, stating that even the *mamakuna* associated with the *panaka* were killed.[37]

Several chroniclers note that the *mamakuna* produced the finest textiles in the empire and that many of those leaving service in Cusco's *akllawasi* became wives or consorts of the Inca ruler, worked to support the mummy cults of the royal *panaka,* or were given in marriage to loyal members of the imperial elite.[38] These women were skilled weavers, knew how to produce the foods and beverages served at the most important imperial festivals, and were initiated into important ritual mysteries related to the state religion. As wives or retainers, these women would enhance the status of those with whom they were paired.

The documentary evidence indicates a wide variety of specialized activities that were organized through the holdings of each *panaka,* or royal lineage. Agricultural production and herding were maximized by bringing in full-time specialists experienced in maize farming and herd management. Wealth production included the care of birds, the processing of salt, and, most importantly, the production of cloth.[39] Specialized laborers were brought to Cusco from the provinces, formally trained, then attached to royal estates to produce wealth goods. The agricultural lands of these estates were also transformed by retainers to produce more ceremonial and exotic products.

The Development of Agricultural "Wealth"

While some important changes took place in the labor structure and management of the heartland economy during the imperial period, the Incas also employed a second means of converting staple production into wealth finance. Besides importing labor specialists—who could consume staples while producing wealth goods—the Incas redefined the symbolic role of certain agricultural goods, some of which could be produced in the Sacred Valley.

The most important of these was maize, which was grown intensively throughout the Cusco region but was particularly productive in the Sacred Valley at elevations between 2800 and 3000 meters. According to Daniel Gade, two kinds of maize predominate the contemporary agriculture in this part of the valley: *paraqay sara*, a large-eared variety used only for food, and *uwina*, a smaller variety that can be used as food or for brewing maize beer (*aqha*).[40] *Paraqay sara* may have been developed in the valley by the Incas as a preferred high-yield variety, and Gade suggests that the conquests of Tawantinsuyu carried this variety as far away as Ecuador and Argentina. *Paraqay sara* might have been one of a few kinds of maize grown on state fields during the period of early state expansion.

Beyond being simply a foodstuff, maize was also an important ceremonial crop, and Spanish eyewitnesses describe the consumption of huge quantities of maize beer during important festivals in Cusco (fig. 10.8).[41] The importance of maize production in the Inca calendar indicates that this crop had a status above other kinds of food that could be produced.[42] As Cusco grew into an imperial capital, its ceremonies became grander, and the importance of maize beer for state ceremonies amplified as larger numbers of provincial people flocked to Cusco to participate in polity-wide ceremonies like the Citua and *qhapaqhucha* (a ritual where boys and girls were selected as sacrificial victims, traveled to Cusco to be sanctified, and returned to provincial regions to be sacrificed). Because certain kinds of maize could be converted from a staple

Fig. 10.8. *Aqha* consumption in Inca ritual. (Redrawn from Guaman Poma de Ayala 1980 [1615].)

product to an important ritual beverage simply by fermenting it, it is possible that maize production in the Sacred Valley focused increasingly on the cultivation of colored and sweet maize varieties for ceremonial use.

Elite women—particularly those associated with the *akllawasi* complex—were responsible for brewing maize beer for state festivals, and large maize storage facilities were located within Cusco's *akllawasi*.[43] While land documents from the Sacred Valley refer repeatedly to women of the royal lineage benefiting from the production of royal estates, they are ambiguous about the role played by different categories of *mamakuna* in state ceremonies. Kathryn Burns notes that the Cusco *akllawasi* possessed lands in the Sacred Valley around Pachar, while Susan Niles cites a 1594 document identifying lands of the *mamakuna* in the Yucay area.[44] Although it does not mention these holdings, the Betancur Collection documents refer to *kamayuqkuna* dedicated to the worship of the sun serving in fields in Yucay.[45] Some female retainers appear to have worked on cloth production, but others probably worked often in the transformation of maize into *aqha*.

In addition to cultivating maize as a ceremonial food, parts of the Sacred Valley appear to have been used to produce exotic crops not available in the Cusco Basin. One of these was chile pepper (*uchu*), which was grown in Yucay on the estate of Huayna Capac, as well as by the natives of Urcon near Calca.[46] Several tributary workers in Yucay testified to having labored in the production of chile peppers.[47] In addition, Inca rulers are said to have introduced the cultivation of fruits and vegetables from provincial regions to Cusco, and colonial documents identify individuals who were associated with maintaining these crops.[48] The cultivation of exotic plants was probably intended for elite use only, and it is doubtful that many of these crops would have grown well in most parts of the Sacred Valley.

Coca Production and the Royal Estates

A final transformation of the agricultural production of the Inca heartland involved the expansion into and development of coca lands (fig. 10.9). Coca leaf can be grown below Machu Picchu in the Urubamba Valley, as well as the Lares and Paucartambo areas.[49] Coca lands were developed by Inca rulers as part of their personal estates, and these lands were worked by people who had a labor obligation to the estate. For example, colonial-period testimony states that Pachacutic Inca Yupanqui

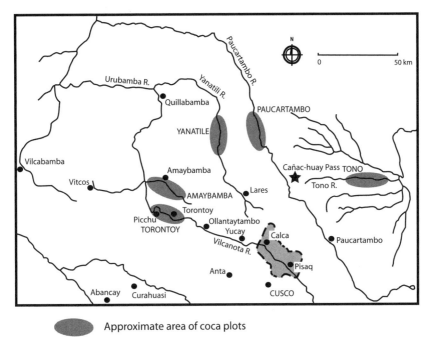

Fig. 10.9. Coca lands near Cusco

possessed several lowland plots in a valley called Tancoa (close to Machu Picchu), including fields named Turuntuy (also Torontoy), Panpa Hugua, Pisca, Chuqui Suso, Macay, Tiobamba, and Guaillanga.[50] While coca leaf is only mentioned peripherally in this document, other sources identify the Cusco *montaña* (including Picchu, Toayma, and Amaybamba) as an important place for cultivating coca.[51]

It appears that coca plots were developed as small, named units, and several Inca rulers often had plots in the same valley, as is the case for Amaybamba.[52] Both Pachacutic Inca Yupanqui and Topa Inca Yupanqui developed coca lands in this valley, and Topa Inca Yupanqui's principal wife, Mama Ocllo, is mentioned as co-owner of the plots pertaining to her husband. Huayna Capac's estate at Yucay probably also had coca lands in the lowlands, in Tono, Paucarbamba, and Yanatile. These locations are mentioned repeatedly as lands claimed by Francisco and Hernando Pizarro for coca cultivation and worked by small numbers of tributary laborers.[53]

While coca cultivation was often conducted by natives of lower-elevation areas (especially Cañaris, Chachapoyas, and a broad category of lowlanders, or "Yungas"), it appears that some of the local ethnic groups of Cusco were dispossessed of their lands and settled in coca-producing areas below Paucartambo. The Pinaguas appear to be one example,[54] and the Cuyos might be another. While some Cuyos were living in the Pisaq area in the early colonial period, they do not appear to have been in the grant of native labor (*encomienda*) of Juan Sierra de Leguizamo—to whom Pisaq was entrusted—but rather in a grant made to Juan de Pancorvo, who possessed some small lowland *encomiendas* with coca fields and perhaps a gold mine.[55] The noble Inca witnesses living in Pisaq testified to Toledo that a group called Chuyos was one of several cannibalistic tribes inhabiting the lowland jungle, an account that might be significant when considering that the only group to give such testimony was the Inca *panaka* that displaced the Cuyos from their traditional lands.[56]

In short, coca cultivation may have provided the Incas with a means of using available labor to produce a valuable ritual and wealth product, as well as a place to send indigenous groups who proved difficult to administer. Permanent settlement in lowland areas was said to be unhealthy for highland groups, both because of climate and lowland diseases like leishmaniasis.[57] For example, a 1571 census in the Betancur Collection lists a Diego Quispe as a forty-year-old *yana* who got sick working in the lowlands ("enfermó en los andes") and died around the time the census was being taken.[58] The census mentions several other tributary laborers who had gotten sick or died while working in the lowlands.[59] The resettlement of problematic groups to the lowlands would benefit the state by producing agricultural wealth and vacating prime *kichwa* lands for state development.

The Estate System and Elite Political Competition

The extension of the estate system to lowland coca plots signals some major changes occurring in the estate system in the imperial period (fig. 10.10).[60] The shift in the valley from intensive cultivation of subsistence goods to a more varied production of prestige and wealth goods also reflects the role of the *panaka* estate in the political system of Tawantinsuyu. When the Spaniards arrived in Cusco in 1533, they were amazed

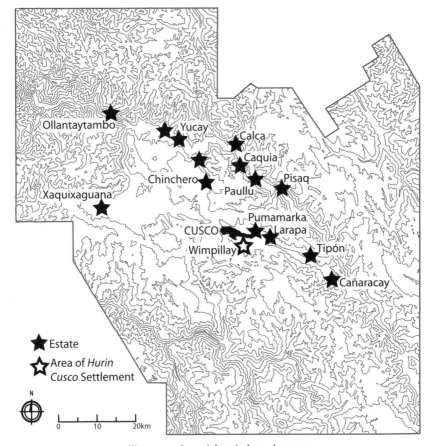

Fig. 10.10. Imperial-period royal estates

by the pomp and grandeur of Inca elite life. Writing years later, Pedro Pizarro describes how the mummies of important Inca women and men formed the basis for the structure and hierarchy of royal Inca interaction. Pizarro observes that living members of the royal *panakakuna* used the dead as an excuse to be supported in lavish fashion on the returns from their estates.[61] Other chroniclers indicate that the royal descent groups were organized by the ruling Inca, who acted to mediate between the groups assigned to the *hanan* and *hurin* moieties.[62] As the productive resources of the *panaka* estates evolved, so too did the relationship between these groups and the government of the empire.[63]

During the imperial period, Inca rulers took multiple wives and consorts from both Cusco and the provinces, and each ruler produced numerous offspring.[64] Juan de Betanzos says that Inca Rocca, a ruler at the time of state formation, had six wives and thirty children, while his successor had twenty wives and fifty children.[65] Pedro Sarmiento de Gamboa claims that Atahuallpa's armies killed eighty sons and daughters of Huascar when they took the city of Cusco.[66] While these numbers cannot be taken as accurate figures for royal offspring, we know that the chronicles mention more than a dozen children of Huayna Capac, even though Atahuallpa had executed as many of his siblings as possible during the Inca civil war.[67] Even if most members of the royal lineages did not practice polygyny, the populations of Cusco's Inca elite would have grown substantially throughout the imperial period.

Under these conditions, the principal wife of the *sapa inka*, as well as his favorite consorts, potentially exercised considerable political power, both officially as administrators and unofficially by forming or supporting political coalitions.[68] For example, the favorite consort of Topa Inca Yupanqui is said to have convinced her husband to give her son (not the legitimate heir) provincial holdings in the Titicaca Basin.[69] Topa Inca Yupanqui's sister-wife Mama Ocllo solved important provincial administrative crises, commanded her own *yanakuna,* and was venerated in women's rituals in Cusco.[70]

The influence wielded by royal wives and consorts promoted factionalism, which became pronounced at times of royal succession. For example, on the death of Topa Inca Yupanqui, two of his secondary wives named Ccuri Ocllo and Chuqui Ocllo rallied the dead emperor's descent group and promoted their relative Ccapac Huari for the Inca rulership.[71] A rival faction and its candidate, Huayna Capac, suppressed this attempt. Interestingly, while the women organizing the coalition are said to have been executed, Ccapac Huari was merely exiled to Topa Inca Yupanqui's estate at Chinchero.

This case illustrates that while estates functioned to provide for the subsistence needs of the Inca elite, they also acted as a means to reduce political competition in Cusco. In the early Inca state, close relatives of the *sapa inka* were useful as provincial governors, military commanders, and religious specialists. The development of decimal administration in many provincial regions would have reduced the number of midlevel bureaucratic offices needing royal staffing,[72] and the burgeoning of the nonruling Inca elite would have had the rapid effect of creating a class

of nobles living in Cusco with no occupation. Several sources associate
the last Cusco ruler, Huascar, with the complaint that the dead—that is,
the descent groups of previous rulers—ate from the best lands of the empire. The civil war that preceded the Spanish invasion was precipitated
in part by the rapid development of top-heavy Inca nobility in the imperial heartland.

Although the estate system was perhaps ultimately unsuccessful, there
is evidence that it was transformed during the imperial period so as to
alleviate some royal Inca political competition by creating areas of elite
recreation outside of the capital. For example, Huayna Capac's estate at
Yucay included gardens and fountains, and personal recreation is frequently mentioned as one of its main functions.[73] As Susan Niles has
pointed out, the estate included lodges in good hunting lands as well.[74]
The estates of some earlier rulers were located in areas to facilitate the
administration of local populations, but Huayna Capac's estate was located at the floor of the Sacred Valley, where its pleasant climate would
induce members of his lineage (Tumipampa Panaka) to remain and enjoy
themselves.

At the time of the civil war between Huascar and Atahuallpa, the
Cusco estate system was not organized uniformly. As has been discussed,
members of the lineages assigned to Hurin Cusco were settled in a cluster of villages located on the south side of the Cusco Basin. The lineages
of Inca Rocca and Yahuar Huaccac each had lands that could be used
for the production of agricultural staples. Conversely, rulers from Viracocha Inca onward had multiple estates that not only were associated
with agricultural production and the administration of tributary groups
but also had elegant ornamental terraces, fine masonry buildings, and a
variety of productive resources stretching into the lowland coca lands.
The estate system appears to have evolved into a system whereby powerful women and their children—royal lineage members who could challenge the accession of a new Inca ruler and thereby encourage provincial
rebellions—could be "retired" and encouraged or forced to reside outside of the city.

Gender and Resource Administration in the Estate System

The importance of women in the estate system is immediately obvious
when looking at the chronicles and archival documents.[75] Major reset-
tlements made by ruling Incas after the conquest of a new province or

suppression of a rebellion formed the labor base for new royal estates, although some Inca rulers are mentioned as providing labor for the estates of their fathers as well. The documents also mention that personal retainers were brought from the provinces to serve the wives and close relatives of the Inca. For example, Martín Capcha was brought from Huánuco to serve Huacco Ocllo, the wife of Huayna Capac,[76] and the Collagua Gómez Condori stated that his father had been brought to serve Amaru Topa Inca, brother of Topa Inca Yupanqui.[77] The father of Francisco Cochachan (or Chachin) had been an important *kuraka* in the Callejón de Huaylas and was brought to Cusco after the death of Huayna Capac to serve his secondary wife, Rahua Ocllo.[78] Land documents from the colonial period indicate that many of the daughters and wives of Huayna Capac held small named plots of land lying within the area of his personal estate.[79] It is likely that such grants were worked by retainers living on the estate, whose labor would have gone to supporting important wives and female relatives of the Inca.

Personal administration of estates and labor resources by Inca women dates at least to the reign of Viracocha Inca. His daughter, Mama Anahuarque, had plots of land in the Quiquijana area that were worked for her.[80] Mama Anahuarque may have been the first daughter of an Inca ruler to marry her brother; she was certainly not the first elite woman in the Cusco region to exercise considerable influence in the administration and politics of the Inca state. Women were not simply passive marriage partners. The Spanish chronicles mention them as political leaders and as initiating alliances between the Incas and groups outside of the Cusco Basin. In the imperial period, women formed coalitions to advance candidates for rulership and are mentioned as canny administrators and important political and ritual figures.[81] Spanish eyewitnesses clearly state that the mummies of important Inca ladies participated in public Inca rituals.[82] The politics of the *panaka* were not controlled solely by its male members.

Inca imperialism did not merely transform provincial regions; the heartland itself was radically altered to respond to internal and external stresses brought by imperial growth. The imperial capital and its hinterland were dominated by an increasingly top-heavy Inca elite, who relied more and more on permanent retainers from the provinces. The mundane subsistence products that were so vital for funding military expansion held secondary importance in a system that increasingly targeted wealth production and catered to elite pleasure. As Inca ethnicity (rather than elite status) became the basis for bureaucratic resettlement, many of Cusco's ethnic groups were sent to live in provincial regions and were replaced by non-Inca retainers. Many of these changes facilitated the imposition of Spanish rule at the top of the Inca system in Cusco.

CHAPTER ELEVEN

Conclusions

Having described a new model of Inca state formation and imperial expansion, let us return to the event-based historic version of Inca imperial origins for some points of comparison. When we reconsider the events that historians interpret as precipitating the sudden appearance of the Inca empire, we see that the new process-based model explains the historical and archaeological evidence more completely and realistically. While stories of the heroics of Pachacutic emphasize his charisma and ambition, they also show that this one Inca ruler alone could not have created the conditions for imperial expansion.

The new radiocarbon dates presented in this book indicate that events linked to Pachacutic's rise to power did not occur around AD 1438, but earlier. Sites said to have been conquered by Pachacutic after he assumed sovereignty actually appear to have been abandoned or in the process of decline by about AD 1400. The dates from Pukara Pantillijlla, Huata, and Chokepukio suggest that Inca campaigns of consolidation in the Cusco region that are said to have followed the Chanca invasion took place as much as fifty years before the traditional date. Such dates would tend to agree with those chronicles that emphasize Pachacutic's father Viracocha Inca as the founder of the Inca imperial order,[1] but for the moment we will not challenge the legacy of Pachacutic as the Inca "great man."

Assuming that Pachacutic came to power by defending Cusco from a historical Chanca invasion, he would not have been protecting the scattered huts of a simple village society. He would have owed his victory to the support of real Inca armies rather than fieldstones animated by the creator deity to assist him. History and archaeology reveal that even before Pachacutic began to rule the Inca polity, the Cusco region had been brought under Inca dominance, with large parts of it directly administered by the state by AD 1400. At the margins of Inca control, some 80 kilometers or so from Cusco, lived several distinct ethnic groups that were either directly ruled by Inca governors or had been reduced to uneasy subordination and indirect rule. Stories of the power of the Inca state would have spread widely throughout the Andean highlands, and emissaries from distant polities would have visited the Inca capital. As they passed through the territory of the Inca state, foreign visitors would have witnessed state representatives using local labor tribute to intensify maize agriculture, to construct royal estates, and to establish infrastructure integrating the Cusco region logistically and economically. A closer inspection of local attitudes toward Inca domination would reveal discontent and unrest among many local elites, particularly the leaders of a few autonomous groups who had held out against Inca expansion.

As they traveled toward Cusco, visitors would see new nucleated settlements established by the state, with improved agricultural lands and storage facilities. Groups living closer to Cusco, like the people of Anta, considered themselves kin of the Inca elite after generations of intermarriage and were loyal supporters even in times of crisis. Upon arriving in the Cusco Basin, travelers would have beheld a valley filled with large villages and towns, with broad expanses of irrigated maize fields. From the hillsides above the valley they would have glimpsed Cusco itself, a large city with palaces, temples, and plazas actively used in the daily governmental and religious life of a centralized state. By the end of the fourteenth century, Cusco had been occupied for two hundred years or more, and the population of the Cusco Basin must have numbered at least in the tens of thousands by this time.

Assuming that our visitors to Cusco were not diplomats or state representatives, but an invading host of Chanca warriors, the forces of the Inca state would have contested their entry into Inca territory and advance on Cusco. An invading army would have to fight experienced warriors who were led by Inca officers with years of experience conquering new territory and putting down local rebellions. The Inca army would be composed of troops drawn from the sizeable Cusco Basin population, as well as more than a dozen loyal ethnic groups. Backed by an army that was well trained, was well supplied, and believed in its divine right to conquer, Pachacutic would have no need for supernatural intervention against an army that was a long distance from home, deep in hostile territory.

Having defeated this Chanca army, Pachacutic would certainly have faced major political and administrative challenges. A foreign invasion would have exacerbated a succession crisis in which the urban elite of

Cusco supported Pachacutic against the wishes of Viracocha Inca, who designated his son Inca Urcon as his successor. The royal Inca lineages would need to be reorganized to diminish the power of opposing factions. Rebellious or disloyal groups that had broken with the Incas during the invasion would need to be conquered and brought permanently under Inca government. By maintaining campaigns of imperialism outside of the heartland, Pachacutic could have facilitated an internal reorganization of Inca Cusco—including a recasting of royal myths and histories. Justifying his role in overturning the existing social order (as a *pachakutiq*) would require considerable force of character, but it would not necessitate the single-handed creation of the imputed new world order.

Intensifying imperial expansion and promoting the Incas and their ethnic neighbors above all other Andean groups would have enabled Inca rulers to undertake the social reorganization of the Inca heartland while reducing internal conflict. Internal elite competition would have been channeled into ongoing campaigns of expansion. Because the Inca state would have begun such conquests a generation or two earlier, the means and ideological justifications were already well developed for continuing the annexation of new territory. Rapid territorial expansion against a wide range of ethnic and political groups—living in all ecological zones found in the Andean region—required the Incas to tailor imperial strategies to local conditions, which was probably the work of a number of knowledgeable Inca local elites and bureaucrats rather than the imperial ruler. The transformation of the heartland was a response to long-term imperial needs that could not have been foreseen when expansion began.

Inca State Formation and Imperial Expansion

This new process-based interpretation of Inca state formation and imperial expansion avoids the pitfalls of a literal historical approach and permits an important body of new archaeological evidence to be placed on equal interpretive footing with the Inca histories. Such an approach informs us of processes about which Spanish writers and their Inca informants were at best only vaguely aware. It allows us to move beyond the personal experiences of individual Andeans—in space as well as time—to look at how the events that are said to have happened were brought about. Some of the processes described here contradict what was asserted to be true in the Spanish chronicles, but our historical and archaeological models are both in agreement regarding general patterns.

We can now see the Incas as an evolving polity, one whose trajectory began hundreds of years before the first Inca armies crossed the Andean highlands. The Cusco Basin was already home to a complex polity when Wari colonists arrived in the seventh century. Although the Wari assumed an indirect role in regional politics, their long occupation of the Lucre Basin widened the scope of elite authority. The decline of the Wari colonies left the Cusco region politically fragmented, with several small polities whose leaders were inclined to compete with each other for control of the region.

While some elites managed diverse herding and farming economies, those living in Cusco used labor tribute to intensify maize production, creating agricultural surpluses that could be used to buffer against environmental fluctuations, to fund ceremonial activities, and to support military conquests and long-distance exchange relationships. When the Cusco region experienced a severe and prolonged drought in the late thirteenth century, the Cusco Basin polity would have had a large population and substantial resource base, and climatic change must have increased competitive pressures between groups. As the state formed in the Cusco Basin, it developed the means for directly administering larger territories and populations, and environmental uncertainty appears to be linked to a period of state expansion that lasted through much of the fourteenth century.

The Inca state used marriage alliances, gift giving, diplomacy, intimidation, and warfare to extend its control over much of the Cusco region. Inca expansion was opportunistic, and the Inca state often chose to administer new subordinates indirectly, leaving local elites in place under the supervision of Inca representatives. The state used local labor tribute to improve the most fertile agricultural lands in the region, which for the first time began to yield massive surpluses. As the state developed infrastructure and increasingly acted as a patron in local affairs, local elites often rebelled (or were accused of plotting rebellion), giving the state an excuse to consolidate administrative control and transform local economic and political systems.

Inca imperial strategies developed out of these processes of state formation and territorial expansion. The archaeological evidence has shown that the Incas did not simply adopt the Wari imperial model, and that Wari colonization in Cusco was much more limited and indirect than has been assumed. It is also clear that the Incas did not begin their imperial campaigns as a village-level society lacking political offices and a centralized government. This book has shown that the strategies of Inca imperialism developed out of processes beginning hundreds of years before Inca imperial expansion overran the Andean region. Recognizing these processes allows us to describe the dynamic nature of Tawantinsuyu and to see it as part of an enduring tradition, rather than the product of a single charismatic individual.

Appendixes

Glossary of Spanish and Quechua Terms Used

This book uses Quechua and Spanish spellings for personal names, toponyms, archaeological sites, and cultural concepts pertaining to social organization, ecology, and kinship. I have elected to use Spanish spellings for people and places mentioned in the Spanish chronicles, following the most commonly accepted form when alternatives exist. For archaeological sites, I use the spellings employed by other archaeologists. For Quechua concepts (e.g., *tinku* and *yana*), I prefer a three-vowel orthography and spellings common to the Cuzco-Collao dialect for most terms and follow entries in the 1976 dictionary of Antonio Cusihuamán where possible. For plural nouns, I have chosen to use the *-kuna* suffix rather than a Spanish ending (e.g., *yana*: retainer; *yanakuna*: retainers). Where colonial dictionaries are referenced, the original spelling is provided. Appendix A provides a glossary defining relevant terminology.

Spanish (Sp.) and Quechua (Q.) terms used in the text are included here. A three-vowel orthography has been used for most Quechua terms, following the 1976 dictionary of Antonio Cusihuamán. Terms from colonial dictionaries follow original spellings.

akllawasi (Q.) (*akllay* "to select or set apart" + *wasi* "house") A restricted complex where young women (*akllakuna*) were taught to spin, weave, and brew *aqha* to support religious and political activities (González Holguin 1989 [1608], 15–16).

amaranth (*Amaranthus caudatus*) A seed-bearing plant originating in Mexico. Called *kiwicha* in Quechua.

apu (Q.) Judge or great lord, but also used for lineage heads or war captains. Also used to refer to important mountains (González Holguin 1989 [1608], 31–32).

aqha (Q.) Maize beer. Also referred to by the Caribe name, *chicha,* or as *azua* (González Holguin 1989 [1608], 18).

ayllu (Q.) A group whose membership shares common descent. The *ayllu* is configured in a number of ways in the ethnographic and ethnohistoric literature (González Holguin 1989 [1608], 39).

cacica/cacique (Caribe) A female/male local political leader. This is a general term applied by Spanish writers to many different kinds of local leaders throughout the Americas. A Quechua equivalent is *kuraka* (González Holguin 1989 [1608]:55).

ccapia (Q.) A soft maize (González Holguin 1989 [1608], 578).

chakrakamayuq (Q.) (*chakra* "agricultural field" + *kamayuq* "specialist") An Inca imperial specialist in constructing agricultural terracing, or someone specialized in a certain kind of agricultural production (González Holguin 1989 [1608], 91).

ch'arki (Q.) Freeze-dried camelid meat (González Holguin 1989 [1608], 98).

chaski (Q.) A person who ran messages along the Inca road system (González Holguin 1989 [1608], 98).

ch'uñu (Q.) Freeze-dried potatoes (González Holguin 1989 [1608], 121).

chuspi sara (Q.) A sweet maize (González Holguin 1989 [1608], 578).

Citua (Q.) An Inca imperial ritual involving the demarcation of the Inca heartland, followed by the required visit to the imperial capital by provincial elites.

coca leaf (Q.) (*Erythroxylon coca*) Ceremonial plant whose leaves are chewed for a mild narcotic effect. Lowland coca lands were owned by Inca rulers, and the use of coca was an elite prerogative.

conquistador (Sp.) A participant in sixteenth-century Spanish conquests in the Americas.

cordillera (Sp.) Mountain range.

culli sara [*kulli sara*] (Q.) A sweet maize (González Holguin 1989 [1608], 578).

encomienda (Sp.) A Spanish colonial grant whereby the *encomendero* was entrusted with the Christianization of a native group, which was in turn required to supply tribute and labor service to support the *encomendero.*

hanan (Q.) "Upper," usually used to refer to the upper moiety of a community (see González Holguin 1989 [1608], 333).

hunu (Q.) A unit of ten thousand (Santo Tomás 1951 [1560], 295).

hurin (Q.) "Lower," usually used to refer to the lower moiety of a community (see González Holguin 1989 [1608], 333).

información (Sp.) A kind of colonial document in which a questionnaire (*interrogatorio*) was read to witnesses, who were given the opportunity to confirm those statements or add relevant information. This was a common technique for collecting information for use in legal proceedings.

intip churin (Q.) "Son of the Sun." A title used by the Inca emperor.

kachikamayuq (Q.) (*kachi* "salt" + *kamayuq* "specialist") A specialist in the processing of salt (see González Holguin 1989 [1608], 44).

kaka [*caca*] (Q.) A category consisting of a man's affinal male relatives. The term has been defined to include (1) mother's brother, (2) wife's father, (3) wife's brother, and (4) mother's brother's son. Not all colonial sources agree on the exact definition.

kamayuq [*camayo*] (Q.) An Inca imperial specialist, literally "one who is characterized by the essence of" a given activity (see González Holguin 1989 [1608], 47–48).

kancha (Q.) An enclosure, often used to describe elite residential compounds (multiple buildings delimiting a restricted central open space). Also, corrals used for herding camelids (González Holguin 1989 [1608], 49).

kañiwa (Q.) (*Chenopodium pallidicaule*) A high-elevation grain, related to quinoa.

khipukamayuq (Q.) An Inca imperial specialist in recording and remembering information through the use of the *khipu,* a series of knotted cords (González Holguin 1989 [1608], 309).

kichwa (Q.) Temperate valley-bottom farmland, and the groups living in this zone (González Holguin 1989 [1608], 300).

kuraka (Q.) A local elite leader, roughly equivalent to a *cacica/cacique.*

llaqtakamayuq (Q.) A low-level Inca imperial bureaucrat, characterized by village-level administration (González Holguin 1989 [1608], 208).

maca [*maka*] (Q.) (*Lepidium meyenii*) A high-elevation tuber.

mamakuna (Q.) Senior women who taught young women in the *akllawasi,* as well as women serving as full-time ritual specialists in the sun cult and other religious orders (González Holguin 1989 [1608], 225).

masa (Q.) A kin category used to include a man's father's kin. *Masa* were work partners and participated in different ritual events than *kaka* kin (González Holguin 1989 [1608], 221).

mashua (Q.) (*Tropaeolum tuberosum*) A high-elevation tuber.

maway (Q.) Early planting lands, particularly lands with a reliable water supply and low frost risk.

mink'a (Q.) Festive or wage labor that is not reciprocated (González Holguin 1989 [1608], 240).

miski sara (Q.) A sweet maize (González Holguin 1989 [1608], 578).

mit'a (Q.) A "turn," as in a system of rotational corvée (see González Holguin 1989 [1608], 243).

mitmaq [*mit'ayuq*] (Q.) A person fulfilling a turn of labor service (see González Holguin 1989 [1608], 243, 244).

montaña (Sp.) The tropical lowlands.

muruchhu sara (Q.) A hard maize variety (González Holguin 1989 [1608], 252).

ñuñas (Q.) (*Phaseolus vulgaris*) Andean "popping beans."

oca [*o'qa*] (Q.) (*Oxalis tuberosa*) A high-elevation tuber.

orejón (Sp.) Literally "big ear." Refers to Inca administrators, who enjoyed the privilege of piercing their ears.

panaka (Q.) One of Cusco's royal Inca *ayllus*.

paraqay sara (Q.) A large-eared high-yield variety of maize (González Holguin 1989 [1608], 279).

puna (Q.) High-elevation grasslands (González Holguin 1989 [1608], 295).

qhapaq (Q.) Paramount ruler of a polity (González Holguin 1989 [1608], 134–35).

qhapaqhucha (Q.) An Inca imperial ritual in which children selected from provincial regions traveled to Cusco to be sanctified, then returned to the provinces to be sacrificed.

qollqa (Q.) An Inca imperial storage structure.

qompi (Q.) Fancy cloth (see González Holguin 1989 [1608], 67).

quinoa [*quinua*] (Q.) (*Chenopodium quinoa*) A high-elevation grain.

reducción (Sp.) A colonial resettlement involving reducing dispersed native settlements into nucleated Spanish-style towns. In Peru, many *reducciones* took place in the early 1570s under the viceroy don Francisco de Toledo.

sapa inka (Q.) See *sapay qhapaq* (see González Holguin 1989 [1608], 78).

sapay qhapaq (Q.) "Peerless Lord," a title used by the Inca ruler (González Holguin 1989 [1608], 661). Similar titles include *sapa inka*.

sara (Q.) Maize (see González Holguin 1989 [1608], 79).

saya (Q.) Moiety.

saywa (Q.) A boundary marker, often between agricultural fields, or on a ridge between two communities (González Holguin 1989 [1608], 325).

selva (Sp.) See *yunka*.

sierra (Sp.) Highlands.

sinchi (Q.) A term used in some chronicles as a title for a temporary war leader. The early dictionary of Santo Tomás (1951 [1560], 263) uses it as an adjective for strength or bravery.

suni (Q.) A farming zone, located in upper *kichwa* elevations.

suyu (Q.) An Inca province. The four principal provinces were Chinchaysuyu, Antisuyu, Qollasuyu, and Cuntisuyu, but other regions are referred to as *suyu* as well (e.g., Colesuyu and Cuyosuyu) (González Holguin 1989 [1608], 333).

suyuruna (Q.) A person pertaining to the Inca imperial provinces (González Holguin 1989 [1608], 333). Used in contrast to *yana*.

thupa (Q.) A prince or lord (González Holguin 1989 [1608], 347). This title sometimes occurs with place names (e.g., Vicchu Topa), perhaps signifying conquest of, or lordship over, a town or region.

tinku (Q.) An ambivalent pairing of two things. Andean dual organization groups moieties or *ayllukuna* in a way that creates a social whole, but one where a certain antagonism is expressed ritually between the two halves (González Holguin 1989 [1608], 342–43).

tukrikuq (Q.) An Inca imperial overseer (González Holguin 1989 [1608], 344).

uchu (Q.) Chile pepper. Also called *ají* (González Holguin 1989 [1608], 349).

ullucu (Q.) (*Ullucus tuberosus*) A high-elevation tuber.

uwina (Q.) A sweet maize, prized for making *aqha* (González Holguin 1989 [1608], 578).

wak'a (Q.) A shrine or sacred object. This term is applied broadly to things sacred or unusual (see González Holguin 1989 [1608], 165–66).

yanakuna (Q.) Retainers in the Inca empire, usually attached to permanent service of royal Inca lineages or the state religion. Singular is *yana* (González Holguin 1989 [1608], 363–64).

ylla (Q.) A rich man, or a talisman thought to bring riches or good luck (González Holguin 1989 [1608], 366–67).

yuca (Sp.) (*Manihot esculenta*) Manioc, a lowland root crop. Called *rumu* in Quechua.

yunka (Q.) Lowland elevations, especially those below about 2700 meters. Also used to refer to people native to such elevations (González Holguin 1989 [1608], 371).

Cusco Regional Chronology

The identification of regional settlement patterns is based on the Cusco regional artifact sequence, which has been presented most recently and thoroughly by Brian Bauer (1999, 2001). This sequence is based on the one first developed by John Rowe (1944), with modifications made to reflect the results of stratigraphic excavations and multiple radiocarbon dates for different periods. In discussing the Cusco artifact sequence and settlement patterns, some problems have arisen in the use of traditional period names. Rowe's system, which was developed in the Ica Valley, is based on a series of *horizons* and *intermediate periods,* implying periods of political centralization and balkanization. Changes in the Cusco region do not correspond well to these periods. Rather than develop a new sequence of local periods and phases, the Cusco sequence follows the basic chronology used in the Titicaca Basin for periods prior to AD 400, using Archaic and Formative periods (Table B.1). For periods after AD 400, periods are named after the dominant regional style, although this does not imply any relationship between contemporaneous pottery styles.

Based on radiocarbon samples from stratigraphic excavations, the development of the Qotakalli pottery style occurred as early as AD 400 (Bauer 2004; Bauer and Jones 2003), a stylistic innovation corresponding to major changes in regional settlement. Qotakalli pottery has been found with incised pottery and a Titicaca Basin-related style called Muyu Urqu, indicating that its production was begun prior to the Wari colonization of the Cusco region (Bauer 2004; Bauer and Jones 2003). Based on the available data, the period from AD 400 to AD 600 is referred to as the Qotakalli Period. Other ceramic styles were produced and used in the Cusco region at this time, but Qotakalli is the dominant style in the area surveyed to date. The best examples of Qotakalli pottery come from the Cusco Basin, and Bauer (1999, 2001) has published numerous photographs and drawings of this pottery.

Radiocarbon dates from excavations at Pikillacta (McEwan 1987) and contemporaneous sites in the Cusco Basin (Bauer and Jones 2003) indicate that Wari colonization began around or after AD 600 and lasted until around AD 1000. Although the occupation of the Lucre Basin and Huaro area does not appear to have had major effects on settlement patterns in areas surveyed, Wari interaction with locals over these centuries was important, and the period from AD 600 to AD 1000 is referred to here as the Wari Period. SVAP settlement patterns for the Wari Period are very similar to those of the preceding Qotakalli Period.

Following the abandonment of the Wari colonies, several ceramic styles were produced and used in the Cusco region, including Killke, Colcha, and Lucre. The period from AD 1000 AD 1400 is referred to as the Killke Period because Killke pottery has the most widespread distribution in the Cusco region at this time. It should be noted that the terminal date of AD 1400 corresponds to the beginning of Inca imperial expansion, rather than the end of Killke pottery use or innovation of the Inca style. Inca and Killke pottery have been found together in excavation strata dating to the fourteenth and fifteenth centuries, making it difficult to mark the end of one period and beginning of the next. The Inca Period (AD 1400–1535) refers to imperial Inca settlement within the Cusco region.

TABLE B.1.   Period Names for the Cusco Region Sequence

Period Name	Other Styles	References
Inca AD 1400–1535	Killke	Kendall 1985
Killke AD 1000–1400	Colcha, "Lucre B," Inca	Bauer 1999, 2001; Dwyer 1971; McEwan 1984
Wari AD 600–1000	Araway, Ccoipa, Qotakalli, "Lucre A"	Bauer 1999, 2001; Glowacki 1996; Bauer and Jones 2003; McEwan 1984, 1987
Qotakalli AD 400–600	Muyu Urqu	Bauer 1999, 2001, 2004; Bauer and Jones 2003
Formative ~2000 BC–AD 400	Marcavalle, Chanapata, Pukara	Bauer 1999, 2001, 2004; Chávez 1980, 1981a, 1981b
Archaic ~7000–2000 BC		Bauer 2004

Notes

Chapter One

1. See, for example, Las Casas 1939 (1550s); Anonymous *Parecer* 1995 (1571); Toledo 1940g (1572), 1940h (1572). Detailed accounts of the Inca past were not widely read by the literate public in Europe but were of great importance in formulating arguments regarding Spanish imperial policy. During the reign of Charles V, Bartolomé de Las Casas wrote an Inca history that challenged the legitimacy of Spanish conquest in the Americas. The reign of Philip II saw the emergence of a reactionary historiography aimed at refuting Las Casas, as well as an increasingly centralized control over the production and publication of chronicles pertaining to the Inca past.

2. These include Juan de Betanzos (1999 [1551–57, bk. 1, chaps. 6–8]) and Pedro Sarmiento de Gamboa (1965 [1572, chaps. 26–28]). Contemporary scholars have also tended to focus on this ruler as the most important force in the innovation of the Inca imperial order (e.g., Bruhns 1994, 331; Davies 1995, 40–63; C. Julien 2000; Schaedel 1978). The story of the Inca empire's rise under Pachacutic may represent the regnant myth of imperial origins in the sixteenth century, but it was one of many conflicting Inca accounts aimed at glorifying competing royal Inca lineages while also promoting the imperial conquest ideology.

3. This name is significant on a number of levels. *Pacha* may be defined as "time," "soil," or "place," while *kutiq* (from the verb *kutiy,* "to return") means "the one who brings a new cycle" (see González Holguin 1989 [1608], 57, 268). In agriculture, a farmer who turns over soil to plant seeds for a new crop could be a *pachakutiq*—Ballón Aguirre et al. (1992,106) define *kutiy* as "to sow once again that which was already sown" (Sembrar de nuevo lo ya sembrado). From the perspective of Inca imperial politics, the term is linked with individuals credited with rearranging social and political organization, as well as the historical narratives that justified the existing order. *Pachakutiq* also reflects a cyclical conceptualization of time and space, the ushering in of a new era.

4. The chronicles of Juan de Betanzos (1999 [1551]), Bartolomé de Las Casas (1939 [1550s]), and Cristóbal de Molina (1989 [1575]) focus on the actions of Pachacutic, but Terence D'Altroy (2001a, 203–4) has noted that other Inca lineages claimed that important imperial expansion began under Viracocha Inca or Topa Inca Yupanqui; cf. C. Julien 2000; Rostworowski 1999; Rowe 1985b. Several of the earliest sources of Inca history emphasize Viracocha—as a mythic or historical figure—as an important early Inca ruler or founding ancestor. Viracocha is mentioned prominently in the accounts of Pascual de Andagoya (1986 [1541/

42]), Pedro de Cieza de León (1986 [1553]), the *khipukamayuqkuna* (1974 [1542/1609]), Ondegardo (1940 [1561]), and Bartolomé de Segovia (1943 [1553]).

5. See Gose 1996; C. Julien 2000. Pachacutic and his great-grandson Atahuallpa are both said to have reorganized the official Inca history, and other modifications by earlier rulers are possible. As Sabine MacCormack (2001a, 331–36) has noted, Inca narratives were composed for specific purposes, and they were reshaped when transcribed in the colonial period by Spanish writers, taking on many features of European narrative structure.

6. The acceptance of Miguel Cabello de Balboa's dates for Inca rulers from Pachacutic onward was first advocated by Rowe (1945, 281). MacCormack (2001a, 330, 334) and other authors have observed a variability in the Inca king lists recorded by different Spanish authors and have argued that the "official" list of twelve rulers and the European calendar dates that accompany it reflect colonial-period influence. David Henige's (1974, 71–94) comparative study of king lists and succession demonstrates that a twelve-generation sequence of unbroken father-son succession is highly unlikely.

7. These are discussed in detail in another work (Covey 2003). It should be noted that many historians object to comparative approaches, preferring instead to consider Inca civilization sui generis. Some anthropologists contest the historicity of the Inca historical narratives, arguing that they should be studied for their structural content alone.

8. These sites are known through the research of Brian Bauer (Bauer and Covey 2002), Edward Dwyer (1971), Arminda Gibaja Oviedo (1973), Mary Glowacki (2002), and Gordon McEwan and colleagues (1995, 2002).

9. The historical evidence supports this conclusion, as has been elaborated in Bauer and Covey 2002.

10. Brian Bauer's Cusco Valley survey has produced the most comprehensive archaeological evidence regarding the internal processes of Inca state formation. Settlement patterns after AD 1000 can be found summarized in Bauer and Covey 2002.

11. The region to the south of the Cusco Basin was surveyed by Brian Bauer (1990, 1992, 1999), who was the first scholar to use regional survey data to hypothesize early Inca state development.

Chapter Two

1. For example, Conrad and Demarest (1984, 138) describe the Inca trajectory as characterized by "stunning abruptness." The Inca achievement was certainly impressive, but as Carla Sinopoli (1994, 162) has observed, rapid territorial expansion is a common feature of early empires.

2. See, for example, Algaze 1993; Bauer and Covey 2002; Berdan et al. 1996; Deagan 2001; Sinopoli and Morrison 1995.

3. This is argued convincingly by Robert Carneiro (2000, 178), but a number of other theoretical perspectives also situate individual action and agency within structures and processes beyond any individual's complete control. For example, Fernand Braudel (1972) focuses on ecological conditions and long-term

macroregional social interactions in creating conditions amenable to the rise of empires; cf. Wallerstein 1974. Anthony Giddens (1984) describes the dialectic between structure and individual agency, a theoretical concept that can be seen in the writings of Antonio Gramsci and other early sociologists.

4. See, for example, Badian 1958; Barker and Rasmussen 2000, 262–96; Gruen 1970. Barker and Rasmussen describe how Roman military success led to the reorganization of local Etruscan lands, the establishment of Roman colonists, and the construction of roads linking colonies to the capital.

5. H. H. Scullard (1980, 136–53) provides a thorough treatment of the Roman consolidation of Italy and the Pyrrhic invasion. William Harris (1979, 175–82) notes that the historical accounts of this period are suspect, but he concludes that by 290 BC Rome had developed an expansion policy aimed at controlling the entire Italian peninsula from the Etruscan, Umbrian, and Picentine territories southward. This involved almost annual warfare.

6. Harris (1979, 182) states that the withdrawal of Pyrrhus led the Roman Senate to begin to consider wars of expansion outside the Italian peninsula in the late 270s BC.

7. Gruen 1970, 3.

8. See essays in Gruen 1970 for some classic treatments of Roman imperialism at this time.

9. One might note that the Inca history of Pedro de Cieza de León (1988 [ca. 1550]) describes many of the same kinds of interregional activities, including interference in disputes outside the area of the Inca heartland (in this case, the Titicaca Basin). Inca and Roman imperial campaigns began as the two polities asserted their influence over areas previously dominated by different ethnic groups (Aymara and Greek speakers, respectively), defeated external invasions, and were forced to devise a means for both administering new subject populations and obviating further invasions.

10. Itzcoatl, the ruler who is credited with overseeing the rise of an independent Aztec polity, is said to have had all histories burned in 1428 so that new ones could be written (Smith 1996, 51).

11. Smith 1996, 38–45; cf. Urton 1990, 1.

12. Smith 1996, 44–49; 2001.

13. Smith 1996, 47–48. Smith notes that one marriage alliance was contracted with an important polity outside the Valley of Mexico, although Mexica military conquests at this time enlarged Tepanec territory rather than that of Tenochtitlan.

14. See essays in Berdan et al. 1996; Smith 1996, 2001.

15. Other examples of rapid expansion include the Achaemenid empire (Kuhrt 2001), the Vijayanagara empire (Sinopoli and Morrison 1995), and the Russian empire. Macedonian and Mongol expansion occurred during the lifetime of a single ruler but was made possible because the expanding culture could place its representatives as rulers of other states and empires throughout a vast region without modifying their political economies radically.

16. See Marcus and Feinman (1998) for a recent bibliographic essay on state formation; cf. Stanish 2001a.

17. The substantial body of literature on state formation is not reviewed here. Classic definitions of the state include those of Morton Fried (1967), Elman Service (1962, 1975), and Henry Wright (1977). Joyce Marcus and Gary Feinman (1998, 6–7) describe a number of possible characteristics that distinguish states from prestate societies: "(1) a change in the settlement hierarchy from three to four levels; (2) a change in the decision-making hierarchy from two to three (or more) levels; (3) a fundamental change in the ideology of stratification and descent, such that rulers were conceded a sacred supernatural origin (establishing their divine right to rule) while commoners were seen as having a separate descent of nondivine origin; (4) the emergence of two endogamous strata, the result of severing the bonds of kinship that had once linked leaders to followers in a branching continuum of relationships; (5) the evolution of the palace as the ruler's official residence; (6) the change from a single centralized leader (e.g., a chief) to a government that employed legal force while denying its citizens the use of personal, individual force; and (7) the establishment of governmental laws and the ability to enforce them."

18. It should be noted that these indicators have traditionally been used to identify the first states that formed in Mesopotamia, Egypt, China, Mesoamerica, and the Andes. Although the Inca empire was the last of several generations of states and empires to develop in the Andes, it formed in a region where earlier states had not implemented centralized regional administration, and many of the processes are analogous to those of first-generation state formation.

19. Johnson 1977, 1980; Wright and Johnson 1975.

20. A caveat should be issued regarding rank-size graphs. As Gregory Johnson (1977, 494–501) has noted, central place theory was developed to address retail production and marketing, not regional settlement in nonurban archaeological cultures. Smith and Schreiber (2004) identify what they consider the misuse of rank-size graphs by Andean archaeologists. I include the rank-size graphs for the Sacred Valley study region because they illustrate a qualitative change in the nature of settlement organization, one that is consistent with other lines of evidence and similar to patterns observed in other cases of state formation; cf. Johnson 1977, 500.

21. Flannery 1998, 21, citing Sanders 1974.

22. See, for example, Chang 1974; Cowgill 1992; Marcus and Flannery 1996; Pollock 2001; Sanders et al. 1979; Spencer and Redmond 2001a, 2001b; Wright 1986; Wright and Johnson 1975.

23. Flannery (1999) argues that individual agency is important in state formation, but his case studies also clearly show that Shaka (Zulu), Osei Tutu (Ashanti), Mir Silim Khan (Hunza), Kamehameha (Hawai'i), and Andrianampoinimerina (Merina) benefited from previous consolidation of power by predecessors and that the success of their states depended on maintaining the integrity of a centralized government following their deaths.

24. Because this process-oriented reading of the Inca past does not consider cultural innovations to reflect the historical actions of actual individuals, it would not be necessary that developmental sequences correspond to the reigns of exactly the same sequence of rulers.

25. Ondegardo 1916a (1571), 51: "estos yngas señorearon por violencia y guerra . . . y así toda la dificultad que hubo fue en conquistar aquellas comarcas del Cuzco, porque luego todos los conquistados iban con ellos y era siempre mucha mas fuerza que los otros." See Ondegardo 1940 (1561), 132.

26. Ondegardo 1916a (1571), 49. Bernabé Cobo also considered the developmental trajectory of the Incas to have lasted approximately four hundred years (1964 [1653], bk. 12, chap. 1). Cobo claims that Inca power extended well beyond the Cusco region prior to the reign of Viracocha Inca, who consolidated Inca control over the many semiautonomous neighboring groups (1964 [1653, bk. 12, chap. 11]).

27. Sarmiento de Gamboa 1965 (1572, chap. 24).

28. The chronicles of Garcilaso de la Vega (1965 [1609]), Felipe Guaman Poma de Ayala (1980 [1615]), and the *khipukamayuqkuna* (1974 [1542/1609]) present a gradualist model of Inca expansion, a trajectory of conquest that begins with Manco Capac (the founding ancestor) controlling the entire Cusco region and expanding outward from the boundaries that were considered the Inca heartland in the imperial period. It should be noted that the lack of information on how the Incas integrated their heartland makes it difficult to use the gradualist chronicles for an anthropological study of Inca state formation.

29. In 1928, Means divided his study of the Spanish chroniclers into "Garcilassans"—those describing gradual expansion—and "Toledans," who were seen as manipulating the Inca past to discredit the Inca achievement. Rowe's early scholarship (1944, 1945, 1946) convincingly demonstrated the lack of concordance between the gradualist perspective and the evidence from Inca provincial regions.

30. In a 1912 paper, Uhle noted that the Spanish chronicles could never explain the relationship between the Inca empire and earlier Andean civilizations because the Incas claimed to be the first civilization to rise in the Andes. Uhle felt at the time that only archaeology could answer such questions.

31. D'Altroy (2002, 46–47) summarizes archaeological research into Inca chronology. He notes that imperial expansion may have begun slightly earlier than historians assume and that the reliance on unprovenanced calendar dates from the Spanish chronicles imparts a false sense of exactness and historicity.

32. Rowe 1946, 203–4.

33. Rowe 1945, 277.

34. Influential studies include Conrad 1981; Conrad and Demarest 1984; Isbell 1978; Lumbreras 1978; Rostworowski 1978, 1988a; Patterson 1985; Schaedel 1978.

35. Among the archaeologists to posit such developments are Bauer 1992; Bauer and Covey 2002; Dwyer 1971; Morris 1998, 294; Moseley 1992, 243–44; Parsons and Hastings 1988, 223–24.

36. Squier 1877; Wiener 1880.

37. Bingham 1915, 1948. See Bauer 2004; Bauer and Stanish 1990; Uhle 1912.

38. Silverman 2002, 884.

39. For example, Valcárcel 1935, 1939.

40. Representative publications include Barreda 1973; Bauer 1999, 2001; Bauer and Jones 2003; Bauer et al. 2001; Chávez 1980, 1981a, 1981b; Dwyer

1971; Gibaja 1982; Glowacki 2002; Kendall 1994; McEwan 1984, 1987, 1996; McEwan et al. 2002; Torres 1989; Zapata Rodríguez 1997, 1998.

41. For example, Dwyer 1971; Kendall 1974, 1985; Rowe 1944, 1967.

42. Bauer 1990, 1992, 1999, 2001; cf. Muelle 1945.

43. Bauer 1990, 1992.

44. In this book, I distinguish between the Cusco Valley and the three basins it comprises (from west to east, the Cusco Basin, Oropesa Basin, and Lucre Basin). The Inca capital is found within the Cusco Basin, where processes of Inca state formation occurred. As discussed in the following, archaeological patterns in the Cusco Basin are quite different from those in the Lucre Basin located at the southeastern extreme of the Cusco Valley. I follow a number of ethnohistoric sources (see chap. 10) to define the Inca heartland (also referred to as the Cusco region) as the area within approximately 50–80 kilometers of Cusco.

45. Bauer 2004; Bauer and Covey 2002.

46. All Cusco surveys used a field methodology based on the one Parsons and colleagues (2000) employed in the central highlands. Crews of three to five members systematically walked all accessible parts of the survey region at intervals of about 50 meters, registering sites based on the presence of surface artifacts or other cultural remains.

47. In this book, I refer to this area as the Sacred Valley study region when discussing project data. Areas downstream from the study region are referred to as the Urubamba Valley, and those upstream as the Vilcanota Valley.

48. Charles Spencer (1990, 1998) has hypothesized that the limits of non-specialized political administration are approximately a half day's walk from a polity's principal settlement. The successful long-term administration of larger territories would thereby require more specialized and hierarchical government.

49. For example, Cosio et al. 1983; Gade 1975.

50. Dwyer 1971; Kendall 1974, 1985; Kendall et al. 1992; Rowe 1944.

51. Dwyer 1971; Espinoza Soriano 1977; Sarmiento de Gamboa 1965 (1572).

Chapter Three

1. For example, Flores 1985; Gade 1975; Cosio et al. 1983; Winterhalder 1993; Zimmerer 1996.

2. For example, Allen 1988; Bolin 1994; Urton 1981, 1990.

3. Parsons et al. 2000, 11.

4. Albórnoz 1989 (1581/85); Pachacuti Yamqui Salcamaygua 1993 (17th century), f. 7v, 15v, 21v.

5. Randall 1982; Sallnow 1987; see Poole 1982.

6. Albórnoz 1989 (1581/85); Pachacuti Yamqui Salcamaygua 1993 (17th century), f. 21v.

7. Flores 1985; Parsons et al. 2000, 28

8. Flannery et al. 1989.

9. Zimmerer 1999.

10. Flores 1985; Rhoades and Nazarea 1999; Zimmerer 1996, 1998.

11. Zimmerer 1999.

12. Goland 1993.

13. Cobo 1964 (1653). María Rostworowski (1962) has published a document that names several corral groups in the Qoricocha *puna*, confirming the practice of herding on behalf of the Inca state or the royal Inca descent groups.

14. Cosio et al. 1983; Zimmerer 1996.

15. Gade 1975.

16. Winterhalder 1993.

17. Gade 1975.

18. Gade 1975.

19. ADC Corregimiento, Causas Ordinarias, L. 1, C. 7 (1568a); Hemming 1970, 367–69; Lizárraga 1968 (1605), 64; Matienzo 1967 (1567), pt. 1, chaps. 55–51.

20. For example, Anonymous *Discurso* 1906 (ca. 1570), 149.

21. Allen 1988; Flores 1985; Webster 1971.

22. See Murra 1960; Zimmerer 1996, 34–44.

23. Sahlins 1972; see Hastorf 1993.

24. Cashdan 1990.

25. For example, Barker and Rasmussen 2000, 25–37; Brush 1977; Forbes 1989; Rhoades and Nazarea 1999, 219; Zimmerer 1996.

26. Winterhalder 1993.

27. Brush 1976, 1992; Cosio et al. 1983; Goland 1993; Rhoades and Nazarea 1999, 220; Zimmerer 1996, 1999.

28. Travel costs can be reduced by sending members of the same kin group (a family or lineage group) to reside in multiple ecozones and exploit different crops directly. John Murra (1972) identifies this pattern of ecological complementarity, calling it a *vertical archipelago*. From this perspective, the limits of diversity involve not only travel costs but also the degree to which kinship or social organization can achieve cultural coherence under conditions of dispersed residence. Prehistoric settlement patterns for the Cusco region include a large number of very small or dispersed settlements, indicating that some sort of transhumance was probably practiced.

29. Goland 1993; see also Winterhalder 1986.

30. Zimmerer (1996, 18) notes that "farmers in the Paucartambo Andes grow crops to yield a variety of foodstuffs in their version of a 'decent life,' an idea that taken broadly also pillars our own lifeways."

31. Rhoades and Nazarea 1999.

32. Brush 1977, 1992; Rhoades and Nazarea 1999, 223.

33. Zimmerer 1996.

34. See Cosio et al. 1983; NAS 1989; Zimmerer 1998.

35. Rhoades and Nazarea 1999, 220–21.

36. Zimmerer 1996, 1998; see also Farrington 1984; Flores 1985.

37. Gade 1975.

38. NAS 1989, 129–61; Repo-Carrasco 1988; Salis 1985.

39. Repo-Carrasco 1988, 18; cf. Parsons et al. 2000, 74.

40. NAS 1989, 181–90.

41. Halstead and O'Shea 1989, 3–4.

42. Zimmerer 1996, 34–40.

43. Murra 1960.

44. For example, Acosta 1940 (1590), bk. 4, chaps. 16–17; Garcilaso de la Vega 1965 (1609), bk. 5, chaps. 1–5; Gasca 1998 (1551–53), f. 8v–9; López de Izturizaga and Román de Baños 1973 (1585); Santillán 1968 (1563), no. 34; Valverde 1959 (1539), 214.

45. See Murra 1980 (1956), 29–44.

46. Cieza de León 1988 (ca. 1550), chap. 75; Cobo 1964 (1653), bk. 14, chap. 8; Garcilaso de la Vega 1965 (1609), bk. 5, chap. 2; see C. Julien 1985.

47. Acosta 1940 (1590), bk. 4, chap. 16; Grobman et al. 1961, 185–89.

48. Grobman et al. 1961, 244–53.

49. See Grobman et al. 1961, 170–75; Zimmerer 1996, 37–38. These varieties are mentioned in colonial dictionaries. For example, Diego González Holguin lists a high-yield white maize (*paraqay sara*), sweet maize (*miski sara, chuspi sara*), and a hard maize for making a lowland variety of *aqha* (*culli sara*). In addition, both González Holguin and the chronicler Garcilaso de la Vega distinguish between hard and soft maize (*muruchhu sara* and *ccapia,* respectively) (Garcilaso de la Vega 1965 [1609], bk. 8, chap. 9).

50. See Murra 1980 [1956].

51. Acosta 1940 (1590), bk. 4, chap. 17; Zimmerer 1996, 38–40; 1998, 446.

52. Bertonio 1956 (1612); González Holguin 1989 (1608).

53. See Gade 1975. Zimmerer (1996, 140–45) discusses early planting practices in the Paucartambo Valley.

54. For example, Espinoza 1973; C. Julien 2001; Rostworowski 1963a, 1963b.

55. See Seltzer and Hastorf 1990; Shimada et al. 1990.

56. Chepstow-Lusty et al. 1996; Thompson et al. 1985; cf. Seltzer and Hastorf 1990.

57. Chepstow-Lusty et al. 1996, 828.

58. Chepstow-Lusty et al. 1996, 827; Chepstow-Lusty et al. 2003, 501.

59. Chepstow-Lusty et al. 1996, 829.

60. Thompson et al. 1985.

61. Thompson et al. 1985, 973.

62. Thompson et al. 1985, 973. See Thompson et al. 1994, 92; cf. Binford et al. 1997.

63. Seltzer and Hastorf 1990, 402.

64. Thompson et al. 1986.

65. Chepstow-Lusty et al. 1996; Thompson et al. 1994, 92; see Thompson et al. 1998.

66. See Binford et al. 1997, 243; Shimada et al. 1990; Williams 2002.

67. We must remember to account for human populations in this discussion. Population growth can generally be expected over time for sedentary farmers, and intensive agriculture sustains higher population densities while requiring far less land per capita than dry-farming. Periods of resource crisis and political competition between groups would tend to increase the costs of diversity-oriented dry-farming, as dispersed farming populations would be more vulnerable and less able to defend their territories from encroachment by larger groups of intensive

agriculturalists. Intensive agricultural systems become increasingly vulnerable to environmental fluctuations as populations grow and become dependent on the maximization of available resources, but intensification appears to be a highly competitive strategy when it is initially implemented.

68. For example, Binford et al. 1997; Moseley 1990; Shimada et al. 1990.

Chapter Four

1. For example, Cieza de León (1986 [1553], chaps. 87, 105) describes the abandoned capitals of the Wari and Tiwanaku, which local informants claimed had been built long before Inca times.

2. Some scholars have hypothesized that the Incas borrowed elements of statecraft from the coastal Chimú empire after they conquered the north coast in the fifteenth century (e.g., Bruhns 1994, 333–34; cf. Conrad 1981; Conrad and Demarest 1984; Rowe 1948). In this scenario, Chimú statecraft was derived from Wari practices (Bruhns 1994, 334; McEwan 1990), then appropriated and codified by Pachacutic. The chronology of Chimú palace construction reveals that this culture probably did not use the same royal estate organization system as the Incas (Kolata 1990, 137; see Ondegardo 1916b [1559], 8–9); the reuse of architectural space at Chan Chan and modification of Chimú oral histories make it difficult to demonstrate that the Incas borrowed elements of Chimú statecraft (Moseley 1992, 256). The archaeological and historical evidence from the Cusco region is consistent with long-term local developments.

3. For example, Gordon McEwan and colleagues (2002, 288) state that "following the Huari collapse (ca. AD 800–900), succeeding local elites in the Valley of Cuzco [the Lucre Basin] appear to have maintained complex social organization based on the Huari model, but on a much smaller scale than that of the Huari Empire. Ultimately, these local organizations formed the core of the Inca regional state and finally the Inca empire"; cf. McEwan 1996, 169. In contrast, Mary Van Buren (2000, 77) argues instead that the centuries-long hiatus in state administration in the central Andean highlands makes it more likely that the Incas "drew on notions of order found in their own as well as many other Andean societies, rather than adopting high culture transmitted by [Wari] inner elites."

4. See Billman 1999; Earle 1972; Stanish 2001a, 53–55. The Moche polity on the north coast was certainly a state, but some researchers argue that the Lima and Gallinazo cultures (and perhaps Nazca, as well) were also organized at the state level at the same time or earlier.

5. Katharina Schreiber (2001, 86–89) discusses variability in the manifestation of the Wari imperial presence, while Charles Stanish (2002, 186–93) provides an overview of the evidence of Tiwanaku control in provincial and peripheral regions.

6. Isbell 1997a; Kolata 1993.

7. For example, Anders 1991; Isbell 1977; Schreiber 1992, 2001.

8. Bermann 1994; Isbell and Burkholder 2002; Janusek 2002; Seddon 1998; Stanish 2002.

9. For example, Anders 1990; J. Topic 1991.

10. Agurto Calvo 1984, 101–18; Anders 1990; Canziani 1992, 107–10.

11. For example, Agurto Calvo 1984, 101–18; Owen 1994; Schreiber 1999; J. Topic 1991.

12. Kolata 1991.

13. Goldstein 1989, 1993, 2000; Higueras-Hare 1996; Stanish 1992; Trimborn 1981.

14. Covey 2000; Goldstein 1993, 1995/96; Rivera 1991.

15. See Schreiber 1992.

16. See Bauer 2001; Bauer and Jones 2003.

17. Barreda 1982; Lumbreras 1978.

18. Bauer and Jones 2003, 15.

19. Bauer 2004.

20. Bauer 2004.

21. Bauer 1999, 126–28; 2004.

22. Bauer 1990, 1992, 1999.

23. Bauer 1987, 1999, 2001.

24. Cf. Jennings and Craig 2001.

25. Bauer 2004; McEwan 1991; Schreiber 2001; Williams 2001.

26. Glowacki 2002; McEwan 1984, 1991; Zapata Rodríguez 1998.

27. McEwan 1991; Zapata 1998.

28. McEwan 1991, 99; Zapata 1997, 1998. It is worth noting that the site of Muyu Urqu in the Cusco Basin also seems to have had early religious architecture but that it does not have a later Wari occupation.

29. McEwan 1991.

30. McEwan 1996, 171–72.

31. McEwan 1984; 1991; 1996, 181–85.

32. McEwan 1998.

33. McEwan 1991, 106–8.

34. McEwan 1991, 98–100.

35. McEwan 1991, 99.

36. McEwan 1991, 99.

37. McEwan 199199.

38. Glowacki 2002.

39. Zapata Rodríguez 1997.

40. Glowacki 2002; Glowacki and Zapata 1998; Lavender 2001.

41. Glowacki and Zapata 1998; see T. Topic and J. Topic 1987.

42. Glowacki 2002, 277–78.

43. See Moseley 1992, 218–19.

44. Bauer 2004; Bauer and Covey 2002; see Urton 1988.

45. Based on ethnographic data from prestate complex polities, Spencer (1998) argues that a radius equivalent to a half day's walk represents an approximate limit to successful prestate political administration. Travel to Wanka from Cusco requires 1400 meters of vertical climbing in each direction and a walk of well over 20 kilometers from the Cusco Basin, meaning that it falls outside that limit.

46. Bauer 1999, 63.

47. Bauer 1999, 63; 2001.
48. Bauer 2001.
49. Bauer 1999, 2001.
50. Montoya et al. 2000.
51. Bauer 1999, 2004.
52. Owen 1994; see Williams 2001; Williams and Nash 2002.
53. Burger et al. 2000 notes that the Wari occupation of the Lucre-Urcos area led to the procurement of obsidian from Wari-controlled sources, although more sourcing of obsidian from non-Wari domestic excavations in the Cusco region would be useful for demonstrating to what extent this pattern extended to local populations.
54. Luis Lumbreras (1978) has hypothesized an indirect Wari influence in the Cusco Basin and Sacred Valley, and the archaeological data appear to support this. Lumbreras also speculates that local Cusco Basin elites were instrumental in resisting Wari imperialism.

Chapter Five

1. See, for example, Bermann 1994; Kolata 1993; Parsons et al. 1997, 337; Schreiber 2001. Central government in the Tiwanaku heartland appears to have disintegrated slightly later than in the Wari heartland, although the abandonment of both polities' provincial centers occurred over a span of several centuries. Recognizing the dynamic and long-term nature of imperial decline, this book uses AD 1000 as an approximate point chronological marker for the balkanization of Wari colonies in the Cusco region.
2. Studies of climate change in the Tiwanaku heartland include Binford et al. 1997 and Ortloff and Kolata 1993. Looking at Tiwanaku provinces in the Moquegua Valley, Patrick Ryan Williams (2002, 371–72) argues that provincial site abandonment began earlier and was precipitated by social unrest rather than climatic perturbations.
3. This includes the major Wari sites in the Cusco region. Mary Glowacki (2002, 275) states that the site of Qoripata was "deserted and then burned, suggesting that there had been a major attempt by local or foreign groups to expel the Huari from Cuzco." Gordon McEwan (1991) has also identified intentional burning associated with the abandonment of Pikillacta.
4. For example, Sutter 2000; Williams 2001.
5. For recent overviews of this period, see Bonavia 1991; Lumbreras 1999; Parsons and Hastings 1988.
6. Albarracin-Jordan and Mathews 1990; Bauer and Stanish 2001, 43–46; Bermann 1994; Bouysse-Cassagne 1986; C. Julien 1983; Stanish et al. 1997.
7. Bauer and Stanish 2001, 154–57; Hyslop 1976; Stanish et al. 1997, 55–57.
8. Albarracin-Jordan and Mathews 1990, 190–92; Bermann 1994, 224–25.
9. Bermann 1994, 224, 235.
10. González-Carré et al. 1997, 90–99.
11. These include the Pampas-Qaracha Basin (Vivanco and Valdez 1993) and the Sondondo Valley (Schreiber 1993).

12. Sufficient data are not available to evaluate this in the Andes, but similar processes occurred throughout Mesoamerica around the same time. During the early Postclassic (ca. AD 950–1150), stratified petty polities coalesced in the Oaxaca Valley, Mixteca Alta, Basin of Mexico, and parts of the Maya lowlands as centralized states declined. There was considerable elite interaction during this period, but this may have actually hindered the consolidation of an entire region under one individual or group (see Marcus 1998). Areas that had never experienced the development of state administrative infrastructure exhibit many of the same characteristics in terms of archaeological settlement patterns but lacked the degree of historically established elite authority and networks of elite interaction.

13. See Conlee and Schreiber 2002; Schreiber 1987, 1993, 2001; Williams 2001.

14. See Bauer 2004; Kolata 1990; Pineda 1989; Sandweiss and Narváez 1995; Shimada 1987, 1990; Topic and Moseley 1983; T. Topic and J. Topic 1987. Local economic self-sufficiency and the development of core area technologies and industries would provide elites with the means of mustering local support to sever weak links with an imperial core that demanded provincial resources to maintain an expensive central administration and elite life at the capital (see Walbank 1953 for a discussion of such features in the Roman imperial decline).

15. D'Altroy 1997; Shimada 1985.

16. Canziani 1992, 110–18.

17. Williams 2001, 81.

18. Covey 2000; Goldstein 1989; Rivera 1991.

19. Owen 1994; Williams 1997, 2002.

20. Sutter 2000, 49–51; but see Williams 2001, 68.

21. Williams and Nash 2002, 259.

22. Sutter 2000, 50–51.

23. See Bermann et al. 1989; Conrad 1993; Rice 1993; Rivera 1991; Sutter 2000.

24. Owen 1994. Our understanding of Tumilaca culture and its relationship to the Wari colonial system will be advanced by work currently being conducted by Kenny Sims.

25. Jessup 1990.

26. McEwan 1991, 1996.

27. McEwan 1996, 183–84.

28. McEwan (1996, 184) implicates local groups in what he describes as a "massive burning episode" at Pikillacta. Within the Cusco Basin, the site of Pucacancha was also burned around the same time (Bauer and Jones 2003, 8–9), and it may be that this burning episode was carried out by local groups.

29. For example, Williams 2001; J. Topic 1991; see Schreiber 2001, 91.

30. Dwyer 1971; Gibaja 1973; McEwan et al. 2002.

31. Bauer and Covey 2002.

32. Heffernan 1989, 1996; Kendall 1994, 1996.

33. Edward Dwyer (1971, 146) notes this difference in the location of Killke Period sites, concluding that "Cuzco was an oasis of tranquillity [sic] surrounded by a disturbed and ravaged buffer zone."

34. Bauer 1992, 1999.

35. See Bauer 1999, 2001; Dwyer 1971; Kendall 1996; Rowe 1944. This book does not attempt to subdivide regional settlement patterns for this period, although some sites are described as having "early Killke Period" occupation, based on continued settlement from the preceding Wari Period (and lack of Inca Period ceramics) or stylistic similarities between surface pottery and materials recovered in early, dated excavation contexts. Evidence of Inca expansion into the Sacred Valley study region (in the last century or so of the Killke Period) includes the presence of Killke Period sites with high percentages of Killke pottery, as well as sites with the remains of rectangular buildings.

36. Covey 2003.

37. For example, Guaman Poma de Ayala 1980 (1615); Ondegardo 1916a (1571).

38. See Mannheim 1991; Fornée 1965 (1586).

39. William Isbell (1997b) discusses the proliferation of aboveground tombs throughout the Andean highlands at this time.

40. Bauer 1999, 2001; Dwyer 1971, 77–78; McEwan 1984; Rivera 1972.

41. For example, Kendall 1985, 1996; McEwan et al. 1995.

42. McEwan 1991.

43. Hastorf (1993, 2001) provides a paleobotanical perspective on pre-Inca diet among the Xauxa, a group living in the central highlands north of the Cusco region. She concludes that local elites consumed more maize than commoners among populations living in high-elevation settlements.

44. For example, Farrington 1984; Kendall 1994.

45. Even though elite leaders may draw on kin ties or labor tribute to intensify agricultural production, the anthropological literature suggests that elites benefit disproportionately from such projects. See, for example, Kirch 1984; Kurella 1998, 198–99; Spencer 1990; Rountree and Turner 1998, 269.

46. Murra 1972, 1976.

47. Brush 1977.

48. Morris 1985. This becomes apparent in the comparison of administrative documents pertaining to two provincial groups in the Inca empire: the Chupaychu of Huánuco and the Lupaqa of Chucuito (Assadourian 1995; C. Julien 1982; Murra 1972). Among the Chupaychu, whose political organization was not centralized prior to Inca conquest, ecological complementarity was maintained through independent exchanges with other groups in intermediate ecozones (i.e., between *puna* and *kichwa,* and between *kichwa* and *montaña*) (Ortiz de Zúñiga 1967 [1562], 1972 [1562]; for archaeological perspectives, see Hastings 1987; Parsons et al. 1997, 2000). Conversely, the pre-Inca *señoríos* of the Titicaca Basin were much more centrally organized and practiced a "horizontal" exchange of altiplano foodstuffs (i.e., camelid meat for tubers), as well as an elite-initiated system where enclaves grew low-elevation foodstuffs far from the natal community (Diez de San Miguel 1964 [1567]; Ondegardo 1916b [1559]; see also Covey 2000; Stanish 1985, 1992).

49. For example, Binford 1980; Wiessner 1982.

50. Ondegardo 1916a (1571), 10.

51. Murra 1980 (1956). For the Xauxa of the upper Mantaro Valley, extensive archaeological research appears to substantiate such interpretations (Hastorf 2001).

52. Sidky (1996) and Spencer (1990) describe cases where the organization of labor for large-scale hydraulic works contributed to the elaboration of leadership positions.

53. See Kuznar 2001 for a study of risk aversion among Andean herders.

54. See Hastorf 2001; Sandefur 2001 for comparisons of status and diet among the pre-Inca Xauxa.

55. Murra 1980 (1956).

56. See Kendall 1994; Heffernan 1989, 1996.

57. Dwyer 1971, 70–78; Gibaja 1973; McEwan et al. 1995. These sites appear to have had more or less continuous occupation from the first millennium BC.

58. See Dwyer 1971, 40–41; cf. McEwan et al. 1995, 11. Although both sites are large, data from intensive surface collections and excavations have not been published, so it is difficult to determine the size of a given phase of occupation with precision.

59. Glowacki 2002.

60. McEwan et al. 2002.

61. McEwan et al. 2002.

62. Bauer and Covey 2002.

63. Dwyer 1971, 74; Hiltunen and McEwan 2004, 253.

64. Bauer 2004; Bauer and Covey 2002; cf. Dwyer 1971; Rowe 1944.

65. Bauer and Covey 2002.

66. Bauer 1990, 1992.

67. Bauer 1999, 13–60; 2001.

68. Bauer 1999, 26.

69. Bauer 1999, 24–25.

Chapter Six

1. Settlement in the Cusco Basin did grow over time, but the Lucre Basin retained a substantial population while fertile farmland between the two areas was abandoned as a buffer zone formed.

2. See Covey 2003.

3. Cabello de Balboa 1951 (1586), bk. 3, chap. 12, p. 283: "governava sus gentes amigable y pacificamente, y con tan loable artificio que con la fama de su benevolencia discrecion y mansedumbre trujo á su obediencia y gracia, muchos Caciques en sus naciones de ellos sugetas: y de los primeros y mas señalados que vinieron fueron Guaman Samo (Cacique y Señor de Guaro) Pachachulla viracocha (hombre de gran discrecion y prudencia) y las naciones Ayarcamas con sus Señores y regentes: Tambo vincais [*sic*]: y Quiliscochas [*sic*], y otros linages circunvecinos, que tubieron noticia de su buen govierno y conversacion." See also Cobo 1964 (1653), bk. 14, chap. 6; Sarmiento de Gamboa 1965 (1572), chap. 16.

4. It should be noted that one feature of this description of early Inca governance—an emphasis on charisma rather than coercion—is not consistent

with the hierarchical settlement pattern of the Cusco Basin after AD 1000. The anthropological literature for persuasive leadership suggests that it is more consistent with autonomous village societies rather than hierarchical polities.

5. Rowe (1960, 419) suggests that Pachachulla Viracocha refers to an important oracle in the Urcos area.

6. For example, Cabello de Balboa 1951 (1586), bk. 3, chap. 10–12; Cieza de León 1986 (1553), chaps. 31–33; Las Casas 1939 (1552), chap. 250; Sarmiento de Gamboa 1965 (1572), chaps. 15–17.

7. Bauer 1992; Bauer and Covey 2002.

8. Bauer and Covey 2002; Covey 2003.

9. Cabello de Balboa 1951 (1586), bk. 3, chap. 12, p. 286; Cieza de León 1988 (ca. 1550), chap. 33; Fernández 1963 (1571), bk. 3, chap. 5.

10. Cobo 1964 (1653), bk. 12, chap. 8.

11. Rountree 1989, 117. This may also be more similar to elite behavior in balkanized petty polities, and it might prove interesting to pursue the analogy of the Anglo-Saxon heptarchy or the succession practices of medieval Castile.

12. Pachacuti Yamqui Salcamaygua (1993 [17th century], f. 14v–15) states that the fifth Inca ruler contended with the principal Cuyo deity, called Cañacguay Yauirca, and was successful in imposing Inca religion on the area. Zuidema (1974–76, 215–16) identifies this as an important sacred place (*wak'a*), while Zimmerer (1996, 45) states that Cañac-huay is the pass through which one travels to reach the Paucartambo coca lands. Repeated campaigns in Paucartambo and the Andes are mentioned for virtually every Inca ruler from the fifth onward, suggesting a continued interest in maintaining access to lowland goods and products.

13. Algaze (1993) and Spencer and Redmond (2001a) describe early state expansion—through military intervention or the establishment of colonies or merchant enclaves—into areas where nonlocal goods could be acquired directly.

14. Cabello de Balboa 1951 (1586), bk. 3, chap. 13, pp. 290–91; Cobo 1964 (1653), bk. 12, chap. 9; Sarmiento de Gamboa 1965 (1572), chap. 19. The development of military hierarchy and a conquest ideology eventually led to the imperial practice of carrying sacred objects (*wak'akuna*) and emblems of the Inca royal dead to war (e.g., Cabello de Balboa 1951 [1586], bk. 3, chap. 22, pp. 374–78; Salomon and Urioste 1991, 114–16; see MacCormack 1991, 134). Betanzos (1999 [1551], pt. 1, chap. 18) states that Pachacutic had a *wak'a* named Caccha made that could be carried into battle as a proxy of the Inca ruler. González Holguin (1989 [1608], 128) defines *Kacchani* as "to strike with terror" (Atemorizar) and *Kac chayacuni* as "to go making courage, or spirit, or with authority" (Yrse haziendo brioso, o animoso, o de autoridad). By carrying royal emblems and sacred objects, Inca armies added a supernatural level to military command, which was closely tied to their expansion ideology. In terms of actual organization of soldiers and command structure, Murra (1986) has noted that military service became more specialized and professional in the imperial period.

15. For example, Murúa 1987 (1590), bk. 1, chap. 13.

16. Sarmiento de Gamboa 1965 (1572), chap. 19.

17. For example, Cieza de León 1988 (ca. 1550), chap. 35; Cobo 1964 (1653), bk. 12, chap. 9; bk. 13, chap. 28; *khipukamayuqkuna* 1974 (1542/1609),

32; Murúa 1987 (1590), bk. 1, chap. 13; Sarmiento de Gamboa 1965 (1572), chap. 19.

18. See Bauer 1998, 92, 93; Cobo 1964 (1653), bk. 12, chap. 9; Murúa 1987 (1590), bk. 1, chap. 13.

19. Murúa 1987 (1590), bk. 1, chap. 13.

20. Manco Capac: ADC Fondo Corregimiento L. 47, C. 17 (1766); ADC Fondo Corregimiento L. 49, C. 29 (1768); Sarmiento de Gamboa 1965 (1572), chap. 14; Toledo 1940d (1571), 81–85; 1940f (1571), 158–67. Sinchi Rocca: Cobo 1964 (1653), bk. 12, chap. 4; Toledo 1940f (1571), 158–67. Lloque Yupanqui: Cobo 1964 (1653), bk. 12, chap. 6; Sarmiento de Gamboa 1965 (1572), chap. 16. Mayta Capac: Sarmiento de Gamboa 1965 (1572), chap. 17. Capac Yupanqui: Cobo 1964 (1653), bk. 12, chap. 8; Sarmiento de Gamboa 1965 (1572), chap. 18.

21. For example, Pachacuti Yamqui Salcamaygua 1993 (17th century), f. 9.

22. Cabello de Balboa 1951 (1586), bk. 3, chap. 13, pp. 290–91; see Cobo 1964 (1653), bk. 12, chaps. 8–9; Guaman Poma de Ayala 1980 (1615), f. 103–4.

23. Cobo 1964 (1653), bk. 12, chap. 8; Pachacuti Yamqui Salcamaygua 1993 (17th century), f. 16v; Sarmiento de Gamboa 1965 (1572), chap. 19.

24. Cobo 1964 (1653), bk. 12, chap. 8.

25. For example, Sarmiento de Gamboa (1965 [1572], chap. 22) mentions that Inca Rocca gave gifts of gold, silver, and cloth to elites in the Anta area.

26. Calancha 1974–82 (1639), bk. 1, chap. 15.

27. For example, *khipukamayuqkuna* 1974 (1542/1609), 31; Oliva 1998 (1598), f. 37v.

28. Sarmiento de Gamboa 1965 (1572), chap. 19.

29. Cieza de León 1988 (ca. 1550), chap. 34; Sarmiento de Gamboa 1965 (1572), chap. 18.

30. *Khipukamayuqkuna* 1974 (1542/1609), 32.

31. Cobo 1964 (1653), bk. 13, chap. 4.

32. There is some confusion about the relationship between this cult and the cult of the sun in the imperial period.

33. Pachacuti Yamqui Salcamaygua 1993 (17th century), f. 14–15.

34. Murúa 1987 (1590), bk. 1, chap. 11.

35. For example, Santillán 1968 (1563), no. 2.

36. Sarmiento de Gamboa 1965 (1572), chap. 17.

37. For example, Argyle 1966, 5; Brown 1979, 121.

38. Sarmiento de Gamboa 1965 (1572), chap. 29. Elite titles are discussed in greater detail in chapter 7.

39. Cabello de Balboa 1951 (1586), bk. 3, chap. 13, p. 294.

40. Sarmiento de Gamboa 1965 (1572), chap. 24; for a discussion of this practice in the imperial period, see MacCormack 2001b.

41. Cabello de Balboa 1951 (1586), bk. 3, chap. 14, p. 298: "Este Viracocha Ynga fue muy inclinado á las armas, y grande amigo de sugetar naciones y ansi se dispuso a no dejar en todos los Circuitos de el Cuzco nacion ninguna fuera del yugo de su mando y obediencia."

42. Sarmiento de Gamboa 1965 (1572), chap. 27.

43. MacCormack 2001b, 428.

44. See Bauer and Covey 2002; Covey 2003.

45. See Bauer and Covey 2002; Bauer 2004.

46. Bauer and Covey 2002; Dwyer 1971; Rowe 1944.

47. Bauer and Covey 2002.

48. Bauer and Covey 2002.

49. See Johnson 1977.

50. Kendall 1996; Kendall et al. 1992; Niles 1980.

51. Kendall et al. 1992, 220.

52. See Castillo and Jurado Chamorro 1996; Kendall et al. 1992; Yépez 1985.

53. For the proxemics of Andean plazas, see Moore 1996. It is tempting to speculate that the outward-facing structures were used—possibly by local elites—for regular interactions with the local Huayllacan populace, while the structure facing the platform was used by Inca administrators during periodic public events.

54. See Betanzos 1999 (1551), bk. 1, chap. 6; Cieza de León 1988 (ca. 1550), chap. 38; Kendall et al. 1992.

55. Brian Bauer, personal communication, 2003.

56. Bauer 1992, 83–88.

57. See also Kendall 1985, 329–34.

58. Bauer 1990, 1992; see Poole 1984. Comparative figures are available from Toledo's *Visita General* in the 1570s (Cook 1975 [1570s]), although these reflect decades of population decline following the Spanish Conquest.

59. Bauer 1999.

60. The Queguars lived to the east of the Paruro River drainage systems near the modern communities of San Juan de Quehuares and Rondocan. To the southeast of the Paruro drainage, across the Apurímac River, lies the region of the Papres near the communities of Pirque, Papre, Sanka, and Curma. Farther to the south, well in the District of Acomayo, were the Acos. The Yanahuaras lived to the southwest, across the Velille River (Poole 1984, 84, 457–68).

61. Bauer 1987; 1992, 124–39; see also Gade and Escobar Moscoso 1982; Poole 1984; Urton 1990.

62. Bauer 1990, 1992.

63. Cf. Cabello de Balboa 1951 (1586), bk. 3, chap. 13, p. 291.

64. Cieza de León 1988 (ca. 1550), chap. 37.

65. Sarmiento de Gamboa 1965 (1572), chap. 35; see Arnold 1993.

66. Bauer 1996.

67. Thompson et al. 1985, 973.

Chapter Seven

1. For example, Albórnoz 1989 (1581/85); Bauer and Barrionuevo Orosco 1998; Ocampo 1999 (1610). Documents in the Betancur Collection (ADC Colección Betancur, vol. 7 [compiled in 1795], f. 445v–46) include colonial resettlement (*reducción*) information on the Xaquixaguana area, identifying towns named Canco, Anta, Cazca, Equeco, Tanboqui, Pomaguanca, Sorite, Lauanqui, and Chiguan Quiliscache. The people of Canco, Equeco, and Conchacalla were

reduced into the town of Anta (ADC Fondo Corregimiento, L. 8, C. 1 [1626]; ADC Fondo Corregimiento, L. 31, C. 9 [1733]; see ADC, Manuscritos 17 [1589]; Cortés de Monroy 1982 [1690], 189–96). The Mayo appear to have lived in (or been reduced into) Zurite (ADC Fondo Corregimiento, L. 2, C. 23 [1595]; Cueva 1982 [1690], 199–203), while several documents refer to the town of Huarocondo continuing to be settled (Olivera y Dolmos 1982 [1689], 184–87). Heffernan (1989, 1996) presents a detailed history of the Limatambo area.

2. Fornée 1965 (1586). Some of this linguistic diversity may have been the product of Inca imperial resettlement projects (see chap. 10).

3. Heffernan 1989, 1996.

4. Bauer and Covey 2002; Kendall 1994; MacCurdy 1923; Rowe 1944; Sarmiento de Gamboa 1965 (1572), chap. 35. The chronicles suggest that the Quilliscache were early Inca allies but that they may not have been reliable ones. For example, Sarmiento de Gamboa (1965 [1572], chaps. 16, 26, 27) identifies their leader as an ally of the third Inca ruler and loyal supporter of Pachacutic during the Chanca invasion, but he also (chap. 35) lists the towns of Cugma and Huata (located in Quilliscache territory) as conquests of Pachacutic. Betanzos (1999 [1551–57], bk. 1, chap. 10) claims that the groups living around Xaquixaguana joined the Chancas and fought against the Incas. The settlement of a Quilliscache village near Xaquixaguana (see n. 1) may indicate that this group was forcibly resettled from its traditional lands following Inca conquest.

5. Farrington 1984; Kendall 1985, 1994, 1996.

6. See Rostworowski 1970b for the most complete ethnohistoric treatment of the Ayarmaca polity (see also AGN Tit. Prop. L. 1, C. 3 [1557]). Rostworowski's study details colonial-period Ayarmaca settlement, which does not appear to have been continuous from the Killke Period. An archaeological survey in the region has identified large villages around Maras, where the chronicles of Sarmiento de Gamboa and Cabello de Balboa situate the principal Ayarmaca settlements. Large villages and a complex settlement hierarchy appear to be absent for the Killke Period around the modern towns of Pucyura and Chinchero, where the Ayarmacas lived in the colonial period.

7. See Sarmiento de Gamboa 1965 (1572) for a discussion of Inca-Ayarmaca relations over time.

8. Archaeological research conducted in this region includes Haquehua Huaman and Maqque Azorsa 1996; Maqque and Haquehua 1993; Rivera 1971a, 1971b, 1972, 1973. The Xaquixaguana Plain Archaeological Survey, which I directed in 2004–5, is developing settlement patterns for a region of more than 500 square kilometers to the west and northwest of Cusco.

9. Cf. Rostworowski 1970b.

10. Bauer and Covey 2002.

11. La Lone (1985) notes that Viracocha Inca conducted the final conquest of the area, establishing a personal estate at Tipón.

12. Sarmiento de Gamboa 1965 (1572), chaps. 19, 23, 24.

13. Cabello de Balboa 1951 (1586), bk. 3, chap. 12, p. 283; Cobo 1964 (1653), bk. 12, chap. 6; Guaman Poma de Ayala 1980 (1615), f. 84; Sarmiento de Gamboa 1965 (1572), chap. 16. Inca kinship has been discussed by C. Julien

(2000), Lounsbury (1986), and Zuidema (1977, 1989), and there is considerable disagreement over the relationship of colonial documentation of commoner marriage practices to those of elites in Cusco at the time of state formation. Colonial sources like Santo Tomás (1995 [1560], f. 69v–70r) and Pérez Bocanegra [1631] do not agree exactly in the definition of important terms, and the dictionaries of González Holguin (1842 [1607], 214–15; 1989 [1608]), Ricardo (1951 [1586], 98), and Santo Tomás (1951 [1560]) leave much room for interpretation. The term *kaka* generally refers to an affine, including father-in-law, mother's brother, or wife's brother; cf. C. Julien 2000, 25; Zuidema 1995, 151–64. Arriaga mentions a ritual participation by *kakakuna* in important initiation events, and his Edict against Idolatry (1999 [1621], 171) defines *kaka* as "uncle," a distinct category from "in-law," or *masa* (see also Guaman Poma de Ayala 1980 [1615], f. 848; Salomon and Urioste 1991, 151 n. 878).

14. Sarmiento de Gamboa 1965 (1572), chap. 23.

15. For example, Sarmiento de Gamboa 1965 (1572), chaps. 23, 25.

16. Rostworowski 1962.

17. Ondegardo 1917 (1571), 46.

18. It should be noted that a few scholars consider the chronicle of Fernando de Montesinos (1882 [1642]) to provide evidence of such a direct transfer of state traditions (Hiltunen 1999; Hiltunen and McEwan 2004). Montesinos wrote his chronicle over a century after the conquest, and his Inca history is copied from a manuscript written by a Spaniard in Ecuador—with heavy editing to fit Montesinos's religious arguments linking Andean civilizations with biblical prophecies. Sabine Hyland's research exposes these and other problems with the Montesinos chronicle (e.g., Hyland n.d.). Bernabé Cobo, a Jesuit who wrote an exhaustive Inca history based on mutiple versions of the Inca past, discounts Montesinos's long sequence of Inca and pre-Inca kings as being at odds with all other source materials that he studied, including the accounts of Inca elites themselves (Cobo 1964 [1653], bk. 12, chap. 2). It should be noted that while Montesinos frequently names places, ethnic groups, and local leaders in Ecuador (e.g., 1882 [1642], chaps. 24–26), almost none are mentioned for the Cusco region. Fewer than a dozen places in the Inca heartland are named—several of which are misspelled— and none of the pre-Inca ethnic groups or their leaders are identified (except as residents of such places as Hillaca [Huayllacan], Choco [Chocco], Muhina [Mohina], and Lima Tambo). Several of the place names refer to the homes of Inca queens, information that may be copied from other chronicles. Even if the ruler list of Montesinos were accurate, his chronicle is virtually useless for understanding Inca state formation processes.

19. Cabello de Balboa 1951 (1586), bk. 3, chap. 12, p. 283; Cobo 1964 (1653), bk. 12, chap. 6; Sarmiento de Gamboa 1965 (1572), chap. 16.

20. Names of early non-Inca leaders include Huaman Samo and Pachachulla Viracocha. These appear to be personal names and not titles. Sarmiento de Gamboa tends to refer to these leaders as *sinchikuna*, but this is part of a deliberate program of downplaying Inca political complexity (Santo Tomás defines *cinchi* as "strong or valiant thing" [fuerte, o valiente cosa], not as a distinct title). Cieza de León (1986 [ca. 1550], chaps. 31–33) refers to non-Inca contemporaries of the

early rulers as "captain" (capitán) or "lord or captain" (señor o capitán). His Quechua informants may have been using the title *apu* (rather than *qhapaq*) to describe such leaders—the early dictionary of Santo Tomás (1951 [1560], 235) uses *apu* for lineage heads, local elites, and military leaders.

21. See Cobo 1964 (1653), bk.12, chap. 25; González Holguin 1989 (1608); Rostworowski 1977b; Santo Tomás 1951 (1560).

22. González Holguin 1989 (1608), 134–35; Santo Tomás 1951 (1560), 96, 192; cf. Betanzos 1999 (1551), bk. 1, chaps. 6, 27; Sarmiento de Gamboa 1965 (1572), chap. 11. In this book, I refer to the office as *qhapaq* but use "ccapac" to spell out titles mentioned in the documents (e.g., Tocay Ccapac).

23. González Holguin 1989 (1608), 31–32.

24. Sarmiento de Gamboa 1965 (1572), chap. 18.

25. González Holguin 1989 (1608), 347.

26. Betanzos 1999 (1551), bk. 1, chap. 27; González Holguin 1989 (1608), 368. In this discussion, I refer to the Inca ruler at the time of state formation as the *qhapaq* or *sapay qhapaq* (see n. 31). When discussing the imperial period, I employ the more commonly used *sapa inka*.

27. Bertonio 1956 (1612), 173; González Holguin 1989 (1608), 366; Ricardo 1951 (1586), 9.

28. It is also possible that Inca rivals developed aspects of state organization to resist Inca expansion. Spencer and Redmond (2001a, 2001b) have described similar processes during state formation in Mexico's Oaxaca Valley.

29. Cf. Santo Tomás 1951 (1560), 96.

30. Cabello de Balboa 1951 (1586), bk. 3, chap. 14, p. 299: "otros principales de menos nombre."

31. For example, Betanzos 1999 (1551), bk. 1, chap. 6. The addition of *sapay* to the *qhapaq* title renders it "peerless king." González Holguin (1989 [1608], 78) observes that *sapay* refers to things that have no partner, as opposed to things that are *missing* a partner, in which case *chulla* is used (e.g., *chullamaqui*, a one-handed person; *chulla çapato*, the one shoe of a pair). By taking this title early in the imperial period, the Inca ruler declared himself to have no partner or equal among others using the *qhapaq* title. This justified and necessitated the conquest of rival *qhapaqkuna*.

32. Betanzos 1999 (1551), bk. 1, chap. 6; Cobo 1964 (1653), bk. 12, chap. 8; *khipukamayuqkuna* 1974 (1542/1609), 33–36.

33. See Lounsbury 1986; Zuidema 1977.

34. Santo Tomás (1951 [1560], 240) defines *cacay* as "grandfather of my mother" (abuelo de mi madre), "revenue, or tribute" (alcauala, o tributo), as well as "contribution" (contribución). González Holguin (1989 [1608], 42) defines *caca* as "the uncle, mother's brother" (el tio, hermano de madre). Some of the stories from the Huarochirí manuscript (e.g., Salomon and Urioste 1991, 57–59) reveal an antagonism between a man and his brother-in-law, which was seen in competitive dancing and drinking, as well as the mobilization of labor for construction projects.

35. Women from other groups appear to have moved to Cusco, where their Inca husbands resided, but they still had claims to labor service in their own com-

munities. Such rights could be passed on to their children, who also appear to have lived in Cusco and were raised as Incas. By contracting multiple marriages, the Inca ruler would have increased the amount of labor tribute available for state projects, and much of the ceremonial or festive reciprocation of such labor would have probably taken place in Cusco, promoting the city to regional prominence.

36. Lounsbury (1986) interprets Inca kinship as being a system of asymmetrical prescriptive alliance, similar to that of the Kachin and other groups; cf. Zuidema 1990, 23–33. It is problematic to apply Inca kinship models addressing the imperial period directly to kinship practices pertaining to earlier periods. Accounts of the period of Inca state formation describe stronger groups demanding women from weaker ones as marriage partners, as well as weaker groups offering women as a sign of their subordinate status in an alliance. Such descriptions are at odds with a recent discussion of Inca kinship (C. Julien 2000).

37. Cobo 1964 (1653), bk. 12, chap. 9.

38. Cobo 1964 (1653), bk. 12, chap. 9.

39. La Lone 1985; Rostworowski 1962.

40. Arriaga 1999 (1621), chap. 6.

41. Guaman Poma de Ayala 1980 (1615), f. 848: "Estos compadres ayudaban en el trabajar, en otras necesidades, y cuando están enfermos y en el comer y beber, y en la fiesta, y en la sementera, y en la muerte a llorar, y después de muerto, y en todos los tiempos mientras que ellos vivieren, y después sus hijos y descendientes, nietos y bisnietos, se servían."

42. Thomas Cummins (2002, 44–52) discusses the transition in Inca festive behavior before and after imperial expansion began.

43. Sarmiento 1965 (1572), chap. 21; see also Las Casas 1939 (1552), chap. 16.

44. Rostworowski 1962; see Zuidema 1986, 192.

45. Fernández (1963 [1571], bk. 3, chap. 5) refers to an uncle of the seventh Inca ruler as Guailla Cancaca (Huayllacan *kaka*), indicating the kinds of affinal relationships and obligations described in this chapter.

46. See Cobo 1964 (1653), bk. 11, chap. 9; Cabello de Balboa 1951 (1586), bk. 3, chap. 13, p. 293; Las Casas 1939 (1552), chap. 16; cf. Gutiérrez de Santa Clara 1963–65 (16th century), chap. 49; Montesinos 1882 (1642), chap. 4.

47. Sarmiento de Gamboa 1965 (1572), chap. 20.

48. Sarmiento de Gamboa 1965 (1572), chap. 20.

49. Cf. Zuidema 1990, 38–44. This story may compress alliance changes occurring over several generations into a single episode. As Catherine Julien has noted (2000, 212), the life history of Yahuar Huaccac is especially difficult to reconstruct. Whether or not events occurred as they are recorded by Sarmiento de Gamboa, there is evidence of intermarriage between the Incas and groups like the Antas and Ayarmacas. In 1571, Pedro Pongo Xiue Paucar appeared before Toledo, stating that he lived in Anta and was the grandson of Viracocha Inca's brother-in-law (Toledo 1940e [1571], 112–18). In the same testimony, don Diego Aucaylle, who lived near Xacxaguana (near Anta), identified himself as a descendant of Yahuar Huaccac and Viracocha Inca. In another presentation of witnesses, don Gonzalo Cusi Roca Inga, the local leader (*cacique principal*) of the town of Ayamarca, also appeared before Toledo (1940f [1571], 167–73), claiming descent from

Tocay Ccapac. He considered himself to be of Inca ethnicity, suggesting intermarriage between the Inca and Ayarmaca nobility.

50. Allegations of illegitimacy in the Spanish chronicles may reflect descent
through a secondary wife, but legitimacy is frequently constructed ex post facto by
one descent group or faction to justify the defeated political ambitions of another
(Henige 1974, 27–33). That the Huayllacans considered themselves more closely
related to one son of Yahuar Huaccac than another indicates that the mother's
identity was of some importance in Inca elite kinship at this time.

51. Sarmiento de Gamboa 1965 (1572), chap. 23; Acosta 1940 (1590), bk. 6,
chap. 20. Descendants of Yahuar Huaccac also lived in Ramay (possibly modern
Lamay, located less than 10 kilometers from modern Paullu) (Toledo 1940f [1571],
149–58). During the colonial period, Huayllacan communities still lived close to
their ancestral lands and were ultimately reduced into the modern town of Coya
(ADC Libro de Matriculas, Industria, Indígenas y Eclesiasticas: Provincia de Calca
[1722]; ADC Colección Betancur, vol. 7 [compiled in 1795], f. 446). Two Huayllacan settlements or descent groups—Pataguayllan and Paulo Guayllacan—are
mentioned in the Betancur documents at the time of the Toledan *reducción* (ADC
Colección Betancur, vol. 7 [compiled in 1795], f. 446).

52. Inca state administration initially functioned by leaving local economies
and kin structures intact, while establishing an additional level of political and religious hierarchy. State representatives interacted with local elites so that state
generosity was communicated, rather than the fulfillment of the obligations of
kinship.

53. Sarmiento de Gamboa 1965 (1572), chap. 23.

54. During the archaeological survey, only areas with continuous architecture
and artifact scatters were considered as part of a habitational site. Therefore,
while the terracing at Qhapaqkancha might cover another 25 hectares or more,
the occupational core is only about 4 hectares.

55. Cobo 1964 (1653), bk. 12, chap. 10. It should be noted that the Incas did
not consider themselves a herding culture but focused on maize cultivation. Inca
origin myths describe the founding ancestors as establishing the cultivation of
suni, kichwa, and even *ceja de montaña* lands, but the myths do not emphasize
herding. This makes marriage alliances with the Huayllacans and Ayarmacas—
two groups said to herd camelids—interesting for considering strategies of political economy, as well as traditional patterns of herder-cultivator relationships.

56. Yépez 1985.

57. Espinoza 1977; Toledo 1940f (1571), 149–58.

58. See Cabello de Balboa 1951 (1586), bk. 3, chap. 13, p. 290; Cobo 1964
(1653), bk. 12, chap. 8; Pachacutic Yamqui 1993 (17th century), f. 14ff.; Sarmiento 1965 (1572), chap. 18.

59. Sarmiento de Gamboa 1965 (1572), chap. 23.

60. See Cabello de Balboa 1951 (1586), bk. 3, chap. 14, p. 300; Cobo 1964
(1653), bk. 12, chap. 8; Pachacutic Yamqui 1993 (17th century), f. 22v–23; Murúa
1987 (1590), bk. 1, chap. 19; Sarmiento de Gamboa 1965 (1572), chap. 34.

61. Murúa 1987 (1590), bk. 1, chap. 19. This is said to have occurred after

Inca sibling marriage had been established in Cusco, at a time when Inca rulers were beginning to marry female relatives to their subordinates.

62. See Cabello de Balboa 1951 (1586), bk. 3, chap. 14, p. 300; Murúa 1987 (1590), bk. 1, chap. 19; Pachacuti Yamqui Salcamaygua 1993 (17th century), f. 22v–23; Sarmiento de Gamboa 1965 (1572), chap. 34.

63. Espinoza 1977; Zuidema and Poole 1982.

64. Murra 1980 (1956), 37–38.

65. Rostworowski 1970a; Rowe 1997.

66. Toledo 1940f (1571), 149–58.

67. The ceramic assemblage at Muyuch'urqu lacks Inca pottery and has very little Killke pottery. It resembles early excavation contexts from Pukara Pantillijlla more closely than later ones. Early contexts at Pukara Pantillijlla have yielded a date of AD 1210–1310, at 86.8 percent confidence (sample AA 47677, BP 733 ± 43).

68. Brian Bauer, personal communication, 2003.

69. See Kendall 1985.

70. Sample AA47669 yielded a date that was calibrated in OxCal v3.5 to a two-sigma range of AD 1210–1330 (81.1 percent probability) or 1340–1400 (14.3 percent). Two other samples (AA47677 and AA47673) came from a nearby semicircular building, in proveniences with Killke Period pottery (with few, if any Cusco Basin shards). These samples respectively returned calibrated two-sigma dates of (1) AD 1210–1310 (86.8 percent probability) or 1350–90 (8.6 percent) and (2) AD 1280–1410. Samples corresponding to the Inca expansion of the site's occupation returned dates in the late thirteenth or fourteenth centuries (AA47670: AD 1240–1410; AA47675: AD 1280–1400).

71. See Angles Vargas 1967; Yépez 1985.

Chapter Eight

1. Sarmiento de Gamboa 1965 (1572), chap. 23. This account states that ten places were conquered by the Inca ruler or his son and military captains during the campaign.

2. Cieza de León 1988 (ca. 1550), chaps. 37, 41–43; cf. Ondegardo 1917 (1571), 46–47. Not only did Inca campaigns become more sustained over time but they appear to have sought more comprehensive territorial control over the Cusco region. In discussing the conquests of Viracocha Inca, Sarmiento de Gamboa mentions three sites whose names are suggestive of herding: Pacaycacha (poss. *pakay* "hidden" + *kancha* "corral or enclosure"), Casacancha (poss. *q'asa* "pass between two mountains" + *kancha*), and Runtucancha (*runtu* "egg, or hailstone" + *kancha*). The conquest and administration of remote herding communities would have been much more difficult to achieve than that of *kichwa* farmers.

3. Ondegardo 1917 (1571), 46–48.

4. See Redmond 1994; cf. Hassig 1988.

5. Cieza de León 1988 (ca. 1550), chap. 38: "y liberalmente les otorgó que pudiesen estar en su tierra poseyendo . . . con tanto que, a tiempo y conforme a

las leyes, tributasen de lo que hobiese en sus pueblos en sus pueblos al Cuzco; y que dellos mismos fuesen luego a la ciudad y le hiciesen dos palacios, uno dentro della y otro en Caqui, para se salir a recrear . . . y para que entendiesen lo que habían de hacer y entre ellos no hobiese disensions, mandó quedar un delegado suyo con poder grande, sin quitar el señorío al señor natural."

6. See Betanzos 1999 (1551), bk. 1, chaps. 9, 10; Kendall et al. 1992.

7. Acuña 1965 (1586), 314; ADC Corregimiento, Causas Ordinarias, L. 1, C. 11 (1572); ADC Educandas 2 (1568b), f. 6; La Lone and La Lone 1987; Rostworowski 1970a, 1993, 168–70; Rowe 1990.

8. See Ondegardo 1916b (1559), 74–75. María Rostworowski (1962) observes that panaka lands tended to be concentrated in the imperial heartland, while newly developed resources in more peripheral regions were more important for supporting imperial administrative apparatus; cf. Conrad and Demarest 1984.

9. AGN Causas Civiles L. 4, C. 26 (1559); Niles 1999; Rostworowski 1962.

10. Farrington 1983; see also AGN Causas Civiles L. 4, C. 26 (1559); Betanzos 1999 (1551), bk. 1, chap. 43; Niles 1999, 133–36; Rostworowski 1962.

11. Gade 1975.

12. Farrington 1983, 226.

13. Bolin (1994, 152–56) estimates that over 1300 hectares of valley-bottom lands could be irrigated by two canal systems in the Urubamba-Yanahuara area alone.

14. Terrace area figures are from Santillana (1999, 91). Assuming a yield of three thousand kilograms/hectare (Santillana 1999, 91), an average caloric content of 3500 kilocalories/kilogram for shelled maize, and a daily caloric intake of 2000 kilocalories (see D'Altroy 1992, 87).

15. Farrington 1983; Kendall 1994; Niles 1999; Protzen 1993.

16. For example, Heffernan 1996.

17. Gasca 1998 (1551–53), 36–37.

18. Bauer 2004; Huaycochea Núñez de la Torre 1994; Morris 1967, 156–70; Niles 1999; Protzen 1993.

19. Vaca de Castro 1908 (1543).

20. Bauer 1992, 136; Kendall et al. 1992.

21. See Parsons et al. 1997.

22. Garcilaso de la Vega 1965 (1609), bk. 5, chap. 3.

23. See Morris 1985, 482; Murra 1972.

24. Sarmiento de Gamboa 1965 (1572), chap. 24: "En viendo la suya, o por muerte del inga que los había vencido, luego tornaban a procurar su libertad, y para ello tomaban las armas y se alzaban. Y así ésta es la causa que decimos muchas veces que un pueblo fué sujetado por diferentes ingas, como de Mohina y Pinagua, que, aunque fueron desterrados y sujectados por Inca Roca, también los oprimió Yaguar Guaca y consiguiente Viracocha y su hijo Inga Yupangui."

25. See Ondegardo 1917 (1571), 47–48.

26. For more on dates for Inca expansion in the Titicaca Basin, see D'Altroy 2002, 47; Pärssinen and Siiriänen 1997; Seddon 1998. Cieza de León (1988 [ca. 1550], chaps. 37, 41–43) describes Inca imperial campaigns beginning under the seventh and eighth rulers.

27. McEwan et al. 2002, 294.

28. Using OxCal v3.5, AA47679 was calibrated to AD 1300–1370 (48.2 percent) or AD 1380–1440 (47.2 percent), while AA 47680 was calibrated to AD 1300–1370 (43.4 percent) or AD 1380–1440 (52 percent).

29. See Flannery 1972.

30. Murra 1980, 37–38.

31. To the extent that local cultures continued to value diverse diets based principally on dry-farmed products, local elites may have continued to be important during the imperial period for organizing the cultivation or acquisition of such foods. With local populations living at lower elevations and laboring on an Inca production schedule, less local labor would be available to put into maintaining crop diversity. Local groups would either embrace the Inca system of food values or be forced to maintain more archipelagic social relationships in order to satisfy pre-Inca culinary norms.

32. For example, Espinoza 1974.

Chapter Nine

1. For example, Cieza de León 1988 (ca. 1550), chaps. 38, 39. See also Santillán 1968 (1563), no. 8.

2. I refer to the Inca empire as Tawantinsuyu throughout this discussion. This name refers to the binding of four principal provincial regions (*suyukuna*) into a political whole.

3. For example, Lynch 1993; Morris and Thompson 1985.

4. *Sensu* Salomon 1985; see Murra 1972, 1976.

5. See Salomon 1986b.

6. Schreiber 1992. It should be noted that any state desiring more than hegemonic control would still have to establish specific bureaucratic and religious offices in polities with unspecialized leadership positions.

7. For example, Covey 2000.

8. Murra 1982.

9. Murra 1986.

10. Cieza de León 1986 (1553); Stanish 1997, 2000.

11. Covey 2000; Hyslop 1976; Stanish 1989, 1992, 1997; Stanish et al. 1997.

12. See Abercrombie 1998, 154–61; Albarracin-Jordan and Mathews 1990, 193; Bauer and Stanish 2001, 51–55; Cieza de León 1986 (1553), chap. 100; 1988 (ca. 1550), chaps. 41–42; Cobo 1964 (1653), bk. 12, chaps. 13–14; Espinoza 1981; C. Julien 1983; Ramos Gavilán 1988 (1589); Sarmiento de Gamboa 1965 (1572), chap. 37; Villamarín and Villamarín 1999.

13. Cieza de León 1988 (ca. 1550), chap. 42.

14. Cieza de León 1988 (ca. 1550), chap. 43.

15. Cieza de León 1988 (ca. 1550), chap. 43.

16. Sarmiento de Gamboa 1965 (1572), chap. 40.

17. Abercrombie 1998, 160–61; Covey 2000; Diez de San Miguel 1964 (1567); Gutiérrez Flores and Ramírez Segarra 1993 (1574); Mercado de Peñalosa 1965 (1586); Ondegardo 1916a (1571); Vázquez de Espinoza 1969 (ca. 1600).

18. For example, Betanzos 1999 (1551); Cobo 1964 (1653); Pachacutic Yamqui 1993 (17th century); Ramos Gavilán 1988 (1589); Sarmiento de Gamboa 1965 (1572).

19. Morris 1985; cf. Pease 1982.

20. Murra 1986, 51.

21. C. Julien 1982, 1988.

22. Hyslop 1976, 1979; C. Julien 1983; Pärssinen and Siiriänen 1997; Stanish 2000; Stanish et al. 1997; Vaca de Castro 1908 (1543).

23. Bauer and Stanish 2001; Stanish and Bauer 2004.

24. The conquest of Llallagua near Copacabana is described by Mercado de Peñalosa 1965 (1586), 338; Ramos Gavilán 1988 (1589), bk. 1, chaps. 12, 19; Sarmiento de Gamboa 1965 (1572), chap. 50.

25. Bauer and Stanish 2001; Salomon and Urioste 1991, 111; Urton 1990, 3.

26. Gyarmati and Varga 1999; C. Julien 1998; Morales 1976 (1556); Wachtel 1982.

27. For example, Trimborn et al. 1975.

28. Cieza de León 1988 (ca. 1550), chap. 48.

29. Cabello de Balboa 1951 (1586), bk. 3, chap. 15, p. 304.

30. Cabello de Balboa 1951 (1586), bk. 3, chap. 15, p. 304; Lavallée 1983; Monzón 1965a (1586), 1965b (1586), 1965c (1586); Sarmiento de Gamboa 1965 (1572); Schreiber 1993; Valdez and Vivanco 1994.

31. Betanzos 1999 (1551), pt. 1, chap. 18; Cieza de León 1988 (ca. 1550), chap. 48; see González-Carré et al. 1981 on Vilcashuamán.

32. Cieza de León 1988 (ca. 1550), chap. 49; D'Altroy 1987, 1992; D'Altroy et al. 2001; González-Carré 1992; Hastorf et al. 1989; Le Blanc 1981; Matos 1994; Parsons et al. 2000.

33. Grosboll 1993; Helmer 1955–56 (1549); C. Julien 1982; Morris and Thompson 1985; Ortíz de Zúñiga 1967 (1562), 1972 (1562); Schreiber 1987, 1993.

34. Costin et al. 1989; D'Altroy et al. 2001; Hastorf 1993; Le Vine 1992; Morris 1967, 1982; Morris and Thompson 1985; Schreiber 1993.

35. Matos 1995.

36. Le Vine 1987; Monzón 1965b (1586).

37. Espinoza 1973; Fornée 1965 (1586); La Lone and La Lone 1987.

38. Morris n.d.

39. For example, Dearborn et al. 1998.

40. For example, Schreiber 1993, 111–12.

41. Salomon 1986b.

42. See Alcina Franch 1978; Bray 1992; Engwall 1995; Pease 1982.

43. Salomon 1986a, 1986b, 1987.

44. Salomon 1986a.

45. Covey and Elson n.d. See Schjellerup 1997 for a discussion of the archaeology and ethnohistory of the Chachapoya region.

46. Murra 1986.

47. See Rowe 1982.

48. Idrovo 1985.

49. Parsons et al. 1997.

50. Morris 1985; Salomon 1986a.

51. For example, Berthelot 1986; Chaumeil and Fraysse-Chaumeil 1982; Earle 1994; C. Julien 1985, 1998; Renard de Casevitz 1981; Saignes 1981, 1986; Salomon 1987; Schjellerup 1997.

52. Schreiber 1992.

53. For example, Morris 2004.

54. Pease 1982; Ramírez 1990.

55. Cieza de León 1988 (ca. 1550), chap. 58.

56. For example, Katterman and Riddell 1994.

57. Canziani 1992; Lumbreras 2001.

58. Castro and Ortega Morejón 1938 (1558), 237.

59. Hyslop 1985.

60. Menzel 1959.

61. Bürgi 1993; Dillehay 1977; Mathews 1989; Ramírez 1990; Van Buren et al. 1993.

62. Hyslop 1984; Morris 1998; Wallace 1998.

63. For example, Conrad 1977; Hayashida 1998; Marcus 1987; Menzel 1959.

64. Menzel 1959.

65. It is possible that the Incas used the Pachacamac shrine network to extend their ideological and religious authority along the central coast. At least eight secondary shrines were said to be relatives of Pachacamac, and the Incas may have increased their authority by dominating Pachacamac and simultaneously sponsoring the veneration of local shrines (Albórnoz 1989 [ca. 1581/85], 190–91; Dávila Briceño 1965 [1586]; Salomon and Urioste 1991, 101–6; Santillán 1968 [1563]). When a Spanish contingent under Hernando Pizarro looted the shrine at Pachacamac, the lords of at least seven coastal polities assembled at Pachacamac to offer their loyalty to the Spaniards, indicating that it had become the most important site for integrating the central coast (see the account of Miguel de Estete, in Xérez 1985 [1534], 138).

66. P. Pizarro 1986 (1571).

67. For example, Conrad 1981; Covey 2000; Hayashida 1998; Marcus 1987; Menzel 1959.

68. The Chimú empire has traditionally served as the cultural place marker for the Late Intermediate Period (ca. AD 1000–1476), while the Inca empire was considered to exemplify the Late Horizon (AD 1476–1532). Such a view is no longer tenable. Theresa Lange Topic (1990) has identified three phases of Chimú development: (1) the poorly understood consolidation of the area immediately surrounding Chan Chan, the Chimú capital (AD 900 to AD 1000 or AD 1050), (2) expansion to incorporate coastal valleys within about 150 kilometers of the capital, in the twelfth and thirteenth centuries, and (3) a second wave of imperial expansion along the coast in the fourteenth century. It now appears that the Inca polity underwent similar developmental phases only about a century or so later than they began on the north coast, and that Inca imperial strategies (the third phase of development) were more successful than those of the Chimú.

69. Sarmiento de Gamboa 1965 (1572), chap. 40.

70. See Rowe 1948.
71. Zárate 1995 (1555), chap. 14, p. 59.
72. Conrad 1981; Ramírez 1990.
73. See Ramírez 1995.
74. See Hayashida 1998; Narváez 1995, 90–101; Sandweiss 1995; Sandweiss and Narváez 1995; Shimada 1990; Willey 1953; Wilson 1988.
75. D. Julien 1993; J. Topic and T. Topic 1993.
76. For example, Berthelot 1986; Millones and Schaedel 1980.
77. Rostworowski 1970c; Salomon 1986a.
78. Salomon 1987.
79. Morris 1985; Murra 1972, 1976; see Stanish 1992.
80. Covey 2000; C. Julien 1985.
81. Dillehay 1977; Flannery et al. 1989, 107–16; Murra 1965; Parsons et al. 2000.
82. Flores 1985; Núñez and Dillehay 1995.
83. D'Altroy 2001b; D'Altroy and Earle 1985; Earle 1994.
84. Sancho de la Hoz 1962 (1534), chap. 17.
85. For example, Berthelot 1986; Blower 2001; Chaumeil and Fraysse-Chaumeil 1982; D'Altroy et al. 2000; Earle 1994; Helmer 1955–56 (1549); Lynch 1993; Saignes 1981; Schjellerup 1997.
86. Dillehay 1977; Rostworowski 1963b, 1988b; Zimmerer 1996.
87. See Murra 1995.
88. C. Julien 1982.
89. Hyslop 1988; Lee 1998; Salomon 1986a, 1986b.
90. Renard de Casevitz 1981; Saignes 1981; cf. Pärssinen 1992.
91. See C. Julien 1998.
92. See D'Altroy et al. 2000; Earle 1994; González 1983.
93. González 1983; León 1981.

Chapter Ten

1. Garcilaso de la Vega 1965 (1609), bk. 1, chap. 17; Guaman Poma de Ayala 1980 (1615).
2. Garcilaso de la Vega 1965 (1609), bk. 1, chaps. 20, 23; Guaman Poma de Ayala 1980 (1615); Pachacuti Yamqui Salcamaygua 1993 (17th century); see Bauer 1992, 19–32; Zuidema 1983.
3. Molina 1989 (1575), 73–96; cf. Cobo 1964 (1653), bk. 11, chap. 29.
4. One noteworthy difference between the Citua boundaries and groups of Incas-of-Privilege is that in the Citua the boundary for the province of Antisuyu was marked at Pisaq, just 20 kilometers from Cusco. While this might signify control over the north side of the Vilcanota Valley, it is interesting to note that the indigenous Cuyos were not Incas-of-Privilege, although more distant Antisuyu groups like the Poques and Lares may have been. This suggests that some *montaña* groups and others living at the edges of the imperial heartland region were not directly involved in the early processes of state formation but were accorded their ethnic status during the imperial period.

5. Ocampo 1999 (1610), 208–9. In the 1570s, much of the native population of the Andean region was forced to abandon villages and settle in new Spanish-style towns for more effective colonial administration.

6. Ocampo 1999 (1610), 209.

7. D'Altroy 1992, 86–93.

8. La Lone and La Lone 1987; Rostworowski 1962.

9. See D'Altroy and Hastorf 1984; Gyarmati and Varga 1999; Le Vine 1992; Morris 1967, 1992.

10. D'Altroy and Earle 1985; see Earle 1994.

11. D'Altroy et al. 2000.

12. P. Pizarro 1986 (1571); see Falcón 1918 (1567), 153.

13. For example, Molina 1989 (1575).

14. Toledo 1940f (1571); ADC Colección Betancur, vol. 7 (compiled in 1795); AGI Patronato 231 N7 R12 (n.d.), f. 1.

15. ADC Libro de Matriculas, Industria, Indígenas y Eclesiasticas: Provincia de Calca (1722); Glave and Remy 1983, 7; Villanueva 1970, 77. Other towns outside the Cusco Basin known to have a *Cusco ayllu* include Accha, Zurite, and Oropesa (Cueva 1982 [1690], 199; Decoster and Bauer 1997, no. 1338; Zamora 1982 [1689], 471).

16. Toledo 1940f (1571).

17. ADC Colección Betancur, vol. 7 (compiled in 1795), f. 446; Espinoza 1977.

18. For example, AGN Tit. Prop. L. 2, C. 17 (1587).

19. Rostworowski 1970a; Rowe 1987; Toledo 1940f (1571), 149–58.

20. See Rostworowski 1962.

21. See Murra 1982; Rowe 1982.

22. See Toledo 1940a–g (1570–72).

23. Toledo 1940e (1571), 108–12; Toledo 1940f (1571), 158–67.

24. ADC Colección Betancur, vol. 7 (compiled in 1795), f. 319v–408.

25. Toledo 1940e (1571), 115.

26. Toledo 1940e (1571), 109.

27. Toledo 1940e (1571), 113; Toledo 1940f (1571), 126.

28. Toledo 1940e (1571), 108.

29. Toledo 1940f (1571), 142–43. Witnesses in a 1569 document attest to keeping birds and fish for Huayna Capac in ponds in the Yucay Valley (ADC Archivo de Urubamba, Varios [1569], f. 8).

30. Toledo 1940e (1571), 114; Toledo 1940f (1571), 159.

31. AGN Tit. Prop. L. 2, C. 17 (1587), f. 31v, 33; ADC Colección Betancur, vol. 7 (compiled in 1795), f. 210v, 353v.

32. See Flannery et al. 1989; Murra 1965.

33. Toledo 1940e (1571), 114–15; Toledo 1940f (1571), 134.

34. Toledo 1940f (1571), 160.

35. Betanzos 1999 (1551), bk. 1, chap. 17.

36. See also Betanzos 1999 (1551), bk. 1, chap. 21; Sarmiento de Gamboa 1965 (1572), chaps. 31, 63.

37. Sarmiento de Gamboa (1965 [1572], chap. 67); Cabello de Balboa (1951 [1586], bk. 3, chap. 31) states that the women still in the *akllawasi* were spared.

38. For example, Anonymous *Relación* 1992, 90–92; Gasca 1998 (1551–53), 36; Guaman Poma de Ayala 1980 (1615), f. 299–301; Molina 'El Almagrista' 1968 (ca. 1553), 82; H. Pizarro 1959 (1533), 81–82; P. Pizarro 1986 (1571).

39. See Murra 1965, 1989.

40. Gade 1975, 114–15, 120.

41. For example, P. Pizarro 1986 (1571).

42. Bauer 1996; Guaman Poma de Ayala 1980 (1615); Murra 1960.

43. Bauer 2004.

44. Burns 1999, 59; Niles 1999, 150.

45. ADC, Colección Betancur, vol. 7 (compiled in 1795), f. 108v, 113v, 119v, 125, 130, 135v, 140v, 146. See Matienzo (1967 [1567], pt. 1, chap. 50)—he defines *camayos* as permanent coca laborers in the *montaña*.

46. ADC Corregimiento, Causas Ordinarias, L. 1, C. 11 (1572).

47. Rostworowski 1962; ADC Colección Betancur, vol. 7 (compiled in 1795), f. 332v, 333v, 334v.

48. For example Rostworowski 1963b.

49. Gade 1975; C. Julien 2001; Zimmerer 1996, 44–55.

50. ADC Educandas 2 (1568b); see Drew 1984.

51. See ADC Corregimiento, Causas Ordinarias, L. 1, C. 11 (1572); Rowe 1987, 1990.

52. Rostworowski 1963b.

53. Gasca 1974 (1549), 541; Rostworowski 1970a, 230–31; ADC Colección Betancur, vol. 7 (compiled in 1795), f. 89v, 107v, 112v, 118, 118v.

54. Espinoza 1974.

55. Cook 1975 (1570s), 113, 114.

56. Toledo 1940f (1571), 149–58.

57. See ADC Corregimiento, Causas Ordinarias, L. 1, C. 7 (1568a); Hemming 1970, 367–69; Lizárraga 1968 (1605), 64; Matienzo 1967 (1567), pt. 1, chaps. 55–51; Rostworowski 1977a, 139.

58. ADC Colección Betancur, vol. 7 (compiled in 1795), f. 320v.

59. For example, f. 345v, f. 356v.

60. See Niles 1993, 146–50.

61. P. Pizarro 1986 (1571), 202–6.

62. See Rowe 1985a. At the time of the Spanish Conquest, the descent groups of Hurin Cusco represented the first five Inca rulers, while those of Hanan Cusco represented those from the sixth Inca ruler onward.

63. See Elson 2003 for a discussion of elite interaction patterns in early state systems.

64. For example, Sarmiento de Gamboa 1965 (1572), chaps. 47, 54, 62.

65. Betanzos 1999 (1551), bk. 1, chap. 5.

66. Sarmiento de Gamboa 1965 (1572), chap. 67.

67. See Niles 1999, 109–13. Hemming (1970, 508–11) lists several of Huayna Capac's children (six sons, five daughters). The sons mentioned in Sarmiento's chronicle include Ninan Cuyoche, Atahuallpa, Huascar, Topa Huallpa, Manco Inca, Paullu Topa, Titu Atauchi, Huanca Auqui, and Topa Atao.

68. See Rostworowski 1960.

69. Cobo 1964 (1653), bk. 14, chap. 15.

70. Cobo 1964 (1653), bk. 11, chap. 13; bk. 14, chap. 15; Sarmiento de Gamboa 1965 (1572), chap. 51.

71. Cabello de Balboa 1951 (1586), bk. 3, chap. 20; Sarmiento de Gamboa 1965 (1572), chap. 55. According to Cieza de León (1988 [ca. 1550], chap. 38), the eighth Inca ruler, Viracocha Inca, was chosen by the Cusco elite on the suggestion of a woman.

72. C. Julien 1982, 1988.

73. For example, López de Velasco 1971 (1574), 245; ADC Colección Betancur, vol. 7 (compiled in 1795), f. 107, 170v.

74. Niles 1999.

75. For example, Rostworowski 1983, 167–73.

76. Toledo 1940f (1571), 141–49. This man served an Inca woman, Catalina Sisa, at the time he gave his testimony.

77. Toledo 1940e (1571), 112–18.

78. Toledo 1940f (1571), 149–58.

79. Covey and Elson n.d.; Rostworowski 1962; Villanueva 1970.

80. Rostworowski 1962.

81. For example, Huayna Capac is said by Cabello de Balboa (1951 [1586], bk. 3, chap. 22) to have sent a statue of his mother, Mama Ocllo, to put down a provincial rebellion.

82. P. Pizarro 1986 (1571).

Chapter Eleven

1. For example, Cobo 1964 (1653), bk. 12, chap. 10; Garcilaso de la Vega 1965 (1609), bk. 4, chaps. 22–23; Murúa 1987 (1590), bk. 1, chap. 19.

References

Archival Documents

Archivo Departamental del Cusco (ADC)

1568a   Corregimiento, Causas Ordinarias, L. 1, C. 7 Autos de información de testigos que presenta don Gonzalo Rodríguez, en nombre de Hernando Illa y demás caciques principales de los indios de Calca, encomendados en don Arias Maldonado, sobre que en la mita de las chácaras de coca de Toayma y Quisquín, han muerto mucha cantidad de indios.

1568b   Educandas 2.

1569   Archivo de Urubamba, Varios.

1572   Corregimiento, Causas Ordinarias, L. 1, C. 11 Autos seguidos sobre las cuentas presentadas por Pedro Alonso Carrasco y García de Melo, donde los comisarios Reales tomaron cuenta de los tributos de la encomienda de don Arias Maldonado.

1589   Manuscritos 17.

1595   Fondo Corregimiento, L. 2, C. 23 Autos sobre la confirmación de bienes hecha por don García Hurtado de Mendoza en la persona de Martín Ataopoma, cacique, segunda persona del repartimiento de San Nicolás de Zurite del ayllu Mayo Hurinsaya, de la encomienda del general Miguel Angel Philipón.

1626   Fondo Corregimiento, L. 8, C. 1 Autos por tierras seguidos por don Francisco Pumaurco Supa, cacique de Anta y de los indios del ayllu Çanco, encomendados en el marqués de Oropesa, contra Juan de Chavarría y Juan de Orosco para que cumplan con la visita y repartición de tierras. . . .

1722   Libro de Matriculas, Industria, Indígenas y Eclesiasticas: Provincia de Calca.

1733   Fondo Corregimiento, L. 31, C. 9 Carta de justicia requisitoria, que presenta el corregidor de Abancay, don Simón Gutiérrez de Caviedes, para que se trabe ejecución de los bienes del maestre de campo don Mateo Quispe Guamán, segunda persona y cacique de los ayllus Anansaya, Urinsaya y Equecoc, reducidas en la villa de Anta . . .

1766   Fondo Corregimiento L. 47, C. 17.

1768   Fondo Corregimiento L. 49, C. 29.
   compiled in 1795 Colección Betancur, vol. 7, Genealogía de la casa, ascendencia y descendencia de Dn Diego Sairetupac Mango Capac Yupangui Ynga . . . [Betancur Collection documents].

Archivo General de Indias (AGI)
    n.d.   Patronato 231 N7 R12 Pleito de don Francisco Marca Yuto sobre casas y chacaras de Paullopata.

Archivo General de la Nación (AGN)
    1557   Tit. Prop. L. 1, C. 3 Títulos de la hacienda y tierras de Amantuy junto al pueblo de Maras, Obispado del Cuzco.
    1559   Causas Civiles L. 4, C. 26 Autos seguidos por don Diego Ataurimache, cacique de Calca, contra el corregidor y justicia mayor de la ciudad del Cuzco, Licenciado Bautista Muñoz.
    1587   Tit. Prop. L. 2, C. 17 Titulo de las tierras de Miscabra en el valle de Vicho, jurisdicción de Pisac, provincia de Calca y Lares, que en 1714 pertenecían a la familia Ramos Cisneros y en sus principios pertenecieron a Domingo Díaz.

Primary Sources

Acosta, José de
    1940 [1590]   *Historia natural y moral de las Indias.* Ed. Edmundo O'Gorman. Mexico City: Fondo de Cultura Económica.

Acuña, Francisco de
    1965 [1586]   Relación fecha por el corregidor de los Chumbibilcas don Francisco de Acuña, por mandado de su Ex.ª del señor don Fernando de Torres y Portugal, visorrey destos reynos, para la discrepción de las Yndias que Su Magestad manda hacer. Biblioteca de Autores Españoles 183:310–25. Madrid: Ediciones Atlas.

Albórnoz, Cristóbal de
    1989 [1581/85]   Instrucción para descubrir todas las guacas del Piru y sus camayos y haziendas. In *Fábulas y mitos de los incas,* ed. Henrique Urbano and Pierre Duviols, 161–98. Madrid: Historia 16.

Andagoya, Pascual de
    1986 [1541/42]   *Relación y documentos,* ed. Adrian Blazquez. Madrid, Historia 16.

Anonymous *Discurso*
    1906 [ca. 1570]   Discurso de la sucesión y gobierno de los Yngas. In *Juicio de límites entre el Perú y Bolivia: prueba peruana presentada al gobierno de la Republica de Argentina, tomo octavo: Chunchos,* ed. Victor M. Maurtua, 149–65. Madrid: Hijos de M.G. Hernández.

Anonymous *Parecer*
    1995 [1571]   Dominio de los yngas en el Perú, y del que Su Majestad tiene en dichos reinos. In *El anónimo de Yucay, frente a Bartolomé de las Casas: Edición crítica del parecer de Yucay (1571),* ed. Isacio Pérez Fernández, 111–71. Cusco: Centro de Estudios Regionales Andinos "Bartolomé de las Casas."

Anonymous *Relación*
    1992   *Relación de las costumbres antiguas de los naturales del Piru.* Ed. Henrique Urbano and Ana Sánchez. Madrid: Historia 16.

Arriaga, Pablo Joesph de
1999 [1621] *La extirpación de la idolatria en el Piru.* Cusco: Centro de Estudios Rurales Andinos "Bartolomé de las Casas."

Bertonio, Ludovico
1956 [1612] *Vocabulario de la lengua aymara.* La Paz: Ediciones CERES.

Betanzos, Juan de
1999 [1551–57] *Suma y narración de los incas.* Cusco: Universidad Nacional de San Antonio Abad del Cusco.

Cabello de Balboa, Miguel
1951 [1586] *Miscelánea antártica, una historia del Perú antiguo,* ed. L. E. Valcárcel. Lima: Universidad Nacional Mayor de San Marcos, Instituto de Etnología.

Calancha, Antonio de la
1974–82 [1639] *Crónica moralizada del Orden de San Agustín en el Perú.* Lima: Universidad Nacional Mayor de San Marcos.

Castro, Cristóbal de, and Diego de Ortega Morejón
1938 [1558] Relaçion y declaraçion del modo que este valle de chincha y sus comarcanos se governavan Antes que / oviese yngas y despues q(ue) los vuo hasta q(ue) los (christian)os e(n)traron en esta tierra. In *Quellen zur Kulturgeschichte des prä Kolumbinischen Amerika,* ed. Hermann Trimborn, 236–46. Stuttgart.

Cieza de León, Pedro de
1986 [1553] *Crónica del Perú, primera parte.* 2nd ed. Lima: Pontificia Universidad Católica del Perú.
1988 [ca. 1550] *El señorío de los incas.* Ed. Manuel Ballesteros. Madrid: Historia 16.

Cobo, Bernabé
1964 [1653] *Obras del P. Bernabé Cobo de la Compañía de Jesus.* Ed. P. Francisco Mateos, vol. 2. Biblioteca de Autores Españoles 92. Madrid: Ediciones Atlas.

Cook, Noble David (ed.)
1975 [1570s] *Tasa de la visita general de Francisco de Toledo.* Lima: Universidad Nacional Mayor de San Marcos.

Cortés de Monroy, Pedro
1982 [1690] Relación de la dotrina de Anta. In *Cvzco 1689: Informes de los párrocos al obispo Mollinedo: Economía y sociedad en el sur andino,* ed. Horacio Villanueva Urteaga, 189–96. Cusco: Centro de Estudios Rurales Andinos "Bartolomé de las Casas."

Cueva, Pedro de la
1982 [1690] Relación de la dotrina de Zurite. In *Cvzco 1689: Informes de los párrocos al obispo Mollinedo: Economía y sociedad en el sur andino,* ed. Horacio Villanueva Urteaga, 199–203. Cusco: Centro de Estudios Rurales Andinos "Bartolomé de las Casas."

Dávila Brizeño, Diego
1965 [1586] Descripción y relación de la provincia de los Yauyos todas. . . .

In *Relaciones geográficas de Indias, t. I, 155–65.* Biblioteca de Autores Españoles 183. Madrid: Ediciones Atlas.

Diez de San Miguel, Garci
1964 [1567] *Visita hecha a la provincia de Chucuito.* Documentos regionales para la etnohistoria Andina 1. Lima: Ediciones de la Casa de la Cultura del Perú.

Falcón, Francisco
1918 [1567] *Representación hecha por el licenciado Francisco Falcón en el concilio provincial, sobre los daños y molestias que se hacen a los Indios.* Colección de Libros y Documentos referentes a la historia del Perú 9:133–76. Lima: Sanmartí.

Fernándcz, Diego "El Palentino"
1963 [1571] *Primera, y segunda Parte de la Historia del Perú.* In *Crónicas del Perú, t. I–II,* ed. Juan Pérez de Tudela Bueso. Biblioteca de Autores Españoles 164–65. Madrid: Ediciones Atlas.

Fornée, Niculoso de
1965 [1586] Breve relación de la tierra del corregimiento de Abancay, de que es corregidor Niculoso de Fornée. Bilbioteca de Autores Españoles 184:16–30. Madrid: Ediciones Atlas.

Garcilaso de la Vega, "El Inca"
1965 [1609] Los comentarios reales de los incas. In *Obras Completas,* ed. Carmelo Sáenz de Santa María. Biblioteca de Autores Españoles 132–35. Madrid: Ediciones Atlas.

Gasca, Pedro de la
1974 [1549] Carta del licenciado Pedro de la Gasca al Consejo de Indias, avisando las disposiciones que se habian adoptado respecto al repartimiento de coca, que tuvo Francisco Pizarro—Los Reyes, 16 de setiembre de 1549. In *Cartas de Indias,* 2:541–44. Biblioteca de Autores Españoles 265. Madrid: Ediciones Atlas.

1998 [1551–53] *Descripción del Perú (1551–1553).* Cusco: Centro de Estudios Regionales Andinos "Bartolomé de las Casas."

González Holguin, Diego
1842 [1607] *Gramática y arte nueva de la lengua general de todo el Perú llamada lengua Qquichua o lengua del Inca.* Genoa: Pagano.

1989 [1608] *Vocabulario de la lengua general de todo el Perú llamada lengua qquichua o del Inca.* Lima: Universidad Nacional Mayor de San Marcos.

Guaman Poma de Ayala, Felipe
1980 [1615] *El primer nueva corónica y buen gobierno.* Ed. J. V. Murra and R. Adorno. Mexico City: Siglo Veintiuno.

Gutiérrez de Santa Clara, Pedro
1963–65 [16th century] *Historia de las guerras civiles del Perú y de otros sucesos de las Indias.* Biblioteca de Autores Españoles 165–67. Madrid: Ediciones Atlas.

Gutiérrez Flores, P., and J. Ramírez Segarra
1993 [1574] Tasa de 1574. In *Toledo y los Lupacas: Las tasas de 1574 y*

1579, ed. C. Julien, K. Angelis, A. Voβ, and A. Hauschild, 1–88. Bonn: Estudios Americanistas de Bonn.

Helmer, Marie
1955–56 [1549]   "La visitación de lo yndios chupachos" inca et encomendero 1549. *Travaux de l'Institut Français d'Études Andines* 5: 3–50.

khipukamayuqkuna (Callapiña, Supno, and others)
1974 [1542/1609]   *Relación de la descendencia, gobierno y conquista de los incas*. Lima: Editorial Jurídica.

Las Casas, Bartolomé de
1939 [1550s]   *Las antiguas gentes del Perú*. Colección de libros y documentos referentes a la historia del Perú, series 2, vol. 11. Lima.

Lizárraga, Reginaldo de
1968 [1605]   Descripción breve de toda la tierra del Perú, Tucumán, Río de la Plata y Chile. Biblioteca de Autores Españoles 216:1–213. Madrid: Ediciones Atlas.

López de Izturizaga, Juan, and Alonso Román de Baños
1973 [1585]   Información sobre las chacras de coca, ají, algodón y otras frutas que cultivaban los mitimaes del valle de Pachachaca en la provincia de Abancay, a pedimento de Juan López de Izturizaga, el nuevo señor de ellos y de Alonso Román de Baños, procurador de los caciques de Ninamarca. In Colonias de mitmas multiples en Abancay, siglos XV y XVI, by Waldemar Espinoza Soriano. Una información inédita de 1575 para la etnohistoria andina. *Revista del Museo Nacional* 39: 267–75.

López de Velasco, Juan
1971 [1574]   *Geografía y descripción universal de las Indias*. Biblioteca de Autores Españoles 248. Madrid: Ediciones Atlas.

Matienzo, Juan de
1967 [1567]   *Gobierno del Perú*. Travaux de l'Institut Français d'Études Andines 11. Lima: Travaux de l'Institut Français d'Études Andines.

Mercado de Peñalosa, P. de
1965 [1586]   Relación de la provincia de los Pacajes. In *Relaciones Geográficas de Indias—Perú*, ed. M. Jiménez de la Espada, 1:334–41. Biblioteca de Autores Españoles 183. Madrid: Ediciones Atlas.

Molina, Cristóbal de, 'El Almagrista' (also attributed to Bartolomé de Segovia)
1968 [ca. 1553]   Relación de muchas cosas acaescidas en el Perú. Biblioteca de Autores Españoles 209:57–95. Madrid: Ediciones Atlas.

Molina, Cristóbal de, 'El Cusqueño'
1989 [1575]   Relación de las fábulas i ritos de los ingas hecha por Cristóbal de Molina, cura de la parroquia de Nuestra Señora de los Remedios, de el Hospital de los naturales de la ciudad de el Cuzco, dirigida al reverendísimo señor Obispo don Sebastián de el Artaum, del consejo de su magestad. In *Fábulas y mitos de los incas*, ed. Henrique Urbano and Pierre Duviols, 47–134. Madrid: Historia 16.

Montesinos, Fernando de
1882 [1642]   *Memorias Antiguas Historiales y Políticas del Perú*. Madrid: Miguel Ginesta.

Monzón, L. de

1965a [1586]   Descripción de la tierra del repartimiento de Atunsora, encomendado en Hernando Palomino, jurisdicción de la ciudad de Guamanga. Año de 1586. In *Relaciones Geográficas de Indias (Perú)*, ed.
M. Jiménez de la Espada, 220–25. Biblioteca de Autores Españoles
183. Madrid: Ediciones Atlas.

1965b [1586]   Descripción de la tierra del repartimiento de San Francisco
de Atunrucana y Laramati, encomendado en Don Pedro de Cor-
dova, jurisdicción de la ciudad de Guamanga. Año de 1586. In *Relaciones Geográficas de Indias (Perú)*, ed. M. Jiménez de la Espada,
226–36. Biblioteca de Autores Españoles 183. Madrid: Ediciones
Atlas.

1965c [1586]   Descripción de la tierra del repartimiento de los Rucanas An-
tamarcas de la corona real, jurisdicción de la ciudad de Guamanga. Año
de 1586. In *Relaciones Geográficas de Indias (Perú)*, ed. M. Jiménez
de la Espada, 237–48. Biblioteca de Autores Españoles 183. Madrid:
Ediciones Atlas.

Morales, Adolfo de

1976 [1556]   Repartimiento de tierras por el Inca Huayna Capac (Testimo-
nio de un documento de 1556). Cochabamba, Bolivia: Universidad
Mayor Boliviano de San Simon, Departamento de Arqueología, Museo
Arqueológico.

Murúa, Martín de

1987 [1590]   *Historia general del Perú*. Madrid: Historia 16.

Ocampo, Baltasar de

1999 [1610]   Account of the Province of Vilcabamba and a Narrative of the
Execution of the Inca Tupac Amaru. In *History of the Incas*, trans. and
ed. Clements Markham, 203–47. Mineola, NY: Dover Publications.

Oliva, Giovanni Anello

1998 [1598]   *Historia del Reino y Provincias del Perú*. Ed. Carlos Gálvez
Peña. Lima: Pontificia Universidad Católica del Perú.

Olivera y Dolmos, Juan de

1982 [1689]   Relación de la doctrina de Huarocondo. In *Cvzco 1689: Informes de los párrocos al obispo Mollinedo: Economía y sociedad en
el sur andino*, ed. Horacio Villanueva Urteaga, 184–87. Cusco: Centro de Estudios Rurales Andinos "Bartolomé de las Casas."

Ondegardo, Polo de

1916a [1571]   Relación de los fundamentos acerca del notable daño que
resulta de no guardar a los Indios sus fueros. Colección de Libros y
Documentos Referentes a la Historia del Perú, series 1, 3:45–188.
Lima: Sanmartí.

1916b [1559]   Lor errores y svpersticiones de los indios, sacadas del tratado
y aueriguación que hizo el licenciado Polo. Colección de Libros y Documentos Referentes a la Historia del Perú, series 1, 3:3–43. Lima:
Sanmartí.

1917 [1571]   Del linage de los Ingas y como conquistaron. Colección de Libros y Documentos Referentes a la Historia del Perú, series 1, 4:45–94. Lima: Sanmartí.

1940 [1561] Informe del Licenciado Juan Polo de Ondegardo al Licenciado Briviesca de Muñatones sobre la perpetuidad de las encomiendas en el Perú. *Revista Histórica* 13: 125–96.

Ortiz de Zúñiga, Iñigo
1967 [1562] *Visita de la Provincia de León de Huánuco.* Vol. 1. Ed. John V. Murra. Huánuco: Universidad Hermilio Valdizán.
1972 [1562] *Visita de la Provincia de León de Huánuco.* Vol. 2. Ed. John V. Murra. Huánuco: Universidad Hermilio Valdizán.

Pachacuti Yamqui Salcamaygua, Joan de Santa Cruz
1993 [17th century] *Relación de antigüedades deste reyno del Piru.* Ed. Pierre Duviols and César Itier. Cusco: Centro de Estudios Rurales Andinos, "Bartolomé del Las Casas."

Pérez Bocanegra, Juan
[1631] *Ritval Formvlario, E Institvcion De Cvras, Para Administrar A Los Natvrales De este Reyno, los sanctos Sacramentos del Baptismo, Confirmacion, Eucaristia, y Viatico, Penitencia, Extremauncion, y Matrimono, Con aduertencias muy necessarias.* Lima.

Pizarro, Hernando
1959 [1533] Letter to the Audiencia de Santo Domingo, 23 November, 1533. In *Cartas del Perú (1524–1543),* ed. Raúl Porras Barrenechea, 77–84. Colección de documentos inéditos para la historia del Perú. Lima: Sociedad de Bibliófilos Peruanos.

Pizarro, Pedro
1986 [1571] *Relación del descubrimiento y conquista de los reinos del Peru.* Ed. Guillermo Lohmann Villena. Lima: Pontificia Universidad Católica del Perú.

Ramos Gavilán, Alonso
1988 [1589] *Historia de Nuestra Señora de Copacabana.* Ed. Ignacio Prado Pastor. Lima: Talleres Gráficos P.L. Villanueva.

Ricardo, Antonio (ed.)
1951 [1586] *Vocabulario y phrasis en la lengua general de los Indios del Perú, llamada Quichua.* Publicaciones del Cuarto Centenario. Lima: Facultad de Letras, Instituto de Historia, Universidad Nacional Mayor de San Marcos.

Salomon, Frank, and George Urioste (eds.)
1991 *The Huarochirí Manuscript: A Testament of Ancient and Colonial Andean Religion.* Austin: University of Texas Press.

Sancho de la Hoz, Pedro
1962 [1534] *Relación de la conquista del Perú.* Madrid: Ediciones J. Porrua Turanzas.

Santillán, Hernando de
1968 [1563] *Relación del orígen, descendencia, política y gobierno de los incas.* Biblioteca de Autores Españoles 209:97–149. Madrid: Ediciones Atlas.

Santo Tomás, Domingo de
    1951 [1560] *Lexicon, o vocabulario de la lengua general del Perú.* Lima:
    Instituto de Historia.
    1995 [1560] *Grammatica, o arte de la lengua general de los indios de los
    reynos del Perú.* Cusco: Centro de Estudios Rurales Andinos "Bar-
    tolomé de las Casas."
Sarmiento de Gamboa, Pedro
    1965 [1572] *Historia de los Incas: Segunda parte de la historia general lla-
    mada índica, la cual por mandado del excelentísimo señor don Fran-
    cisco de Toledo, virrey, gobernador y capitán general de los reinos
    del Perú y mayordomo de la casa real de Castilla, compuso el capitán
    Pedro Sarmiento de Gamboa.* Biblioteca de Autores Españoles 135.
    Madrid: Ediciones Atlas.
Segovia, Bartolomé de
    1943 [1553] See Cristóbal de Molina, 'El Almagrista.'
Toledo, Francisco de
    1940a [1570] Información hecha por orden de Don Francisco de Toledo
    en su visita de las Provincias del Perú . . . Concepción de Xauxa, 20
    Noviembre 1570. In *Don Francisco de Toledo, supremo organizador
    del Perú: Su vida, su obra (1515–1582). Tomo II: Sus informaciones
    sobre los incas (1570–1572),* ed. Roberto Levillier, 14–37. Buenos
    Aires: Espasa-Calpe.
    1940b [1570] Información hecha por orden del Virrey Don Francisco de
    Toledo . . . Guamanga, 14 de Diciembre 1570. In *Don Francisco de
    Toledo, supremo organizador del Perú: Su vida, su obra (1515–1582).
    Tomo II: Sus informaciones sobre los incas (1570–1572),* ed. Roberto
    Levillier, 38–46. Buenos Aires: Espasa-Calpe.
    1940c [1571] Cuatro informaciones levantadas por orden del Virrey Don
    Francisco de Toledo . . . Hechas en Tambo de Vilcas en 27 de Enero,
    en Tambo de Pina en 31 de Enero, en Limatambo en 6 y 7 de Febrero
    y en Tambo de Mayo en 10 de febrero de 1571. In *Don Francisco de
    Toledo, supremo organizador del Perú: Su vida, su obra (1515–1582).
    Tomo II: Sus informaciones sobre los incas (1570–1572),* ed. Roberto
    Levillier, 47–64. Buenos Aires: Espasa-Calpe.
    1940d [1571] Información hecha en el Cuzco por orden del Virrey Toledo
    . . . Cuzco, 13–18 Marzo 1571. In *Don Francisco de Toledo, supremo
    organizador del Perú: Su vida, su obra (1515–1582). Tomo II: Sus in-
    formaciones sobre los incas (1570–1572),* ed. Roberto Levillier, 65–98.
    Buenos Aires: Espasa-Calpe.
    1940e [1571] Información hecha por orden del Virrey Don Francisco de
    Toledo . . . Yucay, Marzo 19–Julio 2 de 1571. In *Don Francisco de
    Toledo, supremo organizador del Perú: Su vida, su obra (1515–1582).
    Tomo II: Sus informaciones sobre los incas (1570–1572),* ed. Roberto
    Levillier, 99–121. Buenos Aires: Espasa-Calpe.
    1940f [1571] Información comenzada en el Valle de Yucay . . . Junio 2–
    Septiembre 6 de 1571. In *Don Francisco de Toledo, supremo organi-
    zador del Perú: Su vida, su obra (1515–1582). Tomo II: Sus infor-*

maciones sobre los incas (1570–1572), ed. Roberto Levillier, 122–77. Buenos Aires: Espasa-Calpe.

1940g [1572]   Información hecha en el Cuzco . . . 4 Enero–27 Febrero de 1572. In *Don Francisco de Toledo, supremo organizador del Perú: Su vida, su obra (1515–1582). Tomo II: Sus informaciones sobre los incas (1570–1572)*, ed. Roberto Levillier, 182–95. Buenos Aires: Espasa-Calpe.

1940h [1572]   Información levantada por orden del Virrey Don Francisco de Toledo . . . Cuzco a 22 de Febrero de 1572. In *Don Francisco de Toledo, supremo organizador del Perú: Su vida, su obra (1515–1582). Tomo II: Sus informaciones sobre los incas (1570–1572)*, ed. Roberto Levillier, 196–204. Buenos Aires: Espasa-Calpe.

Vaca de Castro, Cristóbal
1908 [1543]   Ordenanza de tambos, distancias de unos a otros, modo de cargar los yndios y obligaciones de las justicias respectivas. *Revista Histórica* 3(4): 427–92.

Valverde, fray Vicente de
1959 [1539]   Letter to the Emperor, 20 March 1539. In *Cartas del Perú (1524–1543)*, ed. Raúl Porras Barrenechea, 311–35. Colección de documentos inéditos para la historia del Perú. Lima: Sociedad de Bibliófilos Peruanos.

Vázquez de Espinoza, Antonio
1969 [ca. 1600]   *Compendio y descripción de las Indias Occidentales.* Biblioteca de Autores Espanoles 231. Madrid: Ediciones Atlas.

Villanueva Urteaga, Horacio
1970   Documento sobre Yucay en el siglo XVI. *Revista del Archivo Histórico del Cuzco* 13: 1–148.

Xérez, Francisco de
1985 [1534]   Verdadera relación de la conquista del Perú. . . . In *Verdadera relación de la conquista del Perú*, ed. Concepción Bravo, 57–166. Madrid: Historia 16.

Zamora, Francisco de
1982 [1689]   Relación de la doctrina de Accha Urinsaya. In *Cvzco 1689: Informes de los párrocos al obispo Mollinedo: Economía y sociedad en el sur andino*, ed. Horacio Villanueva Urteaga, 471–76. Cusco: Centro de Estudios Rurales Andinos "Bartolomé de las Casas."

Zárate, Agustín de
1995 [1555]   *Historia del descubrimiento y conquista del Perú.* Ed. Franklin Pease and Teodoro Hampe Martínez. Lima: Pontificia Universidad Católica del Perú.

Secondary Sources

Abercrombie, Thomas A.
1998   *Pathways of Memory and Power: Ethnography and History among an Andean People.* Madison: University of Wisconsin Press.

Adams, R. E. W., and Richard C. Jones
   1981   Spatial Patterns and Regional Growth among Classic Maya Cities. *American Antiquity* 46(2): 301–22.
Agurto Calvo, Santiago
   1984   *Lima prehispánica.* Lima: Municipalidad de Lima.
Albarracin-Jordan, Juan, and James E. Mathews
   1990   *Asentamientos prehispánicos del valle de Tiwanaku.* Vol. 1. La Paz, Bolivia.
Alcina Franch, José
   1978   Ingapirca: Arquitectura y áreas de asentamiento. *Revista de Antropología Americana* 8: 127–46.
Algaze, Guillermo
   1993   Expansionary Dynamics of Some Early Pristine States. *American Anthropologist* 95(2): 304–33.
Allen, Catherine J.
   1988   *The Hold Life Has: Coca and Cultural Identity in an Andean Community.* Washington, DC: Smithsonian Institution Press.
Anders, Martha B.
   1990   Maymi: Un sitio del Horizonte Medio en el valle de Pisco. *Gaceta Arqueológica Andina* 17: 27–40.
   1991   Structure and Function at the Planned Site of Azangaro: Cautionary Notes for the Model of Huari as a Centralized Secular State. In *Huari Administrative Structures: Prehistoric Monumental Architecture and State Government,* ed. William H. Isbell and Gordon F. McEwan, 165–97. Washington, DC: Dumbarton Oaks Research Library and Collection.
Angles Vargas, Victor A.
   1967   *P'isaq, Gran metropoli inca.* Cuzco.
Argyle, W. J.
   1966   *The Fon of Dahomey: A History and Ethnography of the Old Kingdom.* Oxford: Clarendon Press.
Arnold, Dean E.
   1993   *Ecology and Ceramic Production in an Andean Community.* New York: Cambridge University Press.
Assadourian, Carlos Sempat
   1995   Exchange in the Ethnic Territories between 1530 and 1567: The *Visitas* of Huánuco and Chucuito. In *Ethnicity, Markets, and Migration in the Andes,* ed. Brooke Larson and Olivia Harris, 101–34. Durham, NC: Duke University Press.
Badian, E.
   1958   *Foreign Clientelae (264–70 B.C.).* Oxford: Clarendon Press.
Ballón Aguirre, Enrique, Rodolfo Cerrón-Palomino, and Emilio Chambi Apaza
   1992   *Vocabulario razonado de la actividad agraria andina: Terminología agraria quechua.* Cusco: Centro de Estudios Regionales Andinos "Bartolomé de las Casas."
Barker, Graeme, and Tom Rasmussen
   2000   *The Etruscans.* New York: Blackwell.

Barreda Murillo, Luis
    1973   Las culturas inca y pre-inca de Cusco. Thesis, Department of Archaeology, Universidad Nacional de San Antonio Abad del Cusco.
    1982   Asentamiento humano de los Qotakalli del Cuzco. In *Arqueología del Cuzco,* ed. Italo Oberti, 13–21. Cusco: Instituto Nacional de Cultura.
Bauer, Brian S.
    1987   Sistemas andinos de organización rural antes del establecimiento de reducciones: El ejemplo de Pacariqtambo (Perú). *Revista Andina* 9(1): 197–210.
    1990   State Development in the Cusco Region: Archaeological Research on the Incas in the Province of Paruro. Ph.D. dissertation, Department of Anthropology, University of Chicago.
    1992   *The Development of the Inca State.* Austin: University of Texas Press.
    1996   The Legitimization of the Inca State in Myth and Ritual. *American Anthropologist* 98(2): 327–37.
    1998   *The Sacred Landscape of the Inca: The Cuzco Ceque System.* Austin: University of Texas Press.
    1999   The Early Ceramics of the Inca Heartland. *Fieldiana,* Anthropology, new series, 31. Chicago: Field Museum of Natural History.
    2001   *Las antiguas tradiciones alfareras de la región del Cuzco.* Cuzco: Centro de Estudios Regionales Andinas, Bartolome de las Casas.
    2004   *Ancient Cuzco: Heartland of the Inca.* Austin: University of Texas Press.
Bauer, Brian S., and Wilton Barrionuevo Orosco
    1998   Reconstructing Andean Shrine Systems: A Test Case from the Xaquixaguana (Anta) Region of Cusco, Peru. *Andean Past* 5: 73–87.
Bauer, Brian S., and R. Alan Covey
    2002   Processes of State Formation in the Inca Heartland (Cuzco, Peru). *American Anthropologist* 104(3): 846–64.
Bauer, Brian S., and Bradford Jones
    2003   The Early Intermediate and Middle Horizon Ceramic Styles of the Cuzco Valley. *Fieldiana,* Anthropology, new series, 34. Chicago: Field Museum of Natural History.
Bauer, Brian S., and Charles Stanish
    1990   Killke and Killke-Related Pottery from Cuzco, Peru in the Field Museum of Natural History. *Fieldiana,* Anthropology Series 15. Chicago: Field Museum of Natural History.
    2001   *Ritual and Pilgrimage in the Ancient Andes.* Austin: University of Texas Press.
Bauer, Brian, Bradford Jones, and R. Alan Covey
    2001   Early Intermediate and Middle Horizon Ceramic Styles of the Cuzco Valley. Paper presented at the 66th Meeting of the Society for American Archaeology, New Orleans, April 19–22.
Berdan, Frances, Richard Blanton, Elizabeth Boone, Mary Hodge, Michael E. Smith, and Emily Umberger (eds.)
    1996   *Aztec Imperial Strategies.* Washington, DC: Dumbarton Oaks Research Library and Collection.

Bermann, Marc

    1994   *Lukurmata: Household Archaeology in Prehispanic Bolivia.* Princeton, NJ: Princeton University Press.

Bermann, Marc, Paul Goldstein, Charles Stanish, and Luis Watanabe

    1989   The Collapse of the Tiwanaku State: A View from the Osmore Drainage. In *Ecology, Settlement, and History in the Osmore Drainage, Peru,* by D. Rice, C. Stanish, and P. Scarr, 229–85. BAR International Series 545(ii). Oxford: British Archaeological Reports.

Berthelot, Jean

    1986   The Extraction of Precious Metals at the Time of the Inca. In *Anthropological History of Andean Polities,* ed. J. V. Murra, N. Wachtel, and J. Revel, 69–88. New York: Cambridge University Press.

Billman, Brian R.

    1999   Reconstructing Prehistoric Political Economies and Cycles of Political Power in the Moche Valley, Peru. In *Settlement Pattern Studies in the Americas: Fifty Years since Virú,* ed. Brian R. Billman and Gary M. Feinman, 131–59. Washington, DC: Smithsonian Institution Press.

Binford, Lewis R.

    1980   Willow Smoke and Dogs' Tails: Hunter-Gatherer Settlement Systems and Archaeological Site Formation. *American Antiquity* 45(1): 4–20.

Binford, Michael W., Alan L. Kolata, Mark Brenner, John W. Janusek, Matthew T. Seddon, Mark Abbott, and Jason H. Curtis

    1997   Climate Variation and the Rise and Fall of an Andean Civilization. *Quaternary Research* 47: 235–48.

Bingham, Hiram

    1915   Types of Machu Picchu Pottery. *American Anthropologist* 17(2): 257–71.

    1948   *Lost City of the Incas: The Story of Machu Picchu and Its Builders.* New York: Duell, Sloan and Pearce.

Blower, David

    2001   The Many Facets of *Mullu:* More Than Just a *Spondylus* Shell. *Andean Past* 6: 209–28.

Bolin, Inge

    1994   Levels of Autonomy in the Organization of Irrigation in the Highlands of Peru. In *Irrigation at High Altitudes: The Social Organization of Water Control Systems in the Andes,* ed. William P. Mitchell and David Guillet, 141–66, Society for Latin American Anthropology Publication Series 12. Washington, DC: American Anthropological Association.

Bonavia, Duccio

    1991   *Perú: Hombre e historia de los orígenes al siglo XV.* Lima: Edubanco.

Bouysse-Cassagne, Thérèse

    1986   Urco and Uma: Aymara Concepts of Space. In *Anthropological History of Andean Polities,* ed. John V. Murra, Nathan Wachtel, and Jacques Revel, 201–27. New York: Cambridge University Press.

Bradbury, R. E.

    1967   The Kingdom of Benin. In *West African Kingdoms in the Nineteenth*

Century, D. Forde and P. M. Kaberry, 1–35. London: Oxford University Press.

Braudel, Fernand
  1972   *The Mediterranean and the Mediterranean World in the Age of Philip II.* London: William Collins and Sons and Co.

Bray, Tamara L.
  1992   Archaeological Survey in Northern Highland Ecuador: Inca Imperialism and the País Caranqui. *World Archaeology* 24(2): 218–33.

Brown, Mervyn
  1979   *Madagascar Rediscovered: A History from Early Times to Independence.* Hamden, CT: Archon Books.

Bruhns, Karen Olsen
  1994   *Ancient South America.* New York: Cambridge University Press.

Brush, Stephen B.
  1974   El lugar del hombre en el ecosistema andino. *Revista del Museo Nacional* 40: 277–99.
  1976   Man's Use of an Andean Ecosystem. *Human Ecology* 4(2): 147–66.
  1977   *Mountain, Field, and Family: The Economy and Human Ecology of an Andean Village.* Philadelphia: University of Pennsylvania Press.
  1992   Ethnoecology, Biodiversity, and Modernization in Andean Potato Agriculture. *Journal of Ethnobiology* 12(2): 161–85.

Burger, Richard L., Karen L. Mohr Chávez, and Sergio J. Chávez
  2000   Through the Glass, Darkly: Prehispanic Obsidian Procurement and Exchange in Southern Peru and Northern Bolivia. *Journal of World Prehistory* 14(3): 267–362.

Bürgi, Peter
  1993   The Inca Empire's Expansion into the Coastal Sierra Region West of Lake Titicaca. Ph.D. dissertation, Department of Anthropology, University of Chicago.

Burns, Kathryn
  1999   *Colonial Habits: Convents and the Spiritual Economy of Cuzco, Peru.* Durham, NC: Duke University Press.

Canziani A., José
  1992   Patrones de asentamiento en la arqueología del valle de Chincha, Perú. In *II Curso de prehistoria de América hispana,* 87–123. Murcia.

Carneiro, Robert L.
  2000   *The Muse of History and the Science of Culture.* New York: Kluwer Academic/Plenum Publishers.

Cashdan, Elizabeth
  1990   Introduction. In *Risk and Uncertainty in Tribal and Peasant Economies,* ed. Elizabeth Cashdan, 1–16. Boulder, CO: Westview Press.

Castillo Tecsi, Tula, and Katy M. Jurado Chamorro
  1996   El centro urbano prehispánico de Calca. Thesis, Facultad de Ciencias Sociales, Universidad Nacional de San Antonio Abad del Cusco.

Chang, Kwang-chih
  1974   The Emergence of Civilization in North China. In *The Rise and Fall*

of Civilizations: Modern Archaeological Approaches to Ancient Cultures; Selected Readings, ed. Jeremy A. Sabloff and C. C. Lamberg-Karlovsky, 436–67. Menlo Park, CA: Cummings Publishing Co.

Chaumeil, J.-P., and J. Fraysse-Chaumeil

1982 "La Canela y El Dorado": Les indigenes du Napo et du Haut-Amazone—au XVIe siecle. *Bulletin de l'Institut Français de Etudes Andines* 19(3–4): 55–86.

Chávez, Karen Mohr

1980 The Archaeology of Marcavalle, an Early Horizon Site in the Valley of Cuzco, Peru: Part I. *Baessler-Archiv,* neue Folge, 28(2): 203–329.

1981a The Archaeology of Marcavalle, an Early Horizon Site in the Valley of Cuzco, Peru: Part II. *Baessler-Archiv,* neue Folge, 29(1): 107–205.

1981b The Archaeology of Marcavalle, an Early Horizon Site in the Valley of Cuzco, Peru: Part III. *Baessler-Archiv,* neue Folge, 29(1): 241–386.

Chepstow-Lusty, A. J., K. D. Bennett, V. R. Switsur, and A. Kendall

1996 4000 Years of Human Impact and Vegetation Change in the Central Peruvian Andes—with Events Parallelling the Maya Record? *Antiquity* 70: 824–33.

Chepstow-Lusty, Alex, Michael R. Frogley, Brian S. Bauer, Mark B. Bush, and Alfredo Tupayachi Herrera

2003 A Late Holocene Record of Arid Events from the Cuzco Region, Peru. *Journal of Quaternary Science* 18(6): 491–502.

Conlee, Christina A., and Katharina Schreiber

2002 The Role of Local Elites in the Balkanization and Reformation of Post-Wari Society in Nasca, Peru. Paper presented at the 67th Meeting of the Society for American Archaeology.

Conrad, Geoffrey W.

1977 Chiquitoy Viejo: An Inca Administrative Center in the Chicama Valley, Peru. *Journal of Field Archaeology* 4: 1–18.

1981 Cultural Materialism, Split Inheritance, and the Expansion of Ancient Peruvian Empires. *American Antiquity* 46(1): 2–26.

1993 Domestic Architecture of the Estuquiña Phase: Estuquiña and San Antonio. In *Domestic Architecture, Ethnicity, and Complementarity in the South-Central Andes,* ed. Mark Aldenderfer, 55–65. Iowa City: University of Iowa Press.

Conrad, Geoffrey W., and Arthur A. Demarest

1984 *Religion and Empire: The Dynamics of Aztec and Inca Expansionism.* New York: Cambridge University Press.

Cosio, P. et al.

1983 *Diagnóstico técnico agropecuario y socio-económico de las comunidades de Amaru—Paru-Paru—Sacaca y Cuyo Grande, Pisac—Calca—Cusco.* Cusco: IICA-CIID.

Costin, C. L., T. Earle, B. Owen, and G. Russell

1989 The Impact of Inca Conquest on Local Technology in the Upper Mantaro Valley, Peru. In *What's New? A Closer Look at the Process of In-novation,* ed. S. E. van der Leeuw and R. Torrence, 107–39. London: Unwin Hyman.

Covey, R. Alan

2000 Inka Administration of the Far South Coast of Peru. *Latin American Antiquity* 11(2): 119–38.

2003 A Processual Study of Inka State Formation. *Journal of Anthropological Archaeology* 22(4): 333–57.

Covey, R. Alan, and Christina M. Elson

n.d. Ethnicity, Demography, and Estate Management in Sixteenth-Century Yucay. Manuscript under review for publication at *Ethnohistory.*

Cowgill, George

1992 Toward a Political History of Teotihuacan. In *Ideology and Pre-Columbian Civilizations,* ed. Arthur A. Demarest and Geoffrey W. Conrad, 87–114. Santa Fe, NM: School of American Research Press.

Cummins, Thomas B. F.

2002 *Toasts with the Inca: Andean Abstraction and Colonial Images on Quero Vessels.* Ann Arbor: University of Michigan Press.

Cusihuamán, Antonio

1976 *Diccionario quechua: Cuzco-Collao.* Lima: Instituto de Estudios Peruanos.

D'Altroy, Terence N.

1987 Transitions in Power: Centralization of Wanka Political Organization under Inca Rule. *Ethnohistory* 34(1): 78–102.

1992 *Provincial Power in the Inca Empire.* Washington, DC: Smithsonian Institution Press.

1997 Recent Research on the Central Andes. *Journal of Archaeological Research* 5(1): 3–73.

2001a Politics, Resources, and Blood in the Inca Empire. In *Empires: Perspectives from Archaeology and History,* ed. S. E. Alcock, T. N. D'Altroy, K. D. Morrison, and C. M. Sinopoli, 201–26. New York: Cambridge University Press.

2001b From Autonomous to Imperial Rule. In *Empire and Domestic Economy,* ed. Terence N. D'Altroy, Christine A. Hastorf, and Associates, 325–39. New York: Kluwer Academic/Plenum Press.

2002 *The Incas.* New York: Blackwell.

D'Altroy, Terence N., and Timothy K. Earle

1985 Staple Finance, Wealth Finance, and Storage in the Inca Political Economy. *Current Anthropology* 26(2): 187–206.

D'Altroy, Terence N., and Christine A. Hastorf

1984 Distribution and Contents of Inca State Storehouses in the Xauxa Region of Peru. *American Antiquity* 49(2): 334–49.

D'Altroy, Terence N., Ana María Lorandi, Verónica I. Williams, Milena Calderari, Christine A. Hastorf, Elizabeth DeMarrais, and Melissa B. Hagstrum

2000 Inca Rule in the Northern Calchaquí Valley, Argentina. *Journal of Field Archaeology* 27(1): 1–26.

D'Altroy, Terence N., Christine A. Hastorf, and Associates
    2001   *Empire and Domestic Economy.* New York: Kluwer Academic/Plenum
            Press.
Davies, Nigel
    1995   *The Incas.* Niwot: University Press of Colorado.
Deagan, Kathleen
    2001   Dynamics of Imperial Adjustment in Spanish America: Ideology and
            Social Integration. In *Empires: Perspectives from Archaeology and
            History,* ed. S. E. Alcock, T. N. D'Altroy, K. D. Morrison, and C. M.
            Sinopoli, 179–94. New York: Cambridge University Press.
Dearborn, David S. P., Matthew T. Seddon, and Brian S. Bauer
    1998   The Sanctuary of Titicaca: Where the Sun Returns to Earth. *Latin
            American Antiquity* 9(3): 240–58.
Decoster, Jean-Jacques, and Brian S. Bauer
    1997   *Justicia y poder, Cvsco, siglos XVI–XVIII: Catálogo del Fondo Cor-
            regimiento, Archivo Departamental del Cvsco.* Cusco: Centro de Es-
            tudios Rurales Andinos "Bartolomé de las Casas."
Demarest, Arthur, and Geoffrey Conrad
    1983   Ideological Adaptation and the Rise of the Aztec and Inca Empires.
            In *Civilization in the Ancient Americas: Essays in Honor of Gordon
            R. Willey,* ed. R. M. Leventhal, and A. L. Kolata, 373–400. Albu-
            querque: University of New Mexico Press.
Dillehay, Tom D.
    1977   Tawantinsuyu Integration of the Chillon Valley, Peru: A Case of Inca
            Geo-Political Mastery. *Journal of Field Archaeology* 4: 397–405.
Drew, David
    1984   The Cusichaca Project: Aspects of Archaeological Reconnaissance—
            the Lucumayo and Santa Teresa Valleys. In *Current Archaeological
            Projects in the Central Andes: Some Approaches and Results,* ed. Ann
            Kendall, 345–75. BAR International Series 210. Oxford: British Ar-
            chaeological Reports.
Dwyer, Edward B.
    1971   The Early Inca Occupation of the Valley of Cuzco, Peru. Ph.D. dis-
            sertation, Department of Anthropology, University of California,
            Berkeley.
Earle, Timothy K.
    1972   Lurin Valley, Peru: Early Intermediate Period Settlement Develop-
            ment. *American Antiquity* 37(4): 467–77.
    1994   Wealth Finance in the Inca Empire: Evidence from the Calchaquí
            Valley. *American Antiquity* 59(3): 443–60.
Elson, Christina M.
    2003   Elites at Cerro Tilcajete: A Secondary Center in the Vally of Oaxaca,
            Mexico. Ph.D. dissertation, Department of Anthropology, University
            of Michigan.
Engwall, Evan C.
    1995   Turbulent Relations Recast: The Mythohistory of the Cañaris and the

Inca Empire. *Journal of the Steward Anthropological Society* 23(1–2): 345–361.

Espinoza Soriano, Waldemar

1973   Colonias de mitmas multiples en Abancay, siglos XV y XVI: Una información inédita de 1575 para la etnohistoria andina. *Revista del Museo Nacional* 39: 225–99.

1974   El habitat de la etnía Pinagua, siglos XV y XVI. *Revista del Museo Nacional* 40:157–220.

1977   Los cuatro suyus del Cuzco, siglos XV y XVI. *Bulletin de l'Institut Français des Études Andines* 6(3–4): 109–22.

1981   *Los modos de producción en el Imperio de los Incas.* Lima: AMARU Editores.

Farrington, Ian S.

1983   Prehistoric Intensive Agriculture: Preliminary Notes on River Canalization in the Sacred Valley of the Incas. In *Drained Field Agriculture in Central and South America*, ed. J. P. Darch, 221–35. BAR International Series 189. Oxford: British Archaeological Reports.

1984   The Vertical Economy of the Cusichaca Valley (Cuzco, Peru) and Its Prehistoric Implications. In *Social and Economic Organization in the Prehispanic Andes: Proceedings of the 44th International Congress of Americanists, Manchester*, ed. David L. Browman, Richard L. Burger, and Mario A. Rivera, 97–115. BAR International Series 194. Oxford: British Archaeological Reports.

Flannery, Kent V.

1972   The Cultural Evolution of Civilizations. *Annual Review of Ecology and Systematics* 3: 399–426.

1998   The Ground Plans of Archaic States. In *Archaic States*, ed. Gary M. Feinman and Joyce Marcus 15–57. Santa Fe: School of American Research Press.

1999   Process and Agency in Early State Formation. *Cambridge Archaeological Journal* 9(1): 3–21.

Flannery, Kent V., Joyce Marcus, and Robert G. Reynolds

1989   *The Flocks of the Wamani: A Study of Llama Herders on the Punas of Ayacucho, Peru.* San Diego: Academic Press.

Flores Ochoa, Jorge

1985   Interaction and Complementarity in Three Zones of Cuzco. In *Andean Ecology and Civilization*, ed. Shozo Masuda, Izumi Shimada, and Craig Morris, 251–76. Tokyo: University of Tokyo Press.

Forbes, Hamish

1989   Of Grandfathers and Grand Theories: The Hierarchised Ordering of Response to Hazard in a Greek Rural Community. In *Bad Year Economics: Cultural Responses to Risk and Uncertainty*, ed. Paul Halstead and John O'Shea, 87–97. Cambridge: Cambridge University Press.

Fried, Morton

1967   *The Evolution of Political Society.* New York: Random House.

Gade, Daniel W.
  1975   *Plants, Man and the Land in the Vilcanota Valley of Peru*. The Hague: Dr. W. Junk B.V.
Gade, Daniel W., and Mario Escobar Moscoso
  1982   Village Settlement and the Colonial Legacy in Southern Peru. *Geographical Review* 72(4): 430–49.
Gibaja Oviedo, Arminda M.
  1973   Arqueología de Choquepuguio. Thesis, Department of Archaeology, Universidad Nacional San Antonio Abad del Cusco.
  1982   La ocupacion neoinca del valle de Urubamba. In *Arqueología de Cuzco*, ed. Italo Oberti, 81–93. Cuzco: INC.
Giddens, Anthony
  1984   *The Constitution of Society*. Berkeley: University of California Press.
Glave, Luis Miguel, and María Isabel Remy
  1983   *Estructura agraria y vida rural en una región andina: Ollantaytambo entre los siglos XVI y XIX*. Cusco: Centro de Estudios Rurales Andinos "Bartolomé de las Casas."
Glowacki, Mary
  2002   The Huaro Archaeological Site Complex: Rethinking the Huari Occupation of Cuzco. In *Andean Archaeology I: Variations in Sociopolitical Organization*, ed. William H. Isbell and Helaine Silverman, 267–85. New York: Kluwer Academic/Plenum Publishers.
Glowacki, Mary, and Julinho Zapata
  1998   The Wari Occupation of Cuzco: Recent Discoveries from the Huaro Valley. Paper presented at the 38th Annual Meeting of the Institute of Andean Studies, Berkeley.
Goland, Carol
  1993   Cultivating Diversity: Field Scattering as Agricultural Risk Management in Cuyo Cuyo, Department of Puno, Peru. Production, Storage, and Exchange in a Terraced Environment on the Eastern Andean Escarpment Project, Monograph 4. http://www.unc.edu/depts/ecology/winterweb/pse/wp04/wp4_frames.html.
Goldstein, Paul S.
  1989   The Tiwanaku Occupation of Moquegua. In *Ecology, Settlement, and History in the Osmore Drainage, Peru*, ed. D. Rice, C. Stanish, and P. Scarr, 219–55. BAR International Series 545(i). Oxford: British Archaeological Reports.
  1993   Tiwanaku Temples and State Expansion: A Tiwanaku Sunken-Court Temple in Moquegua. *Latin American Antiquity* 4(1): 22–47.
  1995/96 Tiwanaku Settlement Patterns in the Azapa Valley, Chile. *Diálogo Andino* 14/15: 57–73.
  2000   Communities without Borders: The Vertical Archipelago and Diaspora Communities in the Southern Andes. In *The Archaeology of Communities: A New World Perspective*, ed. Marcello A. Canuto and Jason Yaeger, 182–209. New York: Routledge.

González, A. R.
    1983   Inca Settlement Patterns in a Marginal Province of the Empire: Socio-
            cultural Implications. In *Prehistoric Settlement Patterns: Essays in
            Honor of Gordon R. Willey*, ed. E. Z. Vogt and R. Leventhal, 337–60.
            Albuquerque: University of New Mexico Press.
González-Carré, Enrique
    1992   *Historia prehispánica de Ayacucho*. Lima: Universidad Nacional de
            San Cristóbal de Huamanga.
González-Carré, Enrique, Jorge Cosmopolis, and Jorge Lévano
    1981   *La ciudad inca de Vilcashuamán*. Ayacucho: Universidad Nacional de
            San Cristóbal de Huamanga.
González-Carré, Enrique, Jaime Urrutia Ceruti, and Jorge Lévano Peña
    1997   *Ayacucho: San Juan de la Frontera*. Lima: Banco de Crédito del Perú.
Gose, Peter
    1996   Past Is a Lower Moiety: Diarchy, History, and Divine Kingship in the
            Inca Empire. *History and Anthropology* 9(4): 383–414.
Grobman, Alexander, Wilfredo Salhuana, and Ricardo Sevilla
    1961   *Races of Maize in Peru*. National Academy of Sciences—National
            Research Council Publication 915. Washington, DC: National Acad-
            emy of Sciences.
Grosboll, Sue
    1993   . . . And He Said in the Time of the Ynga, They Paid Tribute and Served
            the Ynga. In *Provincial Inca: Archaeological and Ethnohistorical As-
            sessment of the Impact of the Inca State*, ed. M. Malpass, 44–76. Iowa
            City: University of Iowa Press.
Gruen, Erich (ed)
    1970   *Imperialism in the Roman Republic*. New York: Holt, Rinehart and
            Winston.
Gyarmati, J., and A. Varga
    1999   *The Chacras of War: An Inca Estate in the Cochabamba Valley, Bo-
            livia*. Budapest: Museum of Ethnography.
Halstead, Paul, and John O'Shea
    1989   Introduction: Cultural Responses to Risk and Uncertainty. In *Bad
            Year Economics: Cultural Responses to Risk and Uncertainty*, ed.
            Paul Halstead and John O'Shea, 1–7. Cambridge: Cambridge Uni-
            versity Press.
Haquehua Huaman, Wilbert, and Rubén Maqque Azorsa
    1996   Cerámica de Cueva Moqo-Maras. Thesis, Facultad de Ciencias So-
            ciales, Universidad Nacional de San Antonio Abad del Cusco.
Harris, William V.
    1979   *War and Imperialism in Republican Rome, 327–70 B.C.* Oxford:
            Clarendon Press.
Hassig, R. Ross
    1988   *Aztec Warfare: Imperial Expansion and Political Control*. Norman:
            University of Oklahoma Press.

Hastings, Charles M.
  1987   Implications of Andean Verticality in the Evolution of Political Com-
          plexity: A View from the Margins. In *The Origins and Development
          of the Andean State*, ed. Jonathan Haas, Shelia Pozorski, and Thomas
          Pozorski, 145–57. New York: Cambridge University Press.
Hastorf, Christine A.
  1993   *Agriculture and the Onset of Political Inequality before the Inca.*
          Cambridge: Cambridge University Press.
  2001   Agricultural Production and Consumption. In *Empire and Domestic
          Economy,* ed. Terence N. D'Altroy, Christine A. Hastorf, and Asso-
          ciates, 155–78. New York: Kluwer Academic/Plenum Press.
Hastorf, C. A., T. K. Earle, H. E. Wright Jr., L. LeCount, G. Russell, and
E. Sandefur
  1989   Settlement Archaeology in the Jauja Region of Peru: Evidence from
          the Early Intermediate Period through the Late Intermediate Period:
          A Report on the 1986 Field Season. *Andean Past* 2: 81–129.
Hayashida, Frances M.
  1998   Style, Technology, and State Production: Inca Pottery Manufacture in
          the Leche Valley, Peru. *Latin American Antiquity* 10(4): 337–52.
Heffernan, Kenneth
  1989   Limatambo in Late Prehistory: Landscape Archaeology and Docu-
          mentary Images of Inca Presence in the Periphery of Cuzco. Ph.D. dis-
          sertation, Department of Prehistory and Anthropology, Australian
          National University, Canberra.
  1996   *Limatambo: Archaeology, History, and the Regional Societies of Inca
          Cusco.* BAR International Series 644. Oxford: British Archaeological
          Reports.
Hemming, John
  1970   *The Conquest of the Incas.* New York: Harcourt, Brace, Jovanovich.
Henige, David P.
  1974   *The Chronology of Oral Tradition: Quest for a Chimera.* Oxford:
          Clarendon Press.
Herskovits, Melville J.
  1938   *Dahomey: An Ancient West African Kingdom.* Vol. 1. New York: J. J.
          Augustin.
Higueras-Hare, Alvaro
  1996   Prehispanic Settlement and Land Use in Cochabamba, Bolivia. Ph.D.
          dissertation, Department of Anthropology, University of Pittsburgh.
Hiltunen, Juha
  1999   *Ancient Kings of Peru: The Reliability of the Chronicle of Fernando
          de Montesinos.* Biblioteca Histórica 45. Helsinki: Tiedekirjasta.
Hiltunen, Juha, and Gordon F. McEwan
  2004   Knowing the Inca Past. In *Andean Archaeology,* ed. Helaine Silverman,
          237–54. New York: Blackwell.
Huaycochea Núñez de la Torre, Flor de María
  1994   *Qolqas, bancos de reserva andinos: Almacenes incas, arqueología*

de qolqas. Cusco: Universidad Nacional de San Antonio Abad del Cusco.

Hyland, Sabine

    2002   Biblical Prophecy and the Conquest of Peru: Fernando de Montesinos' *Memorias Historiales*. *Colonial Latin American Historical Review* 11(3): 259–78.

Hyslop, John

    1976   An Archaeological Investigation of the Lupaca Kingdom and Its Origins. Ph.D. dissertation, Department of Anthropology, Columbia University.

    1979   El área Lupaca bajo el dominio incaico: Un reconocimiento arqueológico. *Histórica* 3(1): 53–80.

    1984   *The Inca Road System*. New York: Academic Press.

    1985   *Incawasi, the New Cuzco: Cañete, Lunahuaná, Peru*. BAR International Series 234. Oxford: British Archaeological Reports.

    1988   Las fronteras estatales extremas del Tawantinsuyu. In *La frontera del estado Inca*, ed. T. D. Dillehay and P. J. Netherly, 33–51. Quito: Fundación Alexander von Humboldt.

Idrovo, Jaime

    1985   Tomebamba: Primera fase de conquista incásica en los Andes septentrionales. Los cañaris y la conquista incásica del Austro ecuatoriano. In *La frontera del estado Inca*, ed. T. D. Dillehay and P. J. Netherly, 71–84. Quito: Fundación Alexander von Humboldt.

Isbell, William H.

    1977   *The Rural Foundation for Urbanism: Economic and Stylistic Interaction between Rural and Urban Communities in Eighth-Century Peru*. Illinois Studies in Anthropology 10. Urbana: University of Illinois.

    1978   Environmental Perturbations and the Origin of the Andean State. In *Social Archaeology: Beyond Subsistence and Dating*, ed. C. Redman, M. J. Berman, E. V. Curtin, W. T. Langhorne Jr., N. W. Versaggi, and J. C. Wanser, 303–14. New York: Academic Press.

    1997a   Reconstructing Huari: A Cultural Chronology for the Capital City. In *Emergence and Change in Early Urban Societies*, ed. Linda Manzanilla, 181–227. New York: Plenum Press.

    1997b   *Mummies and Mortuary Monuments: A Postprocessual Prehistory of Central Andean Social Organization*. Austin: University of Texas Press.

Isbell, William H., and JoEllen Burkholder

    2002   Iwawi and Tiwanaku. In *Andean Archaeology I: Variations in Sociopolitical Organization*, ed. William H. Isbell and Helaine Silverman, 199–241. New York: Kluwer Academic/Plenum Press.

Janusek, John W.

    2002   Out of Many, One: Style and Social Boundaries in Tiwanaku. *Latin American Antiquity* 13(1): 35–61.

Jennings, Justin, and Nathan Craig

    2001   Polity Wide Analysis and Imperial Political Economy: The Relationship between Valley Political Complexity and Administrative Centers in the Wari Empire of the Central Andes. *Journal of Anthropological Archaeology* 20(4): 479–502.

Jessup, David

1990   Rescate arqueológico en el Museo de Sitio de San Gerónimo, Ilo. In *Trabajos Arqueológicos en Moquegua, Peru,* ed. L. Watanabe, M. Moseley, and F. Cabieses, 3:151–65. Lima: Programa Contisuyu del Museo Peruano de Ciencias de la Salud—Southern Peru Copper Company.

Johnson, Gregory A.

1977   Aspects of Regional Analysis in Archaeology. *Annual Review of Anthropology* 6: 479–508.

1980   Spatial Organization of Early Uruk Settlement Systems. In *L'Archéologie de l'Iraq du début de l'epoque Néolithique a 333 avant notre ere. Perspectives et limites de l'interpretation anthropologique des documents,* Paris, 13–15 juin 1978, 233–63. Colloques Internationaux 580. Paris: Centre National de la Recherche Scientifique.

Julien, Catherine J.

1982   Inca Decimal Administration in the Lake Titicaca Region. In *The Inca and Aztec States, 1400–1800: Anthropology and History,* ed. George A. Collier, Renato I. Rosaldo, and John D. Wirth, 119–51. New York: Academic Press.

1983   *Hatunqolla: A View of Inca Rule from the Lake Titicaca Region.* Publications in Anthropology 15. Berkeley: University of California Press.

1985   Guano and Resource Control in Sixteenth-Century Arequipa. In *Andean Ecology and Civilization,* ed. Shozo Masuda, Izumi Shimada, and Craig Morris, 185–231. Tokyo: University of Tokyo Press.

1988   How Inca Decimal Administration Worked. *Ethnohistory* 35(3): 257–79.

1998   Coca Production on the Inca Frontier: The Yungas of Chuquioma. *Andean Past* 5: 129–60.

2000   *Reading Inca History.* Iowa City: University of Iowa Press.

2001   Inca Estates and the Encomienda: Hernando Pizarro's Holdings in Cusco. *Andean Past* 6: 229–75.

Julien, Daniel

1993   Late Pre-Incaic Ethnic Groups in Highland Peru: An Archaeological-Ethnohistorical Model of the Political Geography of the Cajamarca Region. *Latin American Antiquity* 4(3): 246–73.

Katterman, G. L., and F. A. Riddell

1994   A Cache of Inca Textiles from Rodadero, Acarí Valley, Peru. *Andean Past* 4: 141–67.

Kendall, Ann

1974   *Aspects of Inca Architecture.* Ph.D. dissertation, Institute of Archaeology, University of London.

1985   *Aspects of Inca Architecture: Description, Function and Chronology,* parts 1 and 2. BAR International Series 242. Oxford: British Archaeological Reports.

1994   *Proyecto Arqueológico Cusichaca, Cusco: Investigaciones arqueológicas y de rehabilitación agrícola, tomo I.* Lima: Southern Peru Copper Corporation.

1996   An Archaeological Perspective for Late Intermediate Period Inca Development in the Cuzco Region. *Journal of the Steward Anthropological Society* 24(1/2): 121–56.

Kendall, Ann, Rob Early, and Bill Sillar

1992   Report on Archaeological Field Season Investigating Early Inca Architecture at Juchuy Coscco (Q'aqya Qhawana) and Warq'ana, Province of Calca, Dept. of Cuzco, Peru. In *Ancient America: Contributions to New World Archaeology,* ed. Nicholas J. Saunders, 189–256. Oxbow Monograph 24. Oxford: Oxbow Books.

Kirch, Patrick V.

1984   *The Evolution of the Polynesian Chiefdoms.* New York: Cambridge University Press.

Kolata, Alan L.

1990   The Urban Concept of Chan Chan. In *The Northern Dynasties: Kingship and Statecraft in Chimor,* ed. Michael E. Moseley and Alana Cordy-Collins, 107–44. Washington, DC: Dumbarton Oaks Research Library and Collection.

1991   The Technology and Organization of Agricultural Production in the Tiwanaku State. *Latin American Antiquity* 2(2): 99–125.

1993   *The Tiwanaku: Portrait of an Andean Civilization.* Cambridge: Blackwell.

Kottak, Conrad P.

1980   *The Past in the Present: History, Ecology, and Cultural Variation in Highland Madagascar.* Ann Arbor: University of Michigan Press.

Kuhrt, Amélie

2001   The Achaemenid Persian Empire (c. 550–c. 330 BCE): Continuities, Adaptations, Transformations. In *Empires: Perspectives from Archaeology and History,* ed. S. E. Alcock, T. N. D'Altroy, K. D. Morrison, and C. M. Sinopoli, 93–123. New York: Cambridge University Press.

Kurella, Doris

1998   The Muisca: Chiefdoms in Transition. In *Chiefdoms and Chieftaincy in the Americas,* ed. Elsa M. Redmond, 189–216. Gainesville: University Press of Florida.

Kuznar, Lawrence A.

2001   Risk Sensitivity and Value among Andean Pastoralists: Measures, Models, and Empirical Tests. *Current Anthropology* 42(3): 432–40.

La Lone, Mary B.

1985   Indian Land Tenure in Southern Cuzco, Peru: From Inca to Colonial Patterns. PhD dissertation, Department of Anthropology, University of California, Los Angeles.

La Lone, Mary B., and Darrell E. La Lone

1987   The Inca State in the Southern Highlands: State Administration and Production Enclaves. *Ethnohistory* 34(1): 47–62.

Lavallée, D.

1983   Historia de los Asto. In *Asto: Curacazgo prehispánico de los Andes centrales*, ed. D. Lavallée and M. Julien, 25–47. Lima: Instituto de Estudios Peruanos.

Lavender, Michael

2001   The Huaro Valley Archaeological Survey. Paper presented at the 66th Annual Meeting of the Society for American Archaeology.

Le Blanc, Catherine J.

1981   Late Prehispanic Huanca Settlement Patterns in the Yanamarca Valley, Peru. Ph.D. dissertation, Department of Anthropology, University of California, Los Angeles.

Lee, Vince

1998   Reconstructing the Great Hall at Incallacta. *Andean Past* 5: 35–71.

León, L.

1981   Expansión inca y resistencia indígena en Chile, 1470–1536. *Chungará* 10: 95–115.

Le Vine, Terry Y.

1987   Inca Labor Service at the Regional Level: The Functional Reality. *Ethnohistory* 34(1): 14–46.

1992   *Inca Storage Systems*. Norman: University of Oklahoma Press.

Lounsbury, Floyd G.

1986   Some Aspects of the Inca Kinship System. In *Anthropological History of Andean Polities*, ed. John V. Murra, Nathan Wachtel, and Jacques Revel, 121–36. New York: Cambridge University Press.

Lumbreras, Luis G.

1978   Acerca de la aparición del estado inca. In *Actas y trabajos del III congreso peruano "El hombre y la cultura andina,"* ed. Ramiro Matos M., 1:101–9. Lima: Universidad Nacional Mayor de San Marcos.

1999   Andean Urbanism and Statecraft (C.E. 550–1450). In *The Cambridge History of the Native Peoples of the Americas: Volume III, South America, Part 1*, ed. F. Salomon and S. B. Schwartz, 350–517. New York: Cambridge University Press.

2001   Uhle y los asentamientos de Chincha en el siglo XVI. *Revista del Museo Nacional* 49: 13–87.

Lynch, Thomas

1993   The Identification of Inca Posts and Roads from Catarpe to Río Frío, Chile. In *Provincial Inca: Archaeological and Ethnohistorical Assessment of the Impact of the Inca State*, ed. M. Malpass, 117–42. Iowa City: University of Iowa Press.

MacCormack, Sabine G.

1991   *Religion in the Andes: Vision and Imagination in Early Colonial Peru*. Princeton, NJ: Princeton University Press.

2001a History, Historical Record, and Ceremonial Action: Incas and Spaniards in Cuzco. *Comparative Studies in Society and History* 43(2): 329–63.

2001b Cusco, Another Rome? In *Empires: Perspectives from Archaeology and History,* ed. S. E. Alcock, T. N. D'Altroy, K. D. Morrison, and C. M. Sinopoli, 419–35. New York: Cambridge University Press.

MacCurdy, George G.
  1923 Human Skeletal Remains from the Highlands of Peru. *American Journal of Physical Anthropology* 6(3): 217–329.

Mannheim, Bruce
  1991 *The Language of the Inca since the European Invasion.* Austin: University of Texas Press.

Maqque Azorsa, Rubén, and Wilbert Haquehua Huaman
  1993 Prospección arqueológica de Cueva Moqo-Maras. Informe de prácticas preprofesionales. Facultad de Ciencias Sociales, Universidad Nacional de San Antonio Abad del Cusco.

Marcus, Joyce
  1987 *Late Intermediate Occupation at Cerro Azul, Perú: A Preliminary Report.* University of Michigan Museum of Anthropology Technical Report 20. Ann Arbor: University of Michigan Museum of Anthropology.
  1992 Dynamic Cycles of Mesoamerican States: Political Fluctuations in Mesoamerica. *National Geographic Research and Exploration* 8: 392–411.
  1998 The Peaks and Valleys of Ancient States: An Extension of the Dynamic Model. In *Archaic States,* ed. Gary M. Feinman and Joyce Marcus, 59–94. Santa Fe, NM: School of American Research.

Marcus, Joyce, and Gary M. Feinman
  1998 Introduction. In *Archaic States,* ed. Gary M. Feinman and Joyce Marcus, 3–13. Santa Fe, NM: School of American Research.

Marcus, Joyce, and Kent V. Flannery
  1996 *Zapotec Civilization: How Urban Society Evolved in Mexico's Oaxaca Valley.* New York: Thames and Hudson.

Mathews, James
  1989 Dual Systems of Inca Agricultural Production: Evidence from the Osmore Drainage, Southern Peru. In *Ecology, Settlement, and History in the Osmore Drainage, Peru,* ed. D. Rice, C. Stanish, and P. Scarr, 415–34. BAR International Series 545. Oxford: British Archaeological Reports.

Matos M., Ramiro
  1994 *Pumpú: Centro administrativo Inca de la puna de Junín.* Lima: Editorial Horizonte.
  1995 Los Inca de la sierra central del Perú. *Revista de Arqueología Americana* 8: 159–90.

McEwan, Gordon F.
  1984 Investigaciones en la cuenca del Lucre, Cusco. *Gaceta arqueológica andina* 9: 12–15.
  1987 *The Middle Horizon in the Valley of Cuzco, Peru: The Impact of the Wari Occupation of the Lucre Basin.* BAR International Series 372. Oxford: British Archaeological Reports.
  1990 Some Formal Correspondences between the Imperial Architecture of

the Wari and Chimu Cultures, and Their Implications for the Origins of the Architecture of Chan Chan. *Latin American Antiquity* 1: 97–116.

1991 Investigations at the Pikillacta Site: A Provincial Huari Center in the Valley of Cuzco. In *Huari Administrative Structures: Prehistoric Monumental Architecture and State Government*, ed. William H. Isbell and Gordon F. McEwan, 93–119. Washington, DC: Dumbarton Oaks Research Library and Collection.

1996 Archaeological Investigations at Pikillacta, a Wari Site in Peru. *Journal of Field Archaeology* 23(2): 169–86

1998 The Function of Niched Halls in Wari Architecture. *Latin American Antiquity* 9(1): 68–86.

McEwan, Gordon F., Arminda Gibaja, and Melissa Chatfield
1995 Archaeology of the Chokepukio Site: An Investigation of the Origin of the Inca Civilisation in the Valley of Cuzco, Peru. A Report on the 1994 Field Season. *Tawantinsuyu* 1: 11–17.

McEwan, Gordon F., Melissa Chatfield, and Arminda Gibaja
2002 The Archaeology of Inca Origins: Excavations at Chokepukio, Cuzco, Peru. In *Andean Archaeology I: Variations in Sociopolitical Organization*, ed. William H. Isbell and Helaine Silverman, 287–301. New York: Kluwer Academic/Plenum Press.

Means, Philip Ainsworth
1928 Biblioteca Andina: Part One: The Chroniclers, or, the Writers of the Sixteenth and Seventeenth Centuries Who Treated of the Pre-Hispanic History and Culture of the Andean Countries. *Transactions of the Connecticut Academy of Arts and Sciences* 29: 271–525.

Menzel, Dorothy
1959 The Inca Occupation of the South Coast of Peru. *Southwestern Journal of Anthropology* 15(2): 125–42.

Millones Santagada, L., and Richard P. Schaedel
1980 Plumas para el sol: Comentarios sobre cazadores y cotos de caza en el antiguo Perú. *Bulletin de l'Institut Francais de Etudes Andines* 9(1–2): 59–88.

Montaya, Eduardo, Mary Glowacki, Julinho Zapata, and Pablo Mendoza
2000 A Study of the Production and Distribution of Middle Horizon Pottery of Cuzco, Peru. Final Report for Regional Coordinated Research Program on Nuclear Analytical Techniques in Archaeological Investigations. Washington, DC: International Atomic Energy Agency and Smithsonian Institution.

Moore, Jerry D.
1996 *Architecture and Power in the Ancient Andes: The Archaeology of Public Buildings.* New York: Cambridge University Press.

Morris, Craig
1967 Storage in Tawantinsuyu. PhD dissertation, Department of Anthropology, University of Chicago.

1982 The Infrastructure of Inca Control in the Peruvian Central Highlands. In *The Inca and Aztec States, 1400–1800: Anthropology and History,* ed. G. A. Collier, R. I. Rosaldo, and J. D. Wirth, 153–71. New York: Academic Press.

1985 From Principles of Ecological Complementarity to the Organization and Administration of Tawantinsuyu. In *Andean Ecology and Civilization*, ed. Shozo Masuda, Izumi Shimada, and Craig Morris, 477–90. Tokyo: University of Tokyo Press.

1992 The Technology of Highland Inca Food Storage. In *Inca Storage Systems*, ed. Terry Y. Le Vine, 237–58. Norman: University of Oklahoma Press.

1998 Inca Strategies of Incorporation and Governance. In *Archaic States*, ed. Gary M. Feinman and Joyce Marcus, 293–309. Santa Fe, NM: School of American Research Press.

2004 Enclosures of Power: The Multiple Spaces of Inca Administrative Palaces. Dumbarton Oaks Research Library and Collection. In *Palaces of the Ancient New World: A Symposium at Dumbarton Oaks, 10th and 11th October 1998*, ed. Susan Toby Evans and Joanne Pillsbury, 299–325. Washington, DC: Dumbarton Oaks.

Morris, Craig, and Donald E. Thompson
1985 *Huánuco Pampa: An Inca City and Its Hinterland.* New York: Thames and Hudson.

Moseley, Michael E.
1990 Structure and History in the Dynastic Lore of Chimor. In *The Northern Dynasties: Kingship and Statecraft in Chimor*, ed. Michael E. Moseley and Alana Cordy-Collins, 1–41. Washington, DC: Dumbarton Oaks Research Library and Collection.

1992 *The Incas and Their Ancestors: The Archaeology of Peru.* New York: Thames and Hudson.

Muelle, Jorge C.
1945 Pacarectambo: Apuntes de viaje. *Revista del Museo Nacional* 14: 153–60.

Murra, John V.
1960 Rite and Crop in the Inca State. In *Culture in History: Essays in Honor of Paul Radin*, ed. Stanley Diamond, 393–407. New York: Columbia University Press.

1965 Herds and Herders in the Inca State. In *Man, Culture, and Animals: The Role of Animals in Human Ecological Adjustments*, ed. A. Leeds and A. P. Vayda, 185–216. Publications of the American Association for the Advancement of Science 78. Washington, DC: American Association for the Advancement of Science.

1972 El "control vertical" de un máximo de pisos ecológicos en la economía de las sociedades andinas. In *Visita de la Provincia de León de Huánuco* (1562), ed. John V. Murra, 429–76. Huánuco: Universidad Hermilio Valdizán.

1976 Los límites y las limitaciones del "archipiélago vertical" en los Andes. In *Homenaje al Dr. Gustavo le Paige, SJ*, ed. H. Niemeyer, 141–46. Santiago: Universidad del Norte.

1980 [1956]   *The Economic Organization of the Inca State.* Greenwich, CT: JAI Press.

1982   The Mit'a Obligations of Ethnic Groups to the Inca State. In *The Inca and Aztec States, 1400–1800: Anthropology and History,* ed. G. A. Collier, R. I. Rosaldo, and J. D. Wirth, 237–62. New York: Academic Press.

1986   The Expansion of the Inca State: Armies, Wars, and Rebellions. In *Anthropological History of Andean Polities,* ed. J. V. Murra, N. Wachtel, and J. Revel, 49–58. New York: Cambridge University Press.

1989   Cloth and Its Function in the Inca State. In *Cloth and Human Experience,* ed. A. B. Weiner and J. Schneider, 275–302. Washington, DC: Smithsonian Institution Press.

1995   Did Tribute and Markets Prevail in the Andes before the European Invasion? In *Ethnicity, Markets, and Migration in the Andes,* ed. Brooke Larson and Olivia Harris, 57–72. Durham, NC: Duke University Press.

Narváez V., Alfredo

1995   The Pyramids of Túcume: The Monumental Sector. In *Pyramids of Túcume: The Quest for Peru's Forgotten City,* by Thor Heyerdahl, Daniel Sandweiss, and Alfredo Narváez, 79–130. New York: Thames and Hudson.

NAS (National Academy of Sciences)

1989   *Lost Crops of the Incas: Little-Known Plants of the Andes with Promise for Worldwide Cultivation.* Washington, DC: National Academy Press.

Niles, Susan A.

1980   Pumamarca: A Late Intermediate Period Site near Ollantaytambo. *Ñawpa Pacha* 18: 47–62.

1993   The Provinces in the Heartland: Stylistic Variation and Architectural Innovation near Inca Cuzco. In *Provincial Inca: Archaeological and Ethnohistorical Assessment of the Impact of the Inca State,* ed. M. Malpass, 145–76. Iowa City: University of Iowa Press.

1999   *The Shape of Inca History: Narrative and Architecture in an Andean Empire.* Iowa City: University of Iowa Press.

Núñez, L., and T. D. Dillehay

1995   *Movilidad giratoria, armonía social y desarrollo en los Andes Meridionales: Patrones de Tráfico e interacción económica.* Antofagosta, Chile: Norprint.

Ortloff, Charles L., and Alan L. Kolata

1993   Climate and Collapse: Agro-ecological Perspectives on the Decline of the Tiwanaku State. *Journal of Archaeological Science* 20(2): 195–221.

Owen, Bruce

1994   Were Wari and Tiwanaku in Conflict, Competition, or Complementary Coexistence? Survey Evidence from the Upper Osmore Drainage, Peru. Paper presented at the 59th Annual Meeting of the Society for American Archaeology. http://members.aol.com/OwenBruce/saa94_1.htm.

Parsons, Jeffrey R., and Charles M. Hastings

1988   The Late Intermediate Period. In *Peruvian Prehistory*, ed. Richard W.
        Keatinge, 190–229. Cambridge: Cambridge University Press.

Parsons, Jeffrey R., Charles M. Hastings, and Ramiro Matos M.

1997   Rebuilding the State in Highland Peru: Herder-Cultivator Interaction
        during the Late Intermediate Period in the Tarama-Chinchaycocha
        Region. *Latin American Antiquity* 8(4): 317–41.

2000   *Prehispanic Settlement Patterns in the Upper Mantaro and Tarma
        Drainages, Junín, Peru. Volume* 1: *The Tarama-Chinchaycocha Region,
        Part* 1. Memoirs of the University of Michigan Museum of Anthropol-
        ogy 34. Ann Arbor: University of Michigan Museum of Anthropology.

Pärssinen, Martti

1992   *Tawantinsuyu: The Inca State and Its Political Organization*. Helsinki:
        Societas Historica Finlandiae.

Pärssinen, Martti, and Ari Siiriänen

1997   Inca-Style Ceramics and Their Chronological Relationship to the Inca
        Expansion in the Southern Lake Titicaca Area (Bolivia). *Latin Amer-
        ican Antiquity* 8: 255–71.

Patterson, Thomas

1985   Exploitation and Class Formation in the Inca State. *Culture* 5(1):
        35–42.

Pease G. Y., Franklin

1982   The Formation of Tawantinsuyu: Mechanisms of Colonization and
        Relationship with Ethnic Groups. In *The Inca and Aztec States,
        1400–1800: Anthropology and History*, ed. G. A. Collier, R. I. Ros-
        aldo, and J. D. Wirth, 173–98. New York: Academic Press.

Pineda Quevedo, J.

1989   *Patrones de asentamiento pre-hispánicos en el valle de Condebamba.*
        Lima: CONCYTEC.

Pollock, Susan

2001   The Uruk Period in Southern Mesopotamia. In *Uruk Mesopotamia
        and Its Neighbors: Cross-Cultural Interactions in the Era of State
        Formation*, ed. Mitchell S. Rothman, 181–232. Santa Fe, NM: School
        of American Research Press.

Poole, Deborah

1982   Los santuarios religiosos en la economía regional andina (Cusco).
        Allpanchis 16(19): 79–116.

1984   Ritual Economic Calendars in Paruro: The Structure of Represen-
        tation in Andean Ethnography. Ph.D. dissertation, Department of
        Anthropology, University of Illinois.

Protzen, John-Pierre

1993   *Inca Architecture and Construction at Ollantaytambo.* New York:
        Oxford University Press.

Ramírez, Susan E.

1990   The Inca Conquest of the North Coast: A Historian's View. In *The
        Northern Dynasties: Kingship and Statecraft in Chimor*, ed. M. E.

Moseley and A. Cordy-Collins, 507–37. Washington, DC: Dumbarton Oaks Research Library and Collection.

1995   An Oral History of the Valley of Chicama, circa 1524–1565. *Journal of the Steward Anthropological Society* 23(1–2): 299–342.

Randall, Robert

1982   Qoyllur Rit'i, an Inca Fiesta of the Pleiades: Reflections on Time and Space in the Andean World. *Bulletin de l'Institut Français d'Études Andines* 11(1–2): 37–81.

Redmond, Elsa M.

1994   *Tribal and Chiefly Warfare in South America.* University of Michigan Museum of Anthropology Memoir 28. Ann Arbor: UMMA.

Renard de Casevitz, F.-M.

1981   Las fronteras de las conquistas en el siglo XVI en la montaña meridional del Perú. *Bulletin de l'Institut Français de Etudes Andines* 10(3–4): 113–40.

Repo-Carrasco, Ritva

1988   *Cultivos andinos: Importancia nutricional y posibilidades de procesamiento.* Cuzco: Centro de Estudios Rurales Andinos Bartolomé de las Casas.

Rhoades, Robert E., and Virginia D. Nazarea

1999   Local Management of Biodiversity in Traditional Agroecosystems. In *Biodiversity in Agroecosystems,* ed. Wanda W. Collins and Calvin O. Qualset, 215–36. Boca Raton, FL: CRC Press.

Rice, Don

1993   Late Intermediate Period Domestic Architecture and Residential Organization at La Yaral. In *Domestic Architecture, Ethnicity, and Complementarity in the South-Central Andes,* ed. M. Aldenderfer, 66–82. Iowa City: University of Iowa Press.

Rivera, Mario

1991   The Prehistory of Northern Chile: A Synthesis. *Journal of World Prehistory* 5: 1–47.

Rivera Dorado, Miguel

1971a   La cerámica killke y la arqueología de Cuzco (Perú). *Revista Española de Antropología Americana* 6: 85–124.

1971b   Diseños decorativos en la cerámica killke. *Revista del Museo Nacional* 37: 106–15.

1972   La cerámica de Cancha-Cancha, Cuzco, Peru. *Revista Dominicana de Arqueología y Antropología* 2(2–3): 36–49.

1973   Aspectos tipológicos de la cerámica Cuzqueña del período Intermedio Tardío. In *International Congress of Americanists* (Rome-Genoa): 333–62.

Rostworowski, María

1960   Succession, Cooption to Kingship, and Royal Incest among the Inca. *Southwestern Journal of Anthropology* 16: 417–27.

1962   Nuevos datos sobre tenencia de tierras reales en el incario. *Revista del Museo Nacional* 21: 130–94.

1963a   *Los ascendientes de Pumacahua.* Lima: Imprenta de Universidad Nacional Mayor de San Marcos.

1963b   Dos manuscritos inéditos con datos sobre Manco II, tierras personales de los Incas y mitimaes. *Nueva Corónica* 1: 223–39. Departamento de Historia, Facultad de Letras, Universidad Nacional Mayor de San Marcos.

1970a   El repartamiento de doña Beatriz Coya, en el valle de Yucay. *Historia y Cultura* 4: 153–268.

1970b   Los Ayarmaca. *Revista del Museo Nacional* 36: 58–101.

1970c   Mercaderes del valle de Chincha en la época prehispánica: Un documento y unos comentarios. *Revista Española de Antropología Americana* 5:135–78.

1977a   Algunos comentarios hechos a las ordenanzas del doctor Cuenca. *Historia y Cultura* 9: 119–54.

1977b   La estratificación y el hatun curaca en el mundo andino. *Histórica* 1/2: 249–86.

1978   Una hipótesis sobre el surgimiento del estado inca. In *Actas y trabajos del III congreso peruano "El hombre y la cultura andina,"* ed. Ramiro Matos M., 89–100. Lima: Universidad Nacional Mayor de San Marcos.

1983   *Estructuras andinas del poder: Ideología religiosa y política.* Lima: Insituto de Estudios Peruanos.

1988a   *La historia del Tawantinsuyu.* Lima: Instituto de Estudios Peruanos.

1988b   *Conflicts over Coca Fields in XVIth-Century Peru.* Memoirs of the University of Michigan Museum of Anthropology 21. Ann Arbor: University of Michigan Museum of Anthropology.

1993   *Ensayos de historia andina: Elites, etnías, recursos.* Lima: Instituto de Estudios Peruanos.

1999   *History of the Inca Realm.* Trans. H. Iceland. Cambridge: Cambridge University Press.

Rountree, Helen C.
1989   *The Powhatan Indians of Virginia: Their Traditional Culture.* Norman: University of Oklahoma Press.

Rountree, Helen C., and E. Randolph Turner III
1998   The Evolution of the Powhatan Paramount Chiefdom in Virginia. In *Chiefdoms and Chieftaincy in the Americas,* ed. Elsa M. Redmond, 265–96. Gainesville: University Press of Florida.

Rowe, John H.
1944   An Introduction to the Archaeology of Cuzco. *Papers of the Peabody Museum of American Archaeology and Ethnology* 27(2).

1945   Absolute Chronology in the Andean Area. *American Antiquity* 10(3): 265–84.

1946   Inca Culture at the Time of the Spanish Conquest. In *Handbook of South American Indians, vol. 2: The Andean Civilizations,* ed. Julian Steward, 183–330. Bureau of American Ethnology Bulletin 143. Washington DC: U.S. Government Printing Office.

1948   The Kingdom of Chimor. *Acta Americana* 6: 26–59
1954   Archaeological Explorations in Southern Peru. *American Antiquity* 22(2): 135–51.
1960   The Origins of Creator Worship among the Incas. In *Culture in History: Essays in Honor of Paul Radin,* ed. Stanley Diamond, 408–29. New York: Columbia University Press.
1967   What Kind of Settlement Was Inca Cuzco? *Ñaupa Pacha* 5: 59–75.
1982   Inca Policies and Institutions Relating to the Cultural Unification of the Empire. In *The Inca and Aztec States, 1400–1800: Anthropology and History,* ed. G. A. Collier, R. I. Rosaldo, and J. D. Wirth, 93–118. New York: Academic Press.
1985a   La constitución inca del Cuzco. *Histórica* 9(1): 35–74.
1985b   Probanza de los incas nietos de conquistadores. *Histórica* 9(2): 193–245.
1987   Machupijchu a la luz de los documentos del siglo XVI. *Kuntur* 4: 12–20.
1990   Machu Picchu a la luz de documentos del siglo XVI. *Histórica* 14(1): 139–54.
1997   Las tierras reales de los incas. In *Arqueología, Antropología e Historia en los Andes: Homenaje a María Rostworowski,* ed. Rafael Varón Gabai and Javier Flores Espinoza, 277–87. Lima: Insituto de Estudios Peruanos.

Sahlins, Marshall D.
1972   *Stone Age Economics.* Chicago: Aldine-Atherton.

Saignes, Thierry
1981   El piedmonte Amazónico de los Andes meridionales: Estado de la cuestión y problemas relativas a su ocupación en los siglos XVI y XVII. *Bulletin de l'Institut Français de Etudes Andines* 10(3–4): 141–76.
1986   The Ethnic Groups in the Valleys of Larecaja: From Descent to Residence. In *Anthropological History of Andean Polities,* ed. J. V. Murra, N. Wachtel, and J. Revel, 311–41. New York: Cambridge University Press.

Salis, Annette
1985   *Cultivos andinos: ¿Alternativa alimentaria popular?* Cusco: Centro de Estudios Rurales Andinos "Bartolomé de las Casas."

Sallnow, Michael J.
1987   *Pilgrims in the Andes: Regional Cults in Cusco.* Washington, DC: Smithsonian Institute Press.

Salomon, Frank
1985   The Dynamic Potential of the Complementarity Concept. In *Andean Ecology and Civilization,* ed. S. Masuda, I. Shimada, and C. Morris, 511–31. Tokyo: University of Tokyo Press.
1986a   *Native Lords of Quito in the Age of the Incas: The Political Economy of North-Andean Chiefdoms.* New York: Cambridge University Press.
1986b   Vertical Politics on the Inca Frontier. In *Anthropological History of Andean Polities,* ed. J. V. Murra, N. Wachtel, and J. Revel, 89–117. New York: Cambridge University Press.

1987   A North Andean Status Trader Complex under Inca Rule. *Ethno-history* 34(1): 63–77.

Sandefur, Elsie C.
2001   Animal Husbandry and Meat Consumption. In *Empire and Domestic Economy*, ed. Terence N. D'Altroy, Christine A. Hastorf, and Associates, 179–202. New York: Kluwer Academic/Plenum Press.

Sanders, William T.
1974   Chiefdom to State: Political Evolution at Kaminaljuyú, Guatemala. In *Reconstructing Complex Societies: An Archaeological Colloquium*, ed. C. B. Moore, 97–116. Supplement to the Bulletin of the American Schools of Oriental Research 20. Cambridge, MA.

Sanders, William T., Jeffrey R. Parsons, and Robert S. Santley
1979   *The Basin of Mexico: Ecological Processes in the Evolution of a Civilization.* New York: Academic Press.

Sandweiss, Daniel
1995   Cultural Background and Regional Prehistory. In *Pyramids of Túcume: The Quest for Peru's Forgotten City*, ed. Thor Heyerdahl, Daniel Sandweiss, and Alfredo Narváez, 56–77. New York: Thames and Hudson.

Sandweiss, Daniel, and Alfredo Narváez
1995   Túcume Past. In *Pyramids of Túcume: The Quest for Peru's Forgotten City*, ed. Thor Heyerdahl, Daniel Sandweiss, and Alfredo Narváez, 190–98. New York: Thames and Hudson.

Santillana, Idilio
1999   Andenes, canales, y paisaje. In *Los Incas: Arte y símbolos*, 61–107. Lima: Banco de Crédito del Perú.

Schaedel, Richard P.
1978   Early State of the Incas. In *The Early State*, ed. H. J. M. Claessen and P. Skalník, 289–320. The Hague: Mouton.

Schjellerup, Inge R.
1997   *Incas and Spaniards in the Conquest of the Chachapoyas: Archaeological and Ethnohistorical Research in the North-Eastern Andes of Peru.* GOTARC Series B. Gothenburg Archaeological Theses 7. Göteborg: Göteborg University Department of Archaeology.

Schreiber, Katharina J.
1987   Conquest and Consolidation: A Comparison of the Wari and Inca Occupations of a Highland Peruvian Valley. *American Antiquity* 52: 266–84.

1992   *Wari Imperialism in Middle Horizon Peru.* Anthropological Papers of the Museum of Anthropology, 87. Ann Arbor: University of Michigan Museum of Anthropology.

1993   The Inca Occupation of Andamarca Lucanas, Peru. In *Provincial Inca: Archaeological and Ethnohistorical Assessment of the Impact of the Inca State*, ed. Michael A. Malpass, 77–116. Iowa City: University of Iowa Press.

1999   Regional Approaches to the Study of Prehistoric Empires: Examples from Ayacucho and Nasca, Peru. In *Settlement Pattern Studies in the*

Americas: Fifty Years since Virú, ed. Brian R. Billman and Gary M.
Feinman, 160–71. Washington, DC: Smithsonian Institution Press.

2001   The Wari Empire of Middle Horizon Peru: The Epistemological
Challenge of Documenting an Empire without Documentary Evidence.
In *Empires: Perspectives from Archaeology and History,* ed. S. E. Al-
cock, T. N. D'Altroy, K. D. Morrison, and C. M. Sinopoli, 70–92.
New York: Cambridge University Press.

Scullard, H. H.

1980   *A History of the Roman World, 753 to 146 BC.* 4th ed. New York:
Routledge.

Seddon, Matthew T.

1998   Ritual, Power, and the Development of Complex Society: The Island
of the Sun and the Tiwanaku State. Ph.D. dissertation, Department
of Anthropology, University of Chicago.

Seltzer, Geoffrey O., and Christine A. Hastorf

1990   Climatic Change and Its Effect on Prehispanic Agriculture in the Central Peruvian Andes. *Journal of Field Archaeology* 17: 397–414.

Service, Elman R.

1962   *Primitive Social Organization: An Evolutionary Perspective.* New
York: Random House.

1975   *Origins of the State and Civilization.* New York: Norton.

Shimada, Izumi

1985   Perception, Procurement, and Management of Resources: Archaeological Perspective. In *Andean Ecology and Civilization,* ed. Shozo
Masuda, Izumi Shimada, and Craig Morris, 357–99. Tokyo: University of Tokyo Press.

1987   Horizontal and Vertical Dimensions of Prehistoric States in Northern
Peru. In *The Origins and Development of the Andean State,* ed.
Jonathan Haas, Shelia Pozorski, and Thomas Pozorski, 130–44. New
York: Cambridge University Press.

1990   Cultural Continuities and Discontinuities on the Northern Coast of
Peru, Middle-Late Horizons. In *The Northern Dynasties: Kingship
and Statecraft in Chimor,* ed. Michael E. Moseley and Alana Cordy-
Collins, 297–392. Washington, DC: Dumbarton Oaks Research Library and Collection.

Shimada, Izumi, Crystal Barker Schaaf, Lonnie G. Thompson, and Ellen Mosley-
Thompson

1990   Cultural Impacts of Severe Droughts in the Prehistoric Andes: Appli-
cations of a 1,500-Year Ice Core Precipitation Record. *World Archaeology* 22(3): 247–70.

Sidky, H.

1996   *Irrigation and State Formation in Hunza: The Anthropology of a Hydraulic Kingdom.* Lanham, MD: University Press of America.

Silverman, Helaine

2002   Touring Ancient Times: The Present and Presented Past in Contemporary Peru. *American Anthropologist* 104(3): 881–902.

Sinopoli, Carla
    1994   The Archaeology of Empires. *Annual Review of Anthropology* 23: 159–80.
Sinopoli, Carla, and Kathleen Morrison
    1995   Dimensions of Imperial Control: The Vijayanagara Capital. *American Anthropologist* 97(1): 83–96.
Smith, M. G.
    1967   A Hausa Kingdom: Maradi under Dan Baskore, 1854–75. In *West African Kingdoms in the Nineteenth Century,* ed. D. Forde and P. M. Kaberry, 93–122. Oxford: Oxford University Press.
Smith, Michael E.
    1996   *The Aztecs.* Cambridge, MA: Blackwell.
    2001   The Aztec Empire and the Mesoamerican World System. In *Empires: Perspectives from Archaeology and History,* ed. Susan E. Alcock, Terence N. D'Altroy, Kathleen D. Morrison, and Carla M. Sinopoli, 128–54. New York: Cambridge University Press.
Smith, Michael E., and Katharina J. Schreiber
    2004   New World Complex Societies. Manuscript in press at *Journal of Archaeological Research.*
Spencer, Charles S.
    1990   On the Tempo and Mode of State Formation: Neoevolution Reconsidered. *Journal of Anthropological Archaeology* 9: 1–30.
    1998   A Mathematical Model of Primary State Formation. *Cultural Dynamics* 10(1): 5–20.
Spencer, Charles S., and Elsa M. Redmond
    2001a   Chronology of Conquest: Implications of New Radiocarbon Analyses from the Cañada de Cuicatlán, Oaxaca. *Latin American Antiquity* 12(2): 182–201.
    2001b   Multilevel Selection and Political Evolution in the Valley of Oaxaca, 500–100 B.C. *Journal of Anthropological Archaeology* 20(2): 195–229.
Squier, Ephraim George
    1877   *Peru: Incidents of Travel and Exploration in the Land of the Incas.* New York: Henry Holt.
Stanish, Charles
    1985   Post-Tiwanaku Regional Economies in the Otora Valley, Southern Peru. Ph.D. dissertation, Department of Anthropology, University of Chicago.
    1989   An Archaeological Evaluation of an Ethnohistoric Model in Moquegua. In *Ecology, Settlement and History in the Osmore Drainage,* ed. Don Rice, Charles Stanish, and Philip Scarr, 303–22. Oxford: British Archaeological Reports.
    1992   *Ancient Andean Political Economy.* Austin: University of Texas Press.
    1997   Nonmarket Imperialism in a Prehispanic Context: The Inca Occupation of the Titicaca Basin. *Latin American Antiquity* 8(3): 1–18.
    2000   Negotiating Rank in an Imperial State: Lake Titicaca Basin Elite under Inca and Spanish Control. In *Hierarchies in Action: Cui Bono?*

ed. M. Diehl, 317–39. Southern Illinois University Center for Archaeological Investigations, Occasional Paper 27. Carbondale: Southern
Illinois University Center for Archaeological Investigations.

2001a   The Origin of State Societies in South America. *Annual Review of
Anthropology* 30: 41–64.

2001b   Regional Research on the Inca. *Journal of Archaeological Research*
9(3): 213–41.

2002   Tiwanaku Political Economy. In *Andean Archaeology I: Variations in
Sociopolitical Organization*, ed. William H. Isbell and Helaine Silverman, 169–98. New York: Kluwer Academic/Plenum Press.

Stanish, Charles, and Brian S. Bauer

2004   *Archaeological Research on the Islands of the Sun and Moon, Lake
Titicaca, Bolivia: Final Results from the Proyecto Tiksi Kjarka*. Cot-
sen Institute of Archaeology at UCLA, Monograph 52. Los Angeles:
Cotsen Institute of Archaeology.

Stanish, C., E. de la Vega, L. Steadman, C. Chávez Justo, K. Frye, L. Onofre Ma-
mani, M. Seddon, and P. Calisaya Chuquimia

1997   Archaeological Survey of the Juli-Desaguadero Region of Lake Titicaca Basin, Southern Peru. *Fieldiana Anthropology*, new series, 29.
Chicago: Field Museum of Natural History.

Sutter, Richard

2000   Prehistoric Genetic and Culture Change: A Bioarchaeological Search
for Pre-Inca Altiplano Colonies in the Coastal Valleys of Moquegua,
Peru, and Azapa, Chile. *Latin American Antiquity* 11(1): 43–70.

Thompson, L. G., E. Mosley-Thompson, J. F. Bolzan, and B. R. Koci

1985   A 1500-Year Record of Tropical Precipitation in Ice Cores from the
Quelccaya Ice Cap, Peru. *Science* 229: 971–73.

Thompson, L. G., E. Mosley-Thompson, W. Dansgaard, and P. M. Grootes

1986   The Little Ice Age as Recorded in the Stratigraphy of the Tropical
Quelccaya Ice Cap. *Science* 234: 361–64.

Thompson, Lonnie G., Mary E. Davis, and Ellen Mosley-Thompson

1994   Glacial Records of Global Climate: A 1500-Year Tropical Ice Core
Record of Climate. *Human Ecology* 22(1): 83–95.

Thompson, L. G., M. E. Davis, E. Mosley-Thompson, T. A. Sowers, K. A. Hen-
derson, V. S. Zagorodnov, P.-N. Lin, V. N. Mikhalenko, R. K. Campen, J. F.
Bolzan, and B. Francou

1998   A 25,000-Year Tropical Climate History from Bolivian Ice Cores. *Science* 282: 1858–64.

Topic, John R.

1991   Huari and Huamachuco. In *Huari Administrative Structures: Prehistoric Monumental Architecture and State Government*, ed. William
H. Isbell and Gordon F. McEwan, 141–64. Washington, DC: Dumbarton Oaks Research Library and Collection.

Topic, John R., and Michael E. Moseley

1983   Chan Chan: A Case Study of Urban Change in Peru. *Ñawpa Pacha*
21: 153–82.

Topic, John R., and Theresa Lange Topic
  1993 A Summary of the Inca Occupation of Huamachuco. In *Provincial Inca: Archaeological and Ethnohistorical Assessment of the Impact of the Inca State,* M. Malpass, 17–43. Iowa City: University of Iowa Press.

Topic, Theresa Lange
  1990 Territorial Expansion and the Kingdom of Chimor. In *The Northern Dynasties: Kingship and Statecraft in Chimor,* ed. Michael E. Moseley and Alana Cordy-Collins, 177–94. Washington, DC: Dumbarton Oaks Research Library and Collection.

Topic, Theresa Lange, and John R. Topic
  1987 *Huamachuco Archaeological Project: Preliminary Report on the* 1986 *Field Season.* Trent University Occasional Papers in Anthropology 4. Peterborough, Ontario: Trent University.

Torres Poblete, Nilo
  1989 Sondéo arqueológico de Araway. Thesis, Facultad de Ciencias Sociales, Universidad Nacional de San Antonio Abad del Cusco.

Trimborn, Hermann
  1981 Excavaciones en Sama, 1972 y 1975. In *Sama,* ed. H. Trimborn, 9–28. Collectanea Instituti Anthropos 25. Haus Volker und Kulturen, Anthropos Institut.

Trimborn, H., O. Kleemann, K. Narr, and W. Wurster (eds.)
  1975 *Investigaciones Arqueológicas en los Valles del Caplina y Sama (Dep. Tacna, Perú).* Studia Instituti Anthropos 25. Estella: Editorial Verbo Divino.

Uhle, Max
  1912 Los origenes de los incas. In *Actas del XVII Congreso Internacional de Americanistas,* 302–52. Buenos Aires.

Urton, Gary D.
  1987 *At the Crossroads of Earth and Sky: An Andean Cosmology.* Austin: University of Texas Press.
  1988 Arquitectura pública como texto social: La historia de un muro de adobe en Pacariqtambo, Perú (1915–1985). *Revista Andina* 6(1): 225–61.
  1990 *The History of a Myth: Pacariqtambo and the Origin of the Incas.* Austin: University of Texas Press.

Valcárcel, L.
  1935 Los trabajos arqueológicos en el Departamento de Cuzco. *Revista del Museo Nacional* 4(2): 163–208. (Also four installments of Sacsayhuaman between 1933 and 1935)
  1939 Sobre el orígen del Cuzco. *Revista del Museo Nacional* 8(2): 190–223.

Valdez, Lidio M., and Cirilo Vivanco
  1994 Arqueología de la cuenca del Qaracha, Ayacucho, Perú. *Latin American Antiquity* 5(2): 144–57.

Van Buren, Mary
  2000 Political Fragmentation and Ideological Continuity in the Andean

Highlands. In *Order, Legitimacy, and Wealth in Ancient States,* ed. Janet Richards and Mary Van Buren, 77–87. New York: Cambridge University Press.

Van Buren, M., P. Bürgi, and P. Rice

1993   Torata Alta: A Late Highland Settlement in the Osmore Drainage. In *Domestic Architecture, Ethnicity, and Complementarity in the South-Central Andes,* ed. M. Aldenderfer, 136–46. Iowa City: University of Iowa Press.

Villamarín, Juan, and Judith Villamarín

1999   Chiefdoms: The Prevalence and Persistence of *"Señoríos Naturales,"* 1400 to European Conquest. In *The Cambridge History of the Native Peoples of the Americas, Volume III South America, Part I,* ed. S. Salomon and S. Schwartz, 577–667. New York: Cambridge University Press.

Vivanco, Cirilo, and Lidio M. Valdez

1993   Poblados Wari en la cuenca del Pampas-Qaracha, Ayacucho. *Gaceta Arqueológica Andina* 23: 83–102.

Wachtel, Nathan

1982   The *Mitimas* of the Cochabamba Valley: The Colonization Policy of Huayna Capac. In *The Inca and Aztec States, 1400–1800: Anthropology and History,* ed. G. A. Collier, R. I. Rosaldo, and J. D. Wirth, 199–235. New York: Academic Press.

Walbank, F. W.

1953   *The Decline of the Roman Empire in the West.* New York: Lawrence and Wishart.

Wallace, Dwight T.

1998   The Inca Compound at La Centinela, Chincha. *Andean Past* 5: 9–33.

Wallerstein, Immanuel

1974   *The Modern World System.* Vol. 1. New York: Academic Press

Webster, Stephen S.

1971   An Indigenous Quechua Community in Exploitation of Multiple Ecological Zones. *Revista del Museo Nacional* 37: 174–83.

Wiener, Charles

1880   *Pérou et Bolivie: Récit de voyage suivi d'études archéologiques et ethnographiques et de notes sur l'écriture et les langues des populations indiennes.* Paris: Hachette et cie.

Wiessner, Polly

1982   Beyond Willow Smoke and Dog's Tails: A Comment on Binford's Analysis of Hunter-Gatherer Settlement Systems. *American Antiquity* 47(1): 171–78.

Willey, Gordon R.

1953   *Prehistoric Settlement Patterns in the Viru Valley, Peru.* Bureau of American Ethnology Bulletin 155. Washington, DC: Smithsonian Institution.

Williams, Patrick Ryan

1997   The Role of Disaster in the Development of Agriculture and the Evolution of Social Complexity in the South-Central Andean Sierra. Ph.D. dissertation, Department of Anthropology, University of Florida.

2001   Cerro Baúl, a Wari Center on the Tiwanaku Frontier. *Latin American Antiquity* 12(1): 67–83.

2002   A Re-examination of Disaster Induced Collapse in the Case of the Andean Highland States: Wari and Tiwanaku. *World Archaeology* 33(3): 361–74.

Williams, Patrick Ryan, and Donna Nash

2002   Imperial Interaction in the Andes: Huari and Tiwanaku at Cerro Baúl. In *Andean Archaeology I: Variations in Sociopolitical Organization*, ed. William H. Isbell and Helaine Silverman, 243–65. New York: Kluwer Academic/Plenum Press.

Wilson, David J.

1988   *Prehispanic Settlement Patterns in the Lower Santa Valley, Peru: A Regional Perspective on the Origins and Development of Complex North Coast Society*. Washington, DC: Smithsonian Institution Press.

Winterhalder, Bruce

1986   Diet Choice, Risk, and Food Sharing in a Stochastic Environment. *Journal of Anthropological Archaeology* 5(4): 369–92.

1993   The Ecological Basis of Water Management in the Central Andes: Rainfall and Temperature in Southern Peru. In *Irrigation at High Altitudes: The Social Organization of Water Control Systems in the Andes*, ed. William P. Mitchell and David Guillet, 21–67. Society for Latin American Anthropology Publication Series 12. Washington, DC: American Anthropological Association.

Wright, Henry T.

1977   Recent Research on the Origin of the State. *Annual Review of Anthropology* 6: 379–97.

1986   The Evolution of Civilizations. In *American Archaeology Past and Future: A Celebration of the Society for American Archaeology, 1935–1985*, ed. D. J. Meltzer, D. D. Fowler, and J. A. Sabloff, 323–65. Washington, DC: Smithsonian Institution Press.

1998   Uruk State in Southwestern Iran. In *Archaic States*, ed. Gary M. Feinman and Joyce Marcus, 173–92. Santa Fe, NM: SAR Press.

Wright, Henry T. and Gregory A. Johnson

1975   Population Exchange and Early State Formation in South-Western Iran. *American Anthropologist* 79: 267–89.

Yépez, Wilfredo

1985   Sub-proyecto puesto en valor de moumentos, Dirección de Patrimonio Cultural y Monumental, Obra Pisaq—Q'allaq'asa: Informe Annual—1985. Annual report to the Instituto Nacional de Cultura—Cusco.

Zapata Rodríguez, Julinho

1997   Arquitectura y contextos funerarios wari en Batan Urqu, Cusco. *Boletín de Arqueología PUCP* 1: 165–206.

1998   Los cerros sagrados: Panorama del período Formativo en la cuenca del Vilcanota, Cuzco. *Boletín de Arqueología PUCP* 2: 307–36.

Zimmerer, Karl S.
   1996   *Changing Fortunes: Biodiversity and Peasant Livelihood in the Peruvian Andes.* Berkeley: University of California Press.
   1998   The Ecogeography of Andean Potatoes: Versatility in Farm Regions and Fields Can Aid Sustainable Development. *BioScience* 48(6): 445–54.
   1999   Overlapping Patchworks of Mountain Agriculture in Peru and Bolivia: Toward a Regional-Global Landscape Model. *Human Ecology* 27(1): 135–65.

Zuidema, R. Tom
   1974–76 La imagen del sol y la *huaca* de Susurpuquio en el sistema de los incas en el Cusco. *Journal de la Société des Américanistes* 63: 199–230.
   1977   The Inca Kinship System: A New Theoretical View. In *Andean Kinship and Marriage,* ed. Ralph Bolton and Enrique Mayer, 240–81. Washington, DC: American Anthropological Association.
   1983   Hierarchy and Space in Incaic Social Organization. *Ethnohistory* 30(2): 49–75.
   1986   Inca Dynasty and Irrigation: Another Look at Andean Concepts of History. In *Anthropological History of Andean Polities,* ed. J. V. Murra, N. Wachtel, and J. Revel, 177–200. New York: Cambridge University Press.
   1989   What Does the Equation "Mother's Brother = Wife's Father" Mean in Inca Social Organization? In *Variant Views: Five Lectures from the Perspective of the "Leiden Tradition" in Cultural Anthropology,* ed. Henri J. M. Claessen, 132–56. Leiden: Universiteit van Leiden.
   1990   *Inca Civilization in Cuzco.* Austin: University of Texas Press.
   1995   *El sistema de ceques del Cuzco: La organización social de la capital de los Incas.* Trans. Ernesto Salazar. Lima: Pontificia Universidad Católica del Perú.

Zuidema, Reiner Tom, and Deborah Poole
   1982   Los limites de los cuatro suyus incaicos en el Cuzco. *Bulletin de l'Institut Français des Études Andines* 11(1–2): 83–89.

Index

JUNIATA COLLEGE

2820 9100 103 089 1

WITHDRAWN FROM
JUNIATA COLLEGE LIBRARY